Library of
Davidson College

The United Nations in Bangladesh

The United Nations in Bangladesh

By Thomas W. Oliver

Princeton University Press
Princeton, New Jersey

Copyright © 1978 by Princeton University Press
Published by Princeton University Press, Princeton, New Jersey
In the United Kingdom: Princeton University Press, Guildford, Surrey

All Rights Reserved

Library of Congress Cataloging in Publication Data will
be found on the last printed page of this book

Publication of this book has been aided by a grant from the
Paul Mellon Fund of Princeton University Press
This book has been composed in VIP Electra

Printed in the United States of America
by Princeton University Press, Princeton, New Jersey

Contents

Foreword by Brian Urquhart		vii
Acknowledgments		ix
List of Abbreviations		xi
Map of Transportation Network of Bangladesh		xii
Introduction		xiii
Chapter 1	The Secretary-General's Offer of Assistance: March-June 1971	3
Chapter 2	UNEPRO—The Start-Up: June-July 1971	16
Chapter 3	The Wider Issues: July-August 1971	32
Chapter 4	The Operation Takes Shape: August-November 1971	43
Chapter 5	The Secretary-General's Offer of Good Offices: October-November 1971	61
Chapter 6	UNEPRO—The Attempted Evacuation: December 1971	72
Chapter 7	The End of UNEPRO: December 1971	80
Chapter 8	UNROD—The Early Days: December 1971-February 1972	98
Chapter 9	UNROD—The End of the Beginning: March-April 1972	113
Chapter 10	The Consolidation of the Operation	130
Chapter 11	The Right Road: May-September 1972	142
Chapter 12	UNROD—The Last Six Months: October 1972-March 1973	155
Chapter 13	Winding Up the Operation: April-December 1973	168
Chapter 14	How the Operation Worked	183
Appendix 1	UNEPRO, UNROD, UNROB: A Chronology	203
Appendix 2	Published United Nations Material	207
Notes		211
Index		227

Foreword

by Brian Urquhart, United Nations Under-Secretary-General for Political Affairs

The United Nations Relief Operation in Bangladesh and the humanitarian efforts that preceded it in the same area were among the most ambitious and grand efforts ever undertaken by the world organization to help people in distress.

Efforts to relieve the sufferings of the people of that hard-pressed and disaster-prone area began in 1971 and continued through a period of violent military conflict into the very difficult first years of the newly independent sovereign state of Bangladesh. Despite the extreme difficulties of the situation, the assistance of the international community provided through the United Nations was extraordinarily effective.

Early in 1971, in a time of great political uncertainty and confusion, UN Secretary-General U Thant took personal responsibility for initiating these humanitarian efforts and for securing government support for them. It was a courageous and imaginative initiative open, as U Thant well knew, to all sorts of misinterpretations and criticisms. He took it, however, in the conviction that the United Nations must act to help people in need and to forestall even graver humanitarian disasters. His successor, Kurt Waldheim, continued and enlarged the program, strengthening its structure and its basis of support.

The response of many governments and voluntary agencies was generous, and the effectiveness of the assistance provided was enhanced by a coordinating mechanism at United Nations headquarters and in Bangladesh itself, which was able to call for the kind of contributions needed, to channel them in the right direction, and to work closely with the local authorities in the use of the assistance received. The operation was a happy combination of multilateral and bilateral effort concerted by the United Nations. It was also an example of the whole UN system working as a team and speaking with one voice.

The people who conducted this unprecedented humanitarian

effort worked under extreme pressure and tension and, in the field, often under dangerous conditions. This account of their efforts and of the work of the world organization in an especially sensitive and complicated situation is an encouraging story of what the world community, in the right circumstances and with proper leadership, can do to help a people in distress.

Acknowledgments

This study is an outgrowth of my service as reports officer at UNROD/UNROB headquarters in 1973. It is in no sense an official report on the United Nations operation in Bangladesh. It is a personal attempt to provide a fuller account of the origin and development of a remarkable episode in UN history than can be gleaned from the formal documents.

The information available in published sources has been supplemented by material from internal, private, and unpublished papers, and by interviews with a great many participants in, and observers of, the operation. I cannot hope to name all who assisted me. At the risk of being invidious, I wish, however, to thank particularly Mr. Roberto Guyer, Mr. Paul-Marc Henry, Sir Robert Jackson, Mr. Ismat Kittani, Dr. Victor Umbricht, and Mr. Brian Urquhart for the help they provided. I am grateful also to Mr. Robert Rhodes James, who read the manuscript at an early stage, for his advice and encouragement.

Finally I wish to thank my wife, Marianna, my daughter, Griselda, and my son, Thomas Richard, for their comments, criticism, and assistance in completing the manuscript.

List of Abbreviations

ACC	Administrative Committee on Coordination, United Nations
ECOSOC	Economic and Social Council of the United Nations
FAO	Food and Agriculture Organization of the United Nations
IBRD	International Bank for Reconstruction and Development
ICAO	International Civil Aviation Organization
ICRC	International Committee of the Red Cross
ILO	International Labor Organization
IMF	International Monetary Fund
ITU	International Telecommunication Union
UNDP	United Nations Development Program
UNDRO	United Nations Disaster Relief Office
UNEPRO	United Nations East Pakistan Relief Operation
UNESCO	United Nations Educational, Scientific, and Cultural Organization
UNHCR	United Nations High Commissioner for Refugees
UNICEF	United Nations Children's Fund
UNIDO	United Nations Industrial Development Organization
UNMOGIP	United Nations Military Observer Group in India and Pakistan
UNROB	United Nations Special Relief Office in Bangladesh
UNROD	United Nations Relief Operation in Dacca
USAID	Agency for International Development, United States
WFP	World Food Program
WHO	World Health Organization

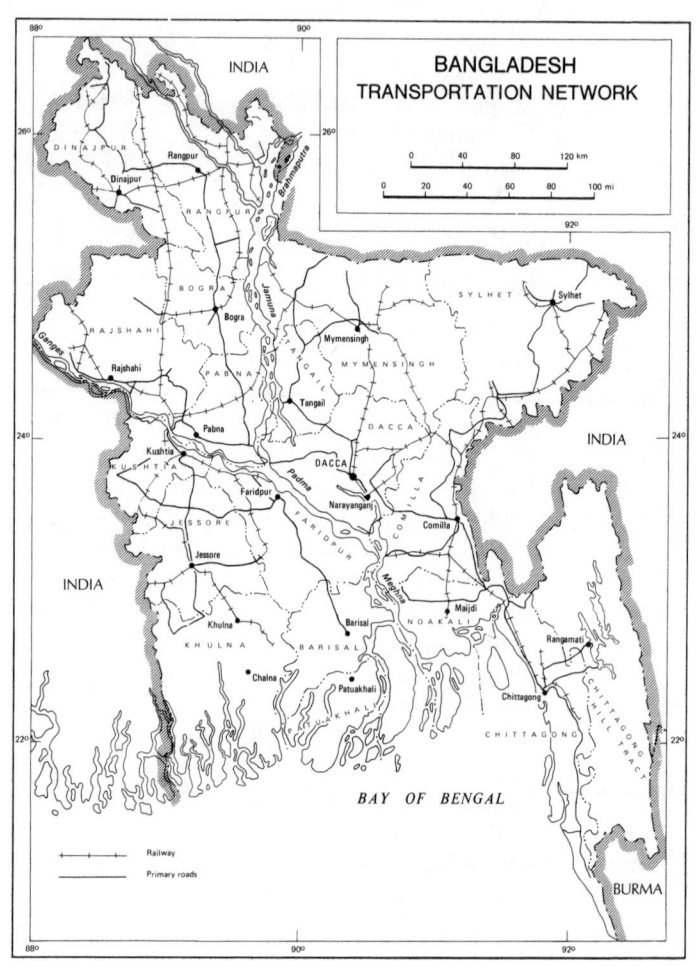

Introduction

The United Nations relief operation in Bangladesh is one of the organization's great unsung success stories. It began in March 1971 with an initiative by then Secretary-General U Thant, which demonstrated both the scope and the limitations of the secretary-general's executive authority. The initiative, like the more directly political ones he took in the course of the year to preserve peace in the subcontinent, was frustrated by events, and brought him more criticism than commendations. The relief operation he started was still struggling to establish itself when war broke out in December and changed the map of the subcontinent. The operation—the United Nations Relief Operation in East Pakistan—did not achieve its objectives. It had, however, mobilized staff, supplies, and equipment that enabled the organization to respond promptly to the emergency relief needs of newly independent Bangladesh. Without UNEPRO, the secretary-general would have been unable to establish UNROD—the United Nations Relief Operation in Dacca—within a week of the surrender of the Pakistan forces in Bangladesh to the joint Bangladesh and Indian command on 16 December 1971.

UNROD, after a period of heroic and sometimes ill-fated improvisation, became the most successful and largest operation of its kind ever mounted by the United Nations. The needs it was intended to meet were unprecedented. "Never before in human history," Secretary-General Kurt Waldheim said, in launching his first appeal for aid to Bangladesh in February 1972, "has international assistance been needed so urgently and in such great amounts." The prospects that confronted the people and provisional government of Bangladesh when they emerged from nine months of bitter struggle in December 1971 and began to rebuild their shattered country were unbelievably bleak. To many outside observers the obstacles seemed insurmountable and some of them predicted disaster. It was clear, a senior Bangalee official has written, that "only a massive effort by the people and government of Bangladesh supported by equally massive inputs of external assistance could bring the new country through its first year without catastrophe."[1]

The grounds for pessimism were solid. Bangladesh is a poor country, a paradigm of the problems of underdevelopment. A Bangalee economist has described it as "a massive concentration of poverty." "Nowhere on earth," he wrote, "is there anything like such extremely low living standards shared by such an enormous mass of population squeezed into so small a geographical area."[2] In terms of population—an estimated 72 million to 75 million in mid-1972—Bangladesh is the eighth largest country in the world. In area—55,000 square miles—it is comparable to Greece or the state of Wisconsin. With over 1,300 inhabitants to the square mile, it is the most densely populated country on earth. Bangladesh is, an American specialist told a congressional subcommittee in 1973, more crowded than the United States would be if the entire world population were settled within its borders.[3]

The population is predominantly rural; 94 percent of the inhabitants live in some 65,000 villages. Between 80 and 90 percent depend on agriculture for their livelihood, the main crops being rice, the country's principal foodstuff, and jute, its most important export. The rice yield is low by international standards. Even after the introduction of better methods, fertilizers, pesticides, irrigation, and high-yield seed, rice production was increasing at a rate of barely 2 percent a year, compared to an estimated population growth rate of about 3 percent. The result was a worsening food shortage, which in the immediate preindependence years required imports of 1.5 million tons of food grain a year. Most of the remainder of the population make a living from fishing, handloom weaving, and other handicrafts. Industry is little developed and there are few mineral resources.

The country's telecommunication and transport systems were archaic and inadequate. Before partition in 1947, the railways were part of the Indian network and were centered on Calcutta, the region's main port. They had been only partly adapted to the needs of East Pakistan as a separate entity. There were two main north-south links, one in the west serving Chalna, the country's

Introduction

second port, and one in the east running north from Chittagong, the country's main port, with transverse links serving Dacca and the central portion of the country. The great rivers that dominate the delta area the country occupies—the Ganges, the Brahmaputra, the Meghna, and their distributaries and affluents—provide a network of natural waterways. They also cause widespread flooding. In the monsoon season an inundation over 100 miles wide spreads over the center of the country, damaging crops and interrupting communications. The rivers and the threat of flooding require the provision of embankments, dikes, ferries, and bridges—over 4,000 on the railway system alone—on a large scale and make the improvement of the road and railway networks costly and difficult.

The statistical evidence is uncertain and challenged in some quarters, but there seems no doubt that in the years preceding independence real per capita income in what is now Bangladesh remained virtually static and probably declined. The stagnation in East Pakistan, which contrasted sharply with the impressive and widely praised growth in West Pakistan, was the outcome of several related factors, among them the development policies of the government of Pakistan. These policies, which were regarded by major donor governments as a model of their kind, were designed to promote development through industrialization. Their effects on the predominantly agricultural economy of East Pakistan were disastrous. Through the operation of the system of multiple exchange rates and import controls, resources were transferred from agriculture, mainly in East Pakistan, to support industrialization, which was concentrated in the West wing. The foreign exchange proceeds of exports of raw jute from East Pakistan were, for example, bought by the government at low rates and used to import capital goods and materials that were sold to industrialists at advantageous prices. The government's development policies had another side-effect. The resources, mostly foreign aid, at the disposal of the government tended to go to West Pakistan rather than East Pakistan, on the ground that investment in the West was more likely to increase the nation's rate of growth as a whole. In the mid-1960s an effort was made to channel more resources to

East Pakistan in order to reduce the political, economic, and social damage that had been done. The results were meager. Many of the projects chosen were, according to international observers, poorly conceived and ill suited to the country's needs, and where they were not, implementation was ineffective.

The problems of underdevelopment and frustrated development, were compounded by the catastrophes of 1970 and 1971. In 1970 the worst cyclone in decades killed hundreds of thousands, destroyed countless homes, and ruined much of the country's agriculture. Only a few months later, on 25 March 1971, internal strife broke out and racked the country for nine months, culminating in civil war and the emergence of independent Bangladesh. The cumulative losses resulting from the nine months of repression, armed struggle, and war were appalling. One estimate puts the total at about $2,000 million—the equivalent of more than 40 percent of a year's Gross National Product (GNP).

Hundreds of thousands were killed or maimed. Villages, schools, and health institutions were destroyed. Millions of people were driven from their homes. Ten million refugees fled to India. Twice that number abandoned their homes and jobs in search of food and safety within the country.

Agricultural losses were heavy. Many of the bullocks used to draw plows and carts were slaughtered. Tools, fishing boats and nets, irrigation pumps and wells were destroyed or damaged. Fields were untilled, and when the farmers returned, stocks of seeds, fertilizers, and pesticides had to be replenished.

The economy was stifled. Foreign exchange reserves, overseas credit facilities, and domestic financial resources were lacking. The transport and communication system was crippled. Thousands of trucks and buses were destroyed, damaged, or removed from the country. On the railways, 296 bridges, including two main links, the Hardinge Bridge over the Padma River and the George VI Bridge over the old Brahmaputra, were destroyed or damaged, severing rail communications from east to central Bangladesh and between the northern and southern parts of the country. Locomotives, rolling stock, stretches of track, and the signaling system were unusable. The telecommunications network was

Introduction   xvii

inoperative. Ferries and inland water craft were sunk or damaged, and the ports—through which food and relief supplies would have to move—were heavily damaged. Channels were mined and movement was restricted by sunken vessels.

After the cessation of imports and the return of the ten million refugees, mass starvation, which had threatened the country for months, now became an immediate concern. A famine repeating or even surpassing the tragedy of 1943 seemed imminent.

There were other dangers. The country had been turned into a no man's land, "a free-for-all with lethal weapons loose through the length and breadth of the land."[4] The collapse of law and order and the massacre of minorities seemed, in the opinion of many foreign observers, certain.

In this situation a new and untried government was faced with the task of converting a provincial administration into a national government, without benefit of any transitional or preparatory period. Most of the senior civil servants in East Pakistan had come from the West wing, and many of the most experienced Bangalee leaders and administrators had been lost or, like Sheikh Mujibur Rahman himself, were still detained in Pakistan. Government departments capable of administering the world's eighth largest nation had to be created from the wreckage of a demoralized and discredited provincial administration that had been accustomed to defer decisions to Islamabad. Sheikh Mujibur and his colleagues succeeded in doing this. A workable administration was established. The pessimists were confounded and the disasters they had predicted were averted. The ten million refugees and the millions of displaced Bangalees were reabsorbed quickly and quietly. Law and order was by and large preserved. The threatened mass slaughter of minorities did not take place. Most important of all, the people were fed.

The credit for this achievement goes in the first place to the people and government of Bangladesh. The people are inured to hardship and to the hazards of cyclone and monsoon. Their spirit of self-reliance, reinforced by the exhilaration of independence, was the primary factor in the survival and recovery of their country. "This tribute," a senior Bangalee official has written, "cannot be quantified. . . . In the nature of things it is not possible to record and tabulate the efforts of millions of farmers to rebuild their homesteads, plow the land, plant the seed, repair the tubewells, find animals and implements, and in general reconstitute their working lives disrupted by occupation, flight and war."[5] The energies of the people could restore a subsistence economy and provide the basis for eventual reconstruction, but much more was needed to avert the threat of famine and disease and economic collapse. The government provided the necessary leadership, and, thanks to the speed with which it established a workable administration, created the conditions in which a successful relief operation could be undertaken.

There was no question that immediate and massive external assistance was essential. The problem was how to mobilize it. A newcomer to the international community, the government of Bangladesh was not recognized by a majority of the world's governments. It was not a member of any of the organizations of the United Nations system and lacked ready access to any of the normal sources of international assistance. In this desperate situation, the United Nations proved acceptable to all concerned for providing the kind of emergency assistance required. The secretary-general's decision, in accordance with the mandate given him by the General Assembly in resolution 2790 (XXVI) and the Security Council in resolution 307 (1971), to continue to furnish humanitarian assistance to the area, enabled the organization to act as the catalyst and coordinator needed to mobilize and deliver assistance. The United Nations operation served as a political umbrella under which donor governments, intergovernmental organizations, and voluntary agencies could work in cooperation with the government of Bangladesh to save the country from disaster.

The response by governments, intergovernmental organizations, and voluntary agencies to the call for assistance was on a scale that matched the needs. By 31 March 1973, when the first phase of the operation ended with the termination of UNROD, the total aid mobilized from all external sources in response to the appeals of the secretary-general and the government of Bangladesh stood at over $1,300 million, two thirds provided bilaterally, one quarter multilaterally through the United Nations system, and the remainder through international voluntary agencies. The volume of aid mobilized is a measure both of the concern and generosity of the international community and of the capacity of the United Nations system to organize and carry out a relief operation of unusual complexity in uniquely difficult political circumstances.

The operation was massive and it was successful. When the first phase of the operation came to an end in March 1973, Bangladesh was, as the development conference convened by the government in Dacca recognized, ready to move from the relief phase into the phase of reconstruction and to begin the long climb to an acceptable level of development. The operation had, as the foreign minister of Bangladesh, Abdus Samad, told Secretary-General Kurt Waldheim during his visit to Dacca in February 1973, tided the war-ravaged country over its initial difficulties and provided a "rare example of international cooperation that has enlarged the scope of constructive United Nations action."[6]

The United Nations in Bangladesh

CHAPTER 1

The Secretary-General's Offer of Assistance: March-June 1971

Until March 1971 events in East Pakistan were, for most observers outside the subcontinent, part of the nagging background of international affairs, one of the many threatening clouds that might blow up into a storm but that might equally well dwindle and disappear over the horizon.

The ingredients for disaster were there. The devastating cyclone of November 1970 had taken a heavy toll of lives, drastically reduced rice production, and made between two million and three million people dependent on external food aid for survival. It also had political repercussions. The government's dilatory response to the emergency confirmed Bangalee suspicions of the insincerity of Islamabad's interest in the welfare of East Pakistan and helped to sweep Sheikh Mujibur Rahman's Awami League to an unexpectedly decisive victory in the elections of December 1970. The Awami League captured all but two of the National Assembly seats in East Pakistan and emerged as the country's majority party. Political negotiations for a new constitution that would satisfy the Awami League's demand for autonomy without dismembering Pakistan and permit the ending of martial law dragged on through January and February 1971. With the announcement on 1 March of President Yahya Khan's decision to postpone the National Assembly scheduled for 3 March, the troubles deepened. Tension increased against a background of civil disobedience, demonstrations, and general strikes in East Pakistan.

Nevertheless, talks continued and were reported to be progressing. The president announced he had decided to convene the National Assembly on 25 March and would visit Dacca for further discussions. Many observers believed—as some still do—that the deadlock between the Awami League and West Pakistan's political leaders could be broken and that a new Pakistan constitution acceptable to all parties could be evolved within the framework of the Awami League's six-point program of regional autonomy. Sheikh Mujib had resisted the call of some of his supporters for independence and, while launching a noncooperation movement, had continued to work for negotiated autonomy. In the talks in Dacca initiated on 15 March, President Yahya Khan also appeared to be opting for compromise.

On 25 March the door was closed to compromise for some time to come. President Yahya Khan broke off the talks and returned to Islamabad. In a broadcast to the nation on 26 March, he explained that he had tolerated "one illegal act after another" in his search for a reasonable solution. Sheikh Mujib's action in starting the noncooperation movement was, he said, "an act of treason," and his followers had continually flouted the government's authority. The president had been forced to conclude that "the man and his party are enemies of Pakistan and . . . want East Pakistan to break away completely from the country." Yahya Khan believed no further progress was possible. When the "law and order situation" returned to normal, he would resume his efforts to transfer power to "the elected representatives of the people." In the meantime he had banned all political activity, imposed complete press censorship, and ordered the armed forces to take action and "fully restore the authority of the government."[1] The army moved at once. Sheikh Mujib was arrested, fighting broke out in Dacca, and the crackdown began. Political confrontation had been transformed into civil strife.

Within forty-eight hours after negotiations between Sheikh Mujib and West Pakistan's political leaders had broken off, Secretary-General U Thant met the permanent representative of Pakistan to the United Nations, Ambassador Agha Shahi, and asked him to inform President Yahya Khan of his concern at the turn of events in Dacca. The secretary-general's immediate preoccupation was humanitarian, to find means of alleviating the human suffering that was bound to ensue. He was also deeply perturbed by the potential threat to peace and stability in the subcontinent. As he later wrote, "these human tragedies have consequences in a far wider sphere. The violent emotions aroused could have repercussions on the relations of religious and ethnic groups on the subcontinent as a whole and the relationship of the governments of India and Pakistan is also a major component of the problem." Moreover, the central issue—the conflict between the right of self-determination and the principle of the territorial integrity of states—was one that had, as the secretary-general wrote, provoked "highly emotional reactions in the international community in recent years," and had often led to "fratricidal strife."[2]

However great the dangers, the secretary-general's possible actions were severely circumscribed. In a note dated 30 March to Ambassador Samar Sen of India, who had visited him the previous day to outline his government's views on the crisis, he explained some of the difficulties. "Both from personal convictions and as secretary-general of the United Nations, I am never neutral on humanitarian issues." There were, however, two obstacles to effective action. The first was "the lack of authoritative information," the second "the claim of governments that the secretary-general has no right to interfere in their internal affairs." His authority was, he said, "limited to what is granted . . . by the consent of member governments."

The first obstacle was to persist throughout the crisis. So far as the second was concerned, the secretary-general could do no more than use the prestige of his office and his powers of persuasion to induce President Yahya Khan to accept humanitarian assistance and to bend his policies in a direction that would permit a political solution to the internal conflict in Pakistan.

The Indian government was understandably anxious that action should be taken to resolve the crisis. Indian public opinion was deeply stirred. On 31 March the Indian Parliament adopted a resolution condemning the Pakistani action in East Pakistan and assuring the people of East Bengal of "the whole-hearted support and sympathy" of the people of India. The resolution, which was moved by Prime Minister Indira Gandhi, was more moderate in tone than many members of the House would have liked, largely because the prime minister insisted that the government must act within "international norms."[3] In a *note verbale* delivered to the secretary-general on 30 March, Ambassador Sen had argued that the international community could and should take suitable action to deal with the situation in East Pakistan. "The scale of human suffering" was, he maintained, such that the situation had ceased "to be a matter of domestic concern of Pakistan alone."[4] It was bound to increase tensions between India and Pakistan and was likely to result in a flow of refugees into the Indian border regions. In response U Thant could only inform the United Nations high commissioner for refugees of India's anxieties concerning a possible influx of refugees and advise the government to discuss with the International Committee of the Red Cross some of the other humanitarian problems that had arisen.

The secretary-general pursued his unpublicized contacts with the permanent representatives of Pakistan, India, and other interested governments, and on 1 April made a public offer of assistance. In response to repeated press inquiries, he authorized his spokesman to announce that "if the government of Pakistan were to request the secretary-general to assist in humanitarian efforts, he would be happy to do everything in his power in this regard. Of course, the secretary-general is very much concerned about the loss of life and human suffering resulting from the recent developments in East Pakistan."

There was no public comment from Islamabad. On 7 April, however, Ambassador Shahi delivered a *note verbale* in which he protested that the position taken by the secretary-general was a violation of article 2, paragraph 7, of the United Nations Charter, which prohibits United Nations intervention in matters essentially within the jurisdiction of any state. The situation was, in any case, he said, returning to normal, despite the fact that India had given proof by deeds of its intention of undermining the national solidarity and territorial integrity of Pakistan. The deeds, the note said, included the Indian Parliament's resolution promising support to East Bengal, intensive propaganda by India, and the infiltration of armed volunteers.[5]

Despite this rebuff, the secretary-general continued his efforts and on 22 April wrote to President Yahya Khan offering humanitarian assistance on behalf of the United Nations system. In the letter, the full text of which was released on 12 May,[6] he reit-

The Secretary-General's Offer of Assistance 7

erated his concern at the situation in East Pakistan in the light of information he had received form various sources, "including reports from United Nations personnel who have recently returned from there," The reports were not identified. They were presumably those of development program staff and other aid officials who had been forced to leave East Pakistan in the aftermath of the 25 March crackdown.

He also addressed himself to the Pakistan government's strongly expressed objection to his earlier public offer of assistance and drew a fine and eminently rational distinction between the Charter injunction against intervention in essentially domestic affairs and the organization's duty under chapter 1 of the Charter "to achieve international cooperation in solving international problems of an economic, social, cultural or humanitarian character" and to be "a center for harmonizing the actions of nations in the attainment of these common ends."

He was, he wrote, "mindful of the position of the Pakistani government" in the matter as conveyed to him by Ambassador Shahi. In the discharge of his responsibilities as secretary-general he had always, he emphasized, "scrupulously observed the provisions of the United Nations Charter, including those of article 2, paragraph 7," and would continue to do so. But, he added, "I am also deeply conscious of the responsibility of the United Nations within the framework of international economic and social cooperation, to help promote and ensure, to all extent possible, human well-being and humanitarian principles."

In the light of these responsibilities, he believed that the United Nations and its specialized agencies had "a most useful role to play, with the consent of your government," in providing emergency assistance to relieve "the widespread misery, hardships and suffering which have befallen the population in East Pakistan as a result of recent events."

He concluded by offering "on behalf of the United Nations family of organizations, all possible assistance to help the government in its task of bringing urgently needed relief for the plight of the population of East Pakistan in the present emergency." "I am," he emphasized, "making this offer prompted purely by humanitarian considerations and sincerely hope that Your Excellency will give a positive response to it."

In the interval between the secretary-general's public offer of assistance of 1 April and his formal letter of 22 April, events moved quickly. The news from East Pakistan was conflicting. There were press reports of continued fighting, but these were denied in official Pakistan government statements, which said that order was being restored and that there had been no "untoward incidents" in various towns in East Pakistan. The formation of the Democratic Republic of Bangladesh was proclaimed on 17 April in Chuadanga, which was designated as the provisional capital. The following day the town was captured by the Pakistan Army, suggesting that the civil war was nearing an end. Whatever the uncertainties of the situation in East Pakistan, there was clear evidence of increasing great-power interest. On 2 April President Nikolai Podgorny of the USSR appealed to President Yahya Khan to end the repression in East Pakistan and to move toward a political settlement. In a 13 April message, Chinese Prime Minister Chou En-lai pledged China's full support to Pakistan and maintained that the crisis was purely internal.[7]

There was evidence too of a developing tragedy that demanded international humanitarian assistance. The flow of refugees from East Pakistan had begun and was gathering momentum. Already there were reports from Indian sources that 600,000 refugees had crossed the border, and the Indian government had indicated through the representative of the United Nations high commissioner for refugees in New Delhi and through direct contacts in New York that it might seek international aid to cope with the influx. On 23 April, the day after the secretary-general's letter to President Yahya Khan, Ambassador Sen delivered the Indian government's formal request for assistance to the secretary-general.

It was clear that the crisis was deepening, and that aid would have to be provided in some form to help restore reasonable conditions of life in East Pakistan and permit the repatriation of the refugees. For the time being normal international assistance to

The Secretary-General's Offer of Assistance 9

the area had virtually ceased. International aid experts had been withdrawn after the crackdown in March and could not return to their posts. Bilateral assistance was also in jeopardy. Apart from the practical difficulties of implementing aid programs, many donor governments were under strong domestic pressure either to suspend assistance or to decline to make further commitments. Strenuous efforts were being made by interested governments, with the assistance of Robert S. McNamara, president of the World Bank, to devise a formula that would permit the continuation of aid to Pakistan and encourage a peaceful solution of the crisis in East Pakistan. By late April they appeared to be nearing success.

On 3 May Ambassador Shahi delivered President Yahya Khan's response to the secretary-general's offer. It was unforthcoming, although much less so than Ambassador Shahi's earlier reaction. It could, U Thant commented to his under-secretary-general for special political affairs, Roberto Guyer, be taken as positive. The president made no reference to article 2, paragraph 7, of the Charter. Instead, he welcomed the secretary-general's offer and expressed his conviction that it was prompted by U Thant's "sincerity and deep personal commitment to humanitarian principles." He was also aware of the organization's responsibilities in the field of economic and social cooperation. There was, however, no immediate need for assistance.

"The present situation in East Pakistan is," the letter said, "that adequate supplies of medicine, foodstuffs and other daily necessities of life are available. No cause for concern has so far been expressed by local authorities. The fact of the matter is that Indian and Western press reports of heavy casualties and widespread destruction and misery are highly exaggerated, if not altogether tendentious. The forces of Pakistan, having restored the situation, are now engaged in assisting the provincial administration in relief and rehabilitation operations."

The Pakistani authorities were assessing the possible need for international assistance and, as soon as the work was completed, would have a clear and comprehensive picture of the requirements. "International assistance, if and when required," the president added, would "be administered by Pakistan's relief agencies, which are well prepared and well equipped to undertake the task."[8]

The president's letter temporarily closed the door to international assistance, but did not lock it. Two weeks later the door was opened. On 17 May M. M. Ahmed, the economic adviser to President Yahya Khan, visited New York after talks in Washington and informed the secretary-general that Pakistan had decided to accept his offer of international assistance.

At a press conference later the same day, Ahmed disclosed his government's intention of working out arrangements with United Nations experts for "a cooperative effort" to deliver aid to East Pakistan, but he did not explain the reasons for the shift in policy. According to newspaper reports, it was the outcome of diplomatic pressures.[9] During discussions in London on 22 and 23 April with British Prime Minister Edward Heath and Foreign Secretary Sir Alec Douglas-Home, McNamara was reported to have secured Britain's agreement to cooperate with the United States in an international economic effort to shore up the Pakistan economy, provided Pakistan agreed to seek an accommodation with the Bangalees and would permit an international relief program in East Pakistan. Ahmed was said to have given assurances during his talks with President Nixon, Secretary of State William Rogers, and Henry Kissinger in Washington that Pakistan would comply with these conditions. As a result, the International Bank for Reconstruction and Development and the International Monetary Fund planned to send a survey team to Pakistan in June and to convene the Pakistan Aid Consortium in Paris later that month.

At the secretary-general's request, Ambassador Shahi confirmed his government's acceptance of the secretary-general's offer of assistance in a letter dated 22 May.[10] The letter detailed Pakistan's preliminary estimate of requirements—250,000 tons of food grain, 100,000 tons of edible oil, 15 coastal vessels and 15 smaller vessels, and 500 vehicles—and confirmed the government's decision that foreign and United Nations experts and personnel who had left East Pakistan during the disturbances could return. The letter accepted the secretary-general's suggestion that

The Secretary-General's Offer of Assistance 11

a representative of the secretary-general should be sent to Pakistan to coordinate the assistance provided. The government would, Ambassador Shahi stated, be willing to receive the secretary-general's representative "on the understanding that his role and activities would be within the framework of humanitarian assistance." There was one potentially troublesome rider to Pakistan's acceptance of a United Nations relief effort: the government still maintained that international assistance would be administered by Pakistan's relief agencies, although it was "prepared to associate UNICEF and World Food Program personnel" in planning and organizing relief programs. In less unusual circumstances, the stipulation need have caused no difficulty. In the situation in East Pakistan, a much greater degree of international control over the use of assistance would be necessary to satisfy donor governments that aid was in fact reaching the people for whom it was intended.

Ambassador Shahi's letter cleared the way for a more direct United Nations contribution to the mitigation of the crisis in East Pakistan. Hitherto, although the secretary-general had taken part in the political and diplomatic consultations that had been in progress in New York and the capitals of the governments concerned since the beginning of the crisis, the organization's role had been peripheral. It had been little more than an instrument that was available if member governments chose to use it. It now became the principal conduit of international efforts to mitigate the effects of the crisis in the hope of reaching a political solution.

The organization had already embarked on what was to develop into a large-scale effort to assist the refugees from East Pakistan in India. In response to the Indian government's request addressed to him on 23 April, the secretary-general had, after consultations with the heads of the United Nations specialized agencies, designated the office of the high commissioner for refugees, Sadruddin Aga Khan, as the focus for coordinating assistance from the organizations and programs of the United Nations system. A team headed by the deputy high commissioner visited India to assess needs, and on 19 May the secretary-general appealed to governments, intergovernmental and nongovernmental organizations, and private contributors for help in meeting the refugees' needs.[11]

That operation was under way. The objective now was to organize a comparable relief effort in East Pakistan. The two operations were to be formally and organizationally separate but were seen from the beginning as related undertakings. Voluntary repatriation of the refugees was the stated goal of all parties and the Indian government's initial estimate of needs had been based on the assumption that the refugees would be able to return to their homes within six months. It was reasonable to suppose that a successful relief operation in East Pakistan, by improving conditions in the country, would increase the chances of halting and eventually reversing the flow of refugees. In the event, these hopes were disappointed. Without a political solution, it was impossible either to organize an effective relief operation in East Pakistan or to effect the return of the Bangalees who had fled to India.

The secretary-general's conversation with M. M. Ahmed and Ambassador Shahi's subsequent letter of confirmation provided the secretary-general with the governmental consent he needed to initiate a relief operation in East Pakistan, but many issues had to be settled prior to this undertaking.

As a first step, after consulting further with Ambassador Shahi, he decided to send Ismat Kittani, his assistant secretary-general for inter-agency affairs, to Islamabad to discuss arrangements for United Nations relief assistance with that government. The secretary-general had earlier designated Kittani's office as the focal point within the secretariat for coordinating United Nations action in natural disasters and similar emergency situations. The main purpose of the mission was to prepare for workable and mutually acceptable arrangements with the Pakistani government for ensuring the most effective mobilization and delivery of relief assistance from and through the United Nations system.

The secretary-general agreed that before traveling to Pakistan Kittani should consult with those United Nations agencies directly concerned and with governments and institutions prepared to participate in the relief operation. On 28 May Kittani accordingly visited Washington, where officials of the World Bank and

The Secretary-General's Offer of Assistance 13

IMF briefed him on the economic and financial situation in Pakistan, and United States officials informed him of the contemplated United States contribution to a relief program. This included the provision of food grains and of coastal vessels. World Bank officials confirmed that Pakistan's financial position—internal and external—was extremely serious.

Kittani had hoped to meet British government officials in London, but was unable to do so because his visit would have coincided with a public holiday. In Geneva he was able to confer with the director-general of WHO, the high commissioner for refugees, the secretary-general of the League of Red Cross Societies, and in Rome—despite a public holiday—with the director-general of FAO and the executive director of WFP.

Kittani arrived in Pakistan on 3 June and the following day had a forty-minute meeting with the president and foreign secretary. The president was, Kittani reported to the secretary-general, "personally very warm" and unequivocally reiterated his desire to let the United Nations provide the auspices for substantial relief operations in East Pakistan. Complying with his instructions, Kittani informed the president of the secretary-general's concern, which was shared by the executive heads of the specialized agencies concerned, that there should be effective coordination in the planning and implementation of the operation at all stages. He particularly emphasized that the United Nations must be able to assure the international community in general, and donors in particular, that relief assistance would reach the intended beneficiaries, the people of East Pakistan. In order to ensure this, and recognizing that the distribution of assistance would have to be undertaken by Pakistani authorities and agencies, he insisted that the United Nations must be associated with all phases of the operation, including the distribution of supplies, and enjoy full freedom of movement. The president accepted all three points and undertook to ensure the full cooperation of his government at all levels.

The other senior officials with whom Kittani conferred were equally friendly and ready to cooperate in the relief operation. They accepted without demur the arrangements for the operation outlined by Kittani. These included the appointment by the government of a counterpart interdepartmental group, which would work in close cooperation with an inter-agency group to be established in Dacca under Bahgat El-Tawil, the United Nations official whom the secretary-general had designated as his representative in East Pakistan.

On 7 June Kittani flew to Karachi with El-Tawil and the following day introduced him as the secretary-general's representative in East Pakistan to the governor, General Tikka Khan, to the chief secretary, to the transportation secretary, and to the relief commissioner. Kittani outlined El-Tawil's terms of reference and the minimum requirements for his mission and was assured of full cooperation at all levels.

With these meetings the first phase of the translation of the secretary-general's offer of humanitarian assistance into practical relief action was completed. The subsequent phases were to prove much more arduous.

When Kittani left Dacca for headquarters on 8 June, he was sanguine about the short-term outlook for United Nations action. He was reasonably confident that the operation to be initiated under United Nations auspices could provide the relief needed to deal with the immediate emergency. Many details remained to be worked out, but the local authorities had accepted the elements considered essential for an effective operation, including the presence of the representative of the secretary-general, freedom of movement for United Nations personnel, the creation of coordinating machinery on both the government and the United Nations side, and the establishment of direct communications with United Nations Headquarters. What was more, the Pakistan officials concerned had shown considerable good will. Members of the World Bank/IMF mission who had begun their survey in East Pakistan confirmed Kittani's impression that the attitude of the civil and military authorities had improved and considered that there were encouraging prospects of mobilizing relief operations through the port of Chittagong. The representatives of donor governments whom Kittani had met in Islamabad and Dacca welcomed both the results of his talks and the projected United Nations operation as a way to facilitate the introduction of assistance by their governments.

The longer-term outlook was more disquieting. With no political resolution of the dispute that underlay the "man-made calamity," as President Yahya Khan had called it, internal tension would continue, and the risk of an international confrontation would grow. It was, Kittani suggested, for Pakistanis to find the formula of national reconciliation that would resolve the crisis. That would, he noted, require boldness, imagination, and a spirit of compromise and reconciliation on all sides. Although there seemed to be a consensus among the diplomats and others with whom he had discussed the situation that the president sincerely desired to transfer powers to the elected representatives of the people, there were, Kittani reported, no political leaders in East Pakistan with whom the government could consult and negotiate.

This was an understatement. Sheikh Mujib was in jail, some leaders were dead, and others had gone underground. One— Justice Abu Syed Chowdhury—was fighting to keep his seat on the United Nations Commission on Human Rights, from which the Pakistan government wished to remove him.[12] The prospects for settling the political conflict were therefore dim. It remained to be seen whether the forthcoming humanitarian effort would help to ease the crisis and whether it could be successfully undertaken in a country torn by internal dissension.

CHAPTER 2

UNEPRO—The Start-Up: June-July 1971

The humanitarian relief operation was taking shape. The pace, in the view of large and articulate segments of public opinion and in the eyes of many governments, was unconscionably slow.

As the sheer scale of the disaster became apparent, the demand for action became more and more insistent, and dissatisfaction with the little the United Nations appeared to be doing more vocal. The flow of refugees to India had become a flood, belying the optimistic view that peace had been restored in East Pakistan and that conditions were returning to normal. At the end of April Indian sources reported that 600,000 refugees had entered India. A month later the figure was 3.5 million. As newspaper, radio, and television reports depicted the human tragedy to millions of readers and viewers, a wave of sympathy and alarm swept many countries.

There was added cause for anxiety. The threat to international peace was becoming evident. In a speech to the Indian Parliament on 24 May, Prime Minister Gandhi spoke of the refugee problem. She welcomed U Thant's appeal for contributions to assist the refugees, although regretting the immoderately long time the world was taking to react. She pleaded with other powers to recognize the need for a political solution that would enable the refugees to return to their homes. "If the world does not take heed," she said, "we shall be constrained to take all measures as may be necessary to ensure our own security and the preservation and development of the structure of our social and economic life."[1]

The situation seemed to demand United Nations action, on humanitarian grounds and to preserve international peace. The organization's response appeared trivial. The crisis had been debated as a side issue in the spring session of the Economic and Social Council, but nothing practical or positive had emerged from the discussion. So far as the public knew, the secretary-

UNEPRO—The Start-Up

general and the United Nations had done no more than launch an appeal for the refugees in India and initiate discussions with Pakistan regarding a relief operation in East Pakistan.

The doubts, anxiety, and exasperation of informed, and usually friendly, public opinion were summed up in a series of three blunt, provocative questions that the president of the United Nations Correspondents Association posed to the secretary-general on 3 June.[2] Louis Foy asked: First, could the secretary-general give an accounting of the cyclone aid channeled through the United Nations to East Pakistan since November 1970? The response to any new appeal might, he suggested, depend on the organization's "credibility" as a coordinator of aid. Second, the millions of refugees entering India were turning military operations in East Pakistan into a potential threat to India's political and economic stability: at what point did the secretary-general think the United Nations might consider the events as ceasing to be an internal matter of Pakistan's? Finally, in the face of events in East Pakistan, the secretary-general and the United Nations had "remained silent, dealing only with peripheral humanitarian problems in a half-hearted way." "Does the United Nations," Louis Foy asked, "deserve public support with such a record?"

U Thant did not answer the first two questions. Instead he reminded correspondents of his offer of United Nations "humanitarian involvement" in late March and of the Pakistan government's eventual positive response. "I very much hope," he said, "that the negotiations now going on between Mr. Kittani and the Pakistani authorities will generate appropriate and effective channels of international aid to the afflicted areas." He also made his own feelings plain. "The happenings in East Pakistan constitute," he said, "one of the most tragic episodes in human history . . . a very terrible blot on a page of human history." He did not however explain the practical and political obstacles to action by the organization or the quiet and unpublicized steps he and concerned governments were taking to deal with the underlying causes or bring about a political solution to the problem. As the summer wore on and the crisis worsened, impatient questions about the United Nations response both to the humanitarian problem and to the underlying political issues were a staple of press conferences and briefings at Headquarters and elsewhere. The answers did little to reassure the public.

Governments were equally concerned at the absence of decisive steps to respond to the disaster in East Pakistan and its tragic repercussions. They conveyed their concern to the secretary-general more discreetly and with greater understanding of the constraints that limited his action. They must have been aware too of the extent to which their own efforts to damp the crisis were hampered by disagreements among themselves and by the obduracy of the parties most closely concerned. In a letter dated 8 June U Thant responded to an inquiry from the British foreign secretary for information about the progress in launching the relief operation. There was, as a British spokesman said in a classic understatement at a press conference at UN headquarters two days later, "a measure of impatience" in Britain and other West European countries at the lack of action. There had been vigorous and well-publicized protests from influential voluntary organizations that "diplomatic niceties" were being allowed to block urgently needed relief action. In his reply the secretary-general reported the progress that had been made. Kittani had had "satisfactory conversations in Islamabad." A representative for the coordination of international humanitarian relief was already in Dacca. "I doubt very much," he wrote, "whether even this much could have been achieved under the circumstances, which are well known to you, without observing the greatest reserve as to publicity." In his experience, a choice had to be made, he said, between "proceeding quickly and allowing a natural desire for favorable publicity to complicate the task at hand." The explanation seems to have satisfied Sir Alec Douglas-Home. On 10 June he told the House of Commons: "The United Nations is our considered choice for the coordination of all the relief work." He said it was the only way of mobilizing the greatest flow of international resources "with the least risk of ulterior political complications."[3]

The United States government, like the United Kingdom government, was committed to the principle of using the United Nations as a neutral vehicle for relief action in East Pakistan and was

UNEPRO—The Start-Up

deeply perturbed by the fumbling that seemed to mark the program's organization. A paper handed to the secretariat in June put the matter bluntly. Realistic planning and prompt efficient action had not, it said, so far been characteristic of United Nations bodies dealing with the present subcontinent situation. The statement was irrefutable, although the secretary-general might well have pointed out in reply that the failure was as much the responsibility of member states and intergovernmental bodies as of their servants in the secretariat. In any event, the United States government continuously pushed for more vigorous action, through its permanent representative and through other channels, and eventually succeeded in making its views known.

Other governments pressed their views on the secretary-general. On 15 June Sardar Swaran Singh, the Indian minister for external affairs, talked with the secretary-general and told a subsequent press conference that he had urged U Thant "to use his tremendous influence" to stabilize conditions in East Pakistan to encourage the refugees to return. Asked why the Security Council was not seized of the matter, he said that it was up to the secretary-general "to make a move." No one asked why India did not avail itself of its right under article 35 of the Charter to bring the situation to the attention of the Security Council. In a statement to the Indian parliament on 20 July, he provided the answer. India, Singh told the House, had raised the Bangladesh issue in the Economic and Social Council in May and would do so in other United Nations organs "provided we are assured of sufficient support for any proposition we expect that organ to adopt."[4] In the meantime the governments of India and Pakistan, through their permanent representatives in New York, were actively seeking the good offices of the secretary-general to secure the safety or repatriation of their officials and nationals in East Pakistan and India respectively.

The secretary-general was pressured from all sides. He was the natural focus for complaints of inactivity and demands for an instant solution, but was without the resources, the political directives, or the consensus among interested governments that would enable him to become a center for effective measures to resolve the crisis. The political complications were in themselves enormous, and there was no prospect of early intergovernmental agreement to remove them. The practical difficulties of mounting a relief operation—even if the political obstacles could have been ignored—were no less forbidding.

The United Nations was not, as U Thant said later in the year, equipped to deal with great humanitarian emergencies.[5] This had been a matter of concern to the secretary-general and to United Nations legislative bodies for many years. In 1964 the Economic and Social Council asked the secretary-general to "take the lead" in setting up "appropriate arrangements" in conjunction with the specialized agencies and the League of Red Cross Societies to provide "rapid and concerted" relief assistance in disaster situations.

The following year the Council gave its imprimatur to a set of proposed arrangements under which a key role was to be played by the resident representatives in developing countries of the United Nations Development Program. In late 1970, the secretary-general, again with the sanction of the Economic and Social Council, took a further step to strengthen the arrangements and appointed the assistant secretary-general for inter-agency affairs to represent him in matters relating to disaster assistance and to provide a focal point from which to exercise more effective coordination.

The appointment filled in the incompleteness of previous arrangements—which had become apparent in the Peruvian earthquake earlier in the year—but seems to have been regarded as an interim measure. In his comprehensive report to the Economic and Social Council on disaster relief issued in May 1971,[6] the secretary-general commented that the establishment of the focal point had made it possible "to improve somewhat" the functioning of the United Nations system in disaster situations, particularly in the matter of the exchange of information on plans and activities and contact with the resident representatives of UNDP, but that the focal point lacked the resources to do more, "no additional posts having been created or credits voted." The secretary-general accordingly proposed the creation of a disaster relief

UNEPRO—The Start-Up

office, with a small staff and a rather imposing array of functions. He was also, he said, in "close agreement" with a United Kingdom proposal for the appointment of a disaster relief coordinator. There were, he said, differences of emphasis: the United Kingdom proposal, for example, stressed the role of the coordinator in organizing relief at the time of a disaster, while the secretary-general gave "no less weight" to the new office's part in promoting the study, prevention, control, and prediction of disasters, predisaster planning and preparedness, and some aspects of relief and rehabilitation. These proposals had yet to be considered by the Economic and Social Council and the General Assembly. For the time being, there was, as the report commented wryly in discussing the East Pakistan cyclone disaster, "a sense of frustration" throughout the international community, a realization that international efforts at times of catastrophe "did not measure up to the techinical capacity and resources of modern society or satisfy the conscience of the world."

In mid-1971 the staff and machinery needed to cope with humanitarian emergencies were lacking, and policies had still to be defined. In this situation the secretary-general could do no more than use his influence—which was less than some observers thought—and attempt to improvise a relief operation in what was an increasingly difficult situation.

On 5 June the secretary-general announced that he had received "further encouraging reports" from his representative in Pakistan and was confident that "in a very short time" the United Nations family of agencies would be able "to contribute substantially to the alleviation of the present situation in East Pakistan."[7] Four days later there was further news of the progress that was being made.[8] Bahgat El-Tawil, the representative of the secretary-general in East Pakistan, had arrived in Dacca on 7 June and had assumed his duties as focal point for international relief assistance. A counterpart Pakistani interdepartmental committee was being set up and would work in close cooperation with a group of specialized agency representatives in Dacca headed by El-Tawil. A direct communications link with headquarters through Rawalpindi and Geneva had been set up by 9 June. Within forty-eight hours Pakistan government approval was obtained and the link was operating, the result both of the cooperative attitude of the Pakistani authorities and of the efficiency of the field service radio staff who had flown to Dacca with El-Tawil. These developments were recapitulated by Kittani at a press conference on 11 June in which he outlined the needs and indicated the type of response that was envisaged. "We are," he told correspondents, "providing an umbrella and we must now make the maximum use of it."

On 16 June the secretary-general took the first public step to make the umbrella more than an ineffectual symbol of international concern by appealing to "governments, intergovernmental and nongovernmental organizations and private institutions and sources" to contribute in cash or kind to alleviate the suffering that had "befallen the people of East Pakistan."[9]

The appeal seems at least in part a gesture intended to reassure those who doubted the organization's will or capacity to act. Only two days earlier Ambassador George Bush of the United States had informed the secretariat that his delegation was disturbed by the slowness with which the operation was developing. The operation launched to assist the refugees in India was, the United States considered, simply a "palliative." The urgent task was to "reverse the flow" by helping to improve the situation in East Pakistan. The appeal dealt indirectly with that point but did little else to indicate either how the operation would be organized or what specifically it would seek to do.

After recounting the steps the secretary-general had taken since 22 April, including the launching of the earlier appeal for assistance to the refugees, the appeal reported that in the discussions between the Pakistani authorities and Assistant Secretary-General Kittani there had been "full agreement on the manner in which the operation should be organized." The government accepted the principle that the United Nations must be in a position to assure the international community and particular donors that all relief assistance would reach the people of East Pakistan, and it was ready to extend "full cooperation at all levels" to the United Nations personnel who would be associated in planning and executing the relief operation.

UNEPRO—The Start-Up

The appeal noted that the secretary-general had appointed a representative in East Pakistan to coordinate the relief work of the United Nations and the specialized agencies but provided no further information on the organizational arrangements envisaged. The operation would be separate from the program of assistance to refugees from East Pakistan in India, although the two operations would, the appeal pointed out, be related "to the extent that as conditions in East Pakistan are improved, there will be a better possibility of arresting and reversing the flow of refugees."

Nor did the appeal list specific relief needs. Instead, it referred to the initial assessment provided by Ambassador Shahi on 22 May and went on to say that the further appraisals of needs being conducted by the government and the United Nations agencies concerned "point to the urgency of mobilizing substantial external resources, notably food and transport, for relief action." The secretary-general concluded by urging governments, intergovernmental and nongovernmental organizations, and private donors to make contributions in cash and in kind, and suggested that they should so far as possible make use of "the established procedures of the United Nations family, particularly those of the World Food Program and UNICEF, whose association in the planning and organization of the task of relief has been expressly welcomed by the government of Pakistan."

The appeal was silent on many points: the actual needs to be met, the shape that the operation was intended to take, or the means by which the United Nations proposed to assure donors that supplies reached intended recipients. The answers to these and other questions were still being worked out. What is surprising in retrospect is not that questions were left unanswered—in the situation in East Pakistan that was understandable—but that the appeal should not have been frankly labeled an interim report that would be supplemented as soon as possible. As it was, the appeal was likely to be dismissed as simply a pious exhortation backed with shadowy promises of coordination of a kind that many observers had found disappointing in the post-cyclone relief operation.

A week later there was a new development that had not been

foreshadowed in the appeal, and which seemed to imply a shift toward more active United Nations participation in the organization of the relief effort. On 21 June the secretary-general announced the appointment of Stephen R. Tripp as "headquarters coordinator, within the framework of the office for inter-agency affairs, for international humanitarian assistance from and through the United Nations to East Pakistan."[10]

There was, the secretary-general said, "an immediate need for an official with extensive experience in large-scale relief operations who will be responsible to headquarters, on a full-time basis, for maintaining constant contacts at the international level with the governments, agencies and other participants in this operation." In particular Tripp was to maintain close liaison with the secretary-general's representative in East Pakistan and his interagency group in Dacca in order to ensure the prompt and effective implementation of relief measures in the area.

Tripp was well qualified. From 1964 to 1971 he had served as disaster relief coordinator with the United States Agency for International Development. He now found himself, however, in a new environment, international instead of national, with no established machinery, confronting a situation in which disaster relief could only theoretically be divorced from political considerations.

In many ways Tripp was a natural choice. His experience in disaster relief and his reputation in Washington—which was bound to be a principal source of assistance—were important assets. On the other hand, he must have been handicapped by his lack of knowledge of the United Nations and of multinational ways of action. The attraction of an outside expert is obvious, particularly when the secretariat is being sharply criticized by major contributors. It might, however, have been better to select an official, perhaps from UNICEF, UNDP, or one of the specialized agencies, who combined experience in field operations with knowledge of the United Nations system. Had such an official been available, some difficulties might have been avoided and more effective headquarters support might have been provided for the relief operation in the field.

UNEPRO—The Start-Up   25

In any event the new coordinator had hardly settled into his job when it was announced that he would move from New York to Geneva, at least for the month of July. Cynics noted that the transfer coincided with the summer session of the Economic and Social Council which takes so many officials to Geneva in July. In fact there were sound operational reasons for the move. Geneva was the center of the refugee operation under the high commissioner for refugees, and in many ways it was the logical base for the parallel operation in East Pakistan.

In Dacca El-Tawil was struggling, with admirable phlegm and pertinacity, to put together the missing pieces of the operation. With only a five-hour briefing in New York, supplemented by talks with Kittani at Karachi airport and on the long flight from Karachi around the coast to Dacca, he was plunged into the task of converting vague directives into realistic, working arrangements that would be credible to potential donors.

He had no professional staff to assist him. Two field service radio technicians accompanied him from Karachi and he was supplied with a field service secretary and a security officer; but, as he later reported, his task would have been easier if he had had professionsl colleagues, if only to act as "sounding boards" for ideas. It would, he later suggested, have helped to have a small backstopping office at headquarters with a full-time working-level staff to organize and analyze information systematically.

An early exchange of cables illustrates his predicament. When, he asked, would the UNICEF and WFP team "whose activities I am to coordinate" arrive; what emergency aid had been approved or was under consideration; and what commitments had been made to donors? The reply must have seemed unhelpful. The UNICEF and WFP staff were said to be already in Dacca. The only emergency assistance approved was a $4 million WFP commitment for cyclone relief, and there was no UN commitment to donors beyond the availability of various agencies to channel assistance in accordance with standard procedures and agreements.

There were other difficulties. After an encouraging series of meetings on 7 June with agency representatives and senior government officials, the Pakistani counterpart committee, one of the principal cogs in the envisaged machinery, proved to be an elusive body. The convener was appointed, and was cooperative, but it was 18 June before the government of East Pakistan announced the constitution of the committee and its terms of reference. It was to "act as the focal point for the UN inter-agency committee at Dacca with a view to receiving and defining the various relief needs that will be channeled through the UN."[11]

The committee convened for the first time on 24 June and even then was slow in getting down to work. A statement of needs was promised for the end of the month. It did not come until July.

Defining the needs was not easy, but the real difficulty was, as El-Tawil later suggested, the "apathy, disaffection and sense of helplessness" of many of the officials concerned. There was, as might have been expected, an uneasy relationship between the civilian officials in East Pakistan and the martial-law authorities. Some Bangalee civil servants, moreover, were still influenced by Sheikh Mujib's call for noncooperation and had, one observer reported, transformed inertia into a fine art. Even civil servants whose loyalties did not lie with the insurgents were nervous and disinclined to do anything that might make their unhappy position worse. At least one official seems to have engaged in quiet sabotage. A list of needs submitted to the headquarters coordinator included a request for "20 prisoners' vans." It is hard to believe that the list was submitted in good faith by a simple-minded soldier.

The relief needs had been stated in broad terms in Ambassador Shahi's letter of 22 May. They were restated by the chief secretary of the government of East Pakistan when he met Kittani and El-Tawil on 7 June, with the addition of a new element, the provision of cash doles for the resettlement of returning refugees and other "affected persons," the millions of people who had fled from the towns to places of refuge in the countryside.

Some observers believed that the government's estimate of food requirements was too low. Many considered that there was an imminent threat of famine, as a result of both the disruption of agriculture and the dislocation of the distribution system. El-Tawil reported that USAID representatives with whom he had

UNEPRO—The Start-Up 27

talked on 19 June were certain that the food shortage for 1971/72 would exceed the estimates. They were also worried about the problem of the equitable distribution of food supplies. There was, they said, a wide discrepancy between Pakistan government policy and its implementation at the local level. The local peace committees, which were responsible for food distribution in some places, were reported to be guilty of bias and the harassment of people suspected of sympathizing with insurgents. Without United Nations staff on the vessels carrying supplies and at the distribution centers, it would, they argued, be impossible to ensure that relief goods reached all sections of the population.

The two issues raised in El-Tawil's conversations with USAID representatives—the possibility of famine in East Pakistan and the organization of effective United Nations supervision of the relief-goods' end-use—were crucial and largely determined the planning of the operation during the remainder of the year.

Famine remained a specter, but it was becoming clear that the presence of the secretary-general's representative in Dacca with a purely coordinating role would neither satisfy donor governments nor provide a framework within which an effective relief operation could be conducted. Glen Haydon, an American disaster-relief expert, who was sent to Dacca in late June to assist El-Tawil, put the alternative bluntly. The choice was, he wrote, between a semi-passive coordination point and a line-type operation. The feeling seemed to be that "everybody, the agencies, should just do their own thing and keep the representatives of the secretary-general informed. Duplication can perhaps be minimized by this method, but there will be no innovative, strong, operational UN leadership. . . ." He was also less hopeful than some of his colleagues about relations with the local authorities. He wrote, "We are being led around by the government, shown what they want us to see." He proposed a strengthened organization in Dacca, which would attempt to weave the various agency activities into an overall United Nations program and would be backed by a network of 19 district liaison officers.

In Geneva Tripp was similarly concerned. The action of the Pakistani armed forces had "so unbalanced the society that its fragile infrastructure is broken," he wrote. The transport system was dislocated—movement by rail was down by 65 to 70 percent. Food supplies were threatened, rice production was estimated by the government to be 12 to 20 percent below normal, and the distribution of relief was thwarted by "the dual system" of military and civil administration. In any case "large areas and populations" were outside government control. East Pakistan faced "famine, epidemics and death." The United Nations must "make good" on the appeal launched by the secretary-general by appointing a "dynamic" administrator to carry out a "joint government/ United Nations plan."

For the time being these questions of organization and direction remained unresolved. Tripp and Haydon were both new to the United Nations, less aware than their colleagues of the political constraints on United Nations action, and still unfamiliar with the convolute processes involved in organizing action by the United Nations system.

In a statement released on 15 July[12] to coincide with the summer session of the Economic and Social Council in Geneva, the secretary-general announced that he had received the first comprehensive review by United Nations officials of the relief needs of East Pakistan. These were estimated to total $28,200,000 for an undefined "initial" period. The needs to be met included food, transport, clothing, blankets, corrugated iron sheets, tents, and medical supplies, and cash to set up a $10 million working fund.

From the statement of needs and the accompanying account of measures being taken by the United Nations system, the voluntary agencies, and donor countries, a diffuse picture emerges of hopeful and well-meaning effort with no clear sense of direction. The release was silent on organizational matters. It said simply that in the month that had elapsed since the secretary-general's appeal "the basic framework for the provision of relief from and through the United Nations system" had been established. No details were given, beyond a statement that the secretary-general's representative in East Pakistan and representatives of FAO, WFP, WHO, and UNICEF were working with the Pakistani government counterpart committee to plan and organize a large-scale

UNEPRO—The Start-Up

international humanitarian effort in East Pakistan. Nothing was said about the threat, real or imagined, of famine, or the way in which the secretary-general proposed to ensure that relief supplies and equipment were not diverted from the uses for which they were intended. Answers to these questions were still being sought.

The following day the Economic and Social Council discussed the two humanitarian efforts initiated by the secretary-general. The debate was curiously muted. Many delegations would have preferred not to discuss the subject. Others insisted that the Council could not ignore the humanitarian crisis in the subcontinent. In the end the Council agreed to devote one meeting to the subject.[13]

The high commissioner for refugees gave a detailed account of what he was doing as "focal point" to assist the refugees in India. As assistant secretary-general for inter-agency affairs, Ismat Kittani reported on the humanitarian operation in East Pakistan. His statement was in the main a straightforward summary of the comprehensive review that had been released the previous day. It deviated from the review in only one respect: Kittani stressed that the operation was still largely at the assessment-and-planning stage.

The discussion ended with a statement by the president of the Council, Ambassador Rachid Driss of Tunisia, which was later interpreted as "expressing full support of the secretary-general's actions in the face of the emergency in the subcontinent."[14] The record shows that Ambassador Driss did not go that far. He voiced the Council's deep concern, expressed its appreciation of the secretary-general's humanitarian spirit, and hoped that all would join in a concerted effort to help the stricken East Pakistanis.

This limited endorsement was the first and, until the General Assembly met later in the year, the only expression of support for the secretary-general's initiative by an intergovernmental body. Its lack of force and clarity reflect the uncertain balance of intergovernmental opinion and the absence of consensus which frustrated the secretary-general's efforts to work toward solving the crisis.

The president's statement was the product of consultations with all the delegations concerned and represented the highest common factor of agreement among them. In dealing with natural disasters, it is the Council's custom to adopt a unanimous resolution calling for assistance from the United Nations system and from the international community. In the case of East Pakistan a decision of that kind was inconceivable. The views of governments on the political conflict underlying the humanitarian crisis were too sharply—and, perhaps, evenly—divided to permit consensus on anything more than a general expression of concern and good will. A more specific statement would have presupposed judgments about the nature of the crisis, the character of the aid required, and the prospects of a solution, and would have resulted in an acrimonious and unproductive debate.

The fact that the secretary-general's comprehensive review was not released until after the Council session had started suggests that he himself doubted the utility of bringing the matter to the Council's notice. The subject was not on the Council's agenda, and several delegations would have preferred not to discuss it. The decision to devote one meeting to the humanitarian aspects of the crisis was reached only at the insistence of the New Zealand representative and a number of his colleagues and was the fruit of lengthy negotiation. The outcome was not impressive. It can be regarded either as an example of the Council's ability to evade thorny issues or as proof of diplomacy's capacity to extract a measure of useful agreement from a welter of conflicting positions. Whichever view is correct, the Council had at least publicly expressed collective governmental concern at the situation and had provided the secretary-general with some degree of legislative support for his initiative.

The occasion was remarkable for another reason. It was the last time that the Council took cognizance of the relief effort. It neither received nor asked for reports on the progress of the operation. It was not told of the inter-agency aspects of the undertaking and apparently did not mind. When it discussed disaster relief coordination in 1971 and again in 1972, it did not attempt to draw lessons from the experience gained in the operation in the subcontinent and did not inquire whether the secretary-general considered that any could be drawn.

Members of the Council were of course aware of the

operation—some of them were its principal supporters—and were undoubtedly influenced by it in considering the secretary-general's comprehensive report on disaster relief.[15] The Council, for example, presumably had the East Pakistan situation in mind when it decided that disaster relief arrangements should extend to man-made as well as natural disasters, or, as the Council's resolution puts it, to "other emergency situations." On the surface, however, the Council confined itself to other issues, to fine-drawn distinctions between coordination and direction and to niceties of inter-agency coordination. After July 1971 the operation ceased to be a matter primarily of inter-agency interest and moved into another realm where the Council chose not to follow.

CHAPTER 3

The Wider Issues: July-August 1971

Throughout June and July the crisis showed no signs of abatement. The faint hopes of a return to normality that had been entertained in late May were apparently illusory. The influx of refugees into India continued and by the end of June had reached over 6 million according to Indian sources. During the next month a million more were reported to have fled East Pakistan. In June international correspondents were readmitted to the country and the press, particularly in the Western countries, was flooded with reports of savage repression and destruction that further aroused public opinion and intensified the demand for international action. Reports from visiting congressmen and parliamentarians—and, of course, propaganda by the supporters of Bangladeshi independence in many capitals—added to the pressure.

In June a bizarre development, indicative of the emotion and even partisanship roused by the situation, further complicated the secretary-general's quiet efforts to bring about a solution. The report, or part of it, by the World Bank survey team that had visited East Pakistan in early June was leaked to the press and appeared to contradict the rather bland assessments of the situation published by the United Nations.[1] The president of the World Bank apologized to the government of Pakistan but did not disown the report.[2] The report's authenticity was not seriously disputed and its judgment—that there were no signs of improvement in the situation in East Pakistan nor any prospect of an early return to normality—was widely accepted as valid.

The report's impact was soon felt. For example, British Foreign Secretary Sir Alec Douglas-Home told the House of Commons on 23 June that an informal meeting of the Pakistan Aid Consortium held two days earlier had considered a report from the IBRD/IMF team, which had visited East Pakistan and Islamabad.

The Wider Issues 33

"No commitments of new aid of any kind were called for, nor were any given, although all expressed their willingness to contribute to humanitarian relief under the effective surveillance of the United Nations." So far as Britain was concerned there could, he said, be no question of new aid to Pakistan until there was "firm evidence that real progress is being made towards a political solution."[3]

President Yahya Khan's announcement, in an interview with the *Financial Times* in July, that Sheikh Mujib would very soon be tried on charges carrying the death penalty, suggested that a political solution was unlikely. The President also touched on some of the other circumstances that were complicating the search for a peaceful outcome. He was highly critical of the United Kingdom which had, he said, "fallen for the cruel, crude propaganda of India," in contrast to the United States which had caused Pakistan "no embarrassment." He charged that there were 24 camps in India to train Bangalee guerillas and warned that Pakistan would declare war if India stepped up its activities, for example, by helping to establish a guerila base area in East Pakistan. He also said that he would "allow United Nations observers into East Pakistan" to supervise the return of the refugees.[4]

These developments touched off a renewed flurry of questions, rumors, and speculations about what the United Nations was, or was not, doing to deal with the situation in East Pakistan and its wider, ever-more threatening repercussions. Speculation reached a peak at the beginning of August with the publication of reports from Washington that the United States had won the agreement of Pakistan and the United Nations to station an international group of 153 relief experts in East Pakistan under United Nations sponsorship.[5] The relief group was referred to as a "United Nations force," presumably analogous to "sales forces," "clerical forces," and the like, and was coupled in much of the speculation with rumors of a United Nations plan to station observers in the area.

On 2 August the secretary-general took steps to correct any misconceptions. In a note to correspondents he explained that "the main purpose of United Nations relief personnel in East Pakistan is to ensure that the most effective possible use is made of the relief made available by the international community." His representative in Dacca, El-Tawil, had submitted an organizational plan for staffing the "relief effort." This had been considered together with the suggestions of a secretariat group which had been consulting representatives of the agencies concerned in Geneva and was being implemented. "The United Nations activity in East Pakistan is," the note emphasized, "solely humanitarian in nature." There was no "peacekeeping" element in its terms of reference, and it was entirely misleading and erroneous to refer to it as a "United Nations force" or a United Nations observer group.[6]

In a press release issued the same day the secretary-general provided information on two separate initiatives that had also been the subject of rumors and speculation.[7]

The first was, the release stressed, "a proposal" made by U Thant to the governments concerned in his capacity as secretary-general after consultation with the high commissioner for refugees. In identical *aide-mémoires* addressed to the permanent representatives of India and Pakistan on 19 July, the secretary-general said that "one possible method" of encouraging "the voluntary repatriation of the refugees in a secure and orderly manner, which takes due account of their welfare" would be "to establish a limited representation of the high commissioner for refugees on both sides of the border." The high commissioner's representatives would be "stationed at collecting points on the Indian side, at border crossing points on both sides, and in reception centers on the Pakistan side." Before applying this arrangement on a large scale, it should be tested, the secretary-general suggested, "in two or three selected areas on both sides of the border, the areas to be suggested by the governments in consultation with the high commissioner. Were this arrangement to prove successful, it would then be possible to expand it gradually to include most, or all, of the repatriation points."

The proposal depended, of course, on the cooperation of the two governments. Pakistan accepted without difficulty. Pakistan had, the government reported on 22 June, declared a general am-

The Wider Issues 35

nesty and set up reception centers. Already 15,000 refugees had returned, and more would do so, President Yahya Khan said in another message to the secretary-general, "if only India desisted from discouraging and hindering their movement." The official Indian reply was delivered on 2 August.[8] It was long, uncompromising, and negative. The government of India expressed "their total opposition" to the suggestion and categorically stated their resentment of "any insinuation that they are preventing the refugees from returning to East Bengal." International observers, including, the *aide-mémoire* said, High Commissioner Sadruddin Aga Khan, had confirmed that India was not obstructing the refugees' return. The secretary-general's suggestion was "unrealistic, unhelpful and even dangerous" and would provide "a façade of action to divert world attention from the root cause of the problem, which is the continuation of military atrocities, leading to a further influx of refugees, and the absence of a political settlement acceptable to the people of East Pakistan and their already elected leaders."

The Indian reply effectively halted the secretary-general's initiative to encourage the repatriation of the refugees. It was the first occasion on which the record shows a note of real acerbity in communications between the secretary-general and the parties most directly concerned. The following day Ambassador Sen communicated a statement made by the Indian minister of external affairs in Parliament. The minister had told members that they might not agree with the secretary-general's judgment, but that "it was not proper to say that he drew inspiration from another country." The message was well meant, but hardly encouraging.

The second initiative was different in kind. The first continued the humanitarian efforts the secretary-general had set in motion in March 1971. The second—a memorandum the secretary-general had addressed to the president of the Security Council on 20 July—was directly political.

He explained the memorandum was intended both to record his own deep concern with the wider dangers of the situation and "to provide an opportunity for an exchange of views among the members of the Security Council on this potentially very grave situation." Under article 99 of the United Nations Charter, the secretary-general can bring to the Security Council's attention any matter that may, in his opinion, threaten the maintenance of international peace and security, and U Thant noted that, apart from his competence under the Charter, the members of the Council had on 2 December 1966 unanimously endorsed a statement fully respecting "his position and his action in bringing basic issues confronting the organization and disturbing developments in many parts of the world to their notice."[9]

The memorandum, the first considered public statement of the secretary-general's position on the political issues, recalled the steps he had taken since the beginning of the crisis, bearing in mind the "dual responsibility of the United Nations, including the secretary-general, under the Charter, both to observe the provisions of its article 2, paragraph 7, and to work, within the framework of international economic and social cooperation, to help promote and ensure human well being and humanitarian principles."

As the weeks had passed since March, the secretary-general had, he said, "become increasingly uneasy and apprehensive at the steady deterioration of the situation." In spite of the international community's response to his appeals for assistance for the refugees from East Pakistan now in India, the money and supplies made available were nowhere near sufficient, and the Indian government still faced "the appalling and disruptive problem of caring, for an unforeseeable period of time, for millions of refugees, whose number is still increasing." In East Pakistan itself international and governmental efforts "to cope with the results of two successive disasters, one of them natural" were "increasingly hampered by the lack of substantial progress towards political reconciliation." Serious food shortages, "even famine," might soon add to the sufferings of the population, unless conditions could be improved sufficiently so that a large-scale relief program could be effective. "Equally serious," the secretary-general said, "is the undoubted fact that reconciliation, an improved political atmosphere and the success of relief efforts are indispensable prerequi-

The Wider Issues

sites for the return of any large proportion of the refugees now in India. The situation is one in which political, economic and social factors had produced a series of vicious circles which largely frustrate the efforts of the authorities concerned and of the international community to deal with the vast humanitarian problems involved."

Turning to the wider consequences of "these human tragedies," the secretary-general noted that the "conflict between the principles of the territorial integrity of states and of self-determination" had often led to "fratricidal strife," and he went on to say:

> . . . In the present case there is an additional element of danger, for the crisis is unfolding in the context of the longstanding and unresolved differences between India and Pakistan—differences which gave rise to open warfare only six years ago. Although there can be no question of the deep desire of both governments for peace, tension between them shows no sign of subsiding. The situation on the borders of East Pakistan is particularly disturbing. Border clashes, clandestine raids and acts of sabotage appear to be becoming more frequent, and this is all the more serious since refugees must cross this disturbed border if repatriation is to become a reality. Nor can any of us here in the United Nations afford to forget that a major conflict in the subcontinent could all too easily expand.
>
> In tragic circumstances such as those prevailing in the subcontinent, it is all to easy to make moral judgments. It is far more difficult to face up to the political and human realities of the situation and to help the peoples concerned to find a way out of their enormous difficulties. It is this latter course which, in my view, the United Nations must follow.

The secretary-general said he had concluded that the international community could no longer stand by "watching the situation deteriorate and hoping that relief programs, humanitarian efforts and good intentions will be enough to turn the tide of human misery and potential disaster." He wrote, "It seems to me that the present tragic situation, in which humanitarian, economic and political problems are mixed in such a way as almost to defy any distinction between them, presents a challenge to the United Nations as a whole which must be met. Other situations of this kind may well occur in the future. If the organization faces up to such a situation now, it may be able to develop the new skill and the new strength required to face future situations of this kind."

For these reasons, he was taking the unusual step, he said, of reporting to the president of the Security Council on a question that had not been inscribed on the Council's agenda. "The political aspects of this matter are of such far-reaching importance that the secretary-general is not in a position to suggest precise courses of action before the members of the Security Council have taken note of the problem. I believe, however, that the United Nations, with its long experience in peacekeeping and with its varied resources for conciliation, must, and should, now play a more forthright role in attempting both to mitigate the human tragedy which has already taken place and to avert the further deterioration of the situation."

The Security Council was in a position to consider the situation, he suggested, and "to reach some agreed conclusions as to measures which might be taken." Naturally, it was for the members of the Council to decide whether such consideration should take place formally or informally, in public or in private. His primary purpose was to provide an opportunity for such discussions to take place and to express his grave concern "that all possible ways and means should be explored which might help to resolve this tragic situation."

In spite of its eloquence and compelling common sense, the secretary-general's memorandum, like his attempt to ease the repatriation of the refugees, came to nothing. The members of the Security Council went on discussing the situation informally as they had done in the past. For the time being nothing indicated that the Council would be in a position to make a decision that would help alleviate the crisis. Views were too far apart, political—and moral—judgments too disparate, and interests too divergent to provide basis for consensus.

In general terms, governments agreed only that a way must be

The Wider Issues

found to reconcile Bangalee demands for autonomy with Pakistan's insistence on the preservation of national unity, end the crisis in East Pakistan, and eliminate the threat of war between India and Pakistan. There the agreement stopped. By mid-1971 some governments accepted the view that the civil war was as good as over and believed that President Yahya Khan's willingness, once the rebellion was suppressed, to grant East Pakistan a measure of regional autonomy would suffice to end the crisis. As they saw it, the insurgents were a spent force, sustained only by India's increasingly overt support. Other governments saw the situation in terms that were much closer to the position of the Indian government, which had made its support for the Awami League clear and which obviously would not accept the defeat of the East Pakistan guerillas as a solution to the crisis.

The situation was complicated by the announcement of President Nixon's impending visit to Peking. The fact that Henry Kissinger's secret preliminary journey to China was made by way of Islamabad strengthened Indian and other suspicions that Washington's attitude in the crisis was governed by its desire to improve relations with Peking, and that the United States was leaning decisively toward Pakistan. It is far from certain that this was the case, at any rate at this stage.[10] Whether it was the case or not, relations between India and the United States worsened, and, with the conclusion on 9 August of a treaty of peace, friendship, and cooperation between India and the Soviet Union, there could be no doubt that a discussion of the East Pakistan situation in the Security Council would find the permanent members on opposite sides of the fence. The near certainty that the longstanding battle over Chinese representation in the United Nations would be settled within the next few months was a further deterrent to Security Council action.

The crucial issue was a political settlement inside East Pakistan. It was not, in these circumstances, one that lent itself to constructive discussion in the Security Council, the members of which, apart from other considerations, attached differing weights to the competing claims of the principles of territorial integrity and self-determination. The strictures of article 2, paragraph 7 of the Charter presumably deterred the secretary-general from laboring this point or suggesting possible solutions—which must in any case already have occurred to the many governments seeking a settlement outside the Security Council. One way out might have been mediation between the Awami League and the government of Pakistan. There would have been difficulties, if only because a provisional government of Bangladesh had been proclaimed and was in a state of war with the central authorities in Islamabad. Nevertheless in the course of July, the high commissioner for refugees had suggested, when asked at a press conference whether he would mediate between India and Pakistan, that it was not for him to do so and that in any event mediation was needed not between New Delhi and Islamabad, but between Islamabad and Dacca. The heavens did not fall, and the high commisioner's usefulness was undiminished. It is, however, one thing to make suggestions at a press conference and another to propose actions to a legislative body for which there is no evidence of widespread support. It was the settled opinion of the Pakistan government that its efforts to bring about a settlement were being frustrated by India, which had "created a situation in which normalcy cannot return." It would, the Pakistan government told the secretary-general in a note of 13 August, be unreasonable to seek a political solution acceptable to the insurgents who were "committing sabotage" and "bent upon bringing about famine in East Pakistan."[11] So long as these views prevailed and were confirmed by the action of the rebels, an offer of mediation was likely to be no more than an empty and futile gesture.

And it was likely to be misunderstood in many quarters. Many governments, particularly in the third world, saw the situation as essentially a part of the long, drawn-out Indo-Pakistan conflict. President Idi Amin Dada of Uganda, for example, in forwarding a contribution to the high commissioner's refugee program, had suggested that the United Nations should also address itself "to the wider issue of bringing the two countries together to work for a peaceful settlement by discussion."[12] An effort to explain that the crisis was primarily an internal crisis that had gravely affected a neighboring country would have been unproductive and would have seemed to be hewing unreasonably close to the Indian line. There are possibly situations in which the secretary-general might be authorized to intervene in a civil war, but this was not one of them. The only hope was that governments, particularly those represented in the Pakistan Aid Consortium, could persuade the government of Pakistan to seek an accommodation and induce its adversaries to accept something less than the total independence to which many of them were committed.

In his memorandum to the president of the Security Council, U Thant deprecated easy moral judgments. He was not, however, content to follow the advice of the Irish priest who urged his flock to tread carefully the narrow path that divides right from wrong.[13] Where moral judgments were called for and might have an effect, he did not hesitate to express his views. On 3 August, in a personal message to President Yahya Khan, he expressed his concern at the impending trial of Sheikh Mujib and "earnestly appealed that nothing be done . . . which might further increase tension and emotion." He had, he said, talked to many representatives, and "in their view the chances of the restoration of peace and normalcy in the region are remote unless some kind of accommodation is reached."

A week later, in reply to questions, a United Nations spokesman said the secretary-general considered that the trial of Sheikh Mujib was "an extremely delicate and sensitive matter which falls within the domestic competence of a member state—in this case, Pakistan. It is also a matter of extraordinary interest and concern in many quarters, from a humanitarian as well as a political point of view. . . . The secretary-general shares the feelings of many representatives that any developments concerning the fate of Sheikh Mujibur Rahman will inevitably have repercussions outside the borders of Pakistan."[14] The statement did not mention the personal message to President Yahya Khan. Nor did it mention the private approaches U Thant had made to influential leaders, among them Tungku Abdul Rahman, the secretary-general of the Islamic secretariat. Pakistan's response was predictable. On 16 August Ambassador Shahi, upon the instructions of his government, regretted Secretary-General U Thant's statement which, he complained, exceeded "both the bounds of humanitarian concern and the competence of the United Nations" under the Charter. His government could not accept "any attempt to interfere in Pakistan's internal affairs or to dictate the kind of political accommodation it should reach in its eastern region."[15]

The secretary-general's endeavors to facilitate the repatriation of the refugees, to mobilize the institutional strength available in the Security Council, and to exercise moral persuasion had all been frustrated. In the circumstances he could only return to the exacting, easily misunderstood but ultimately more productive path of quiet diplomacy. In a note to Sardar Swaran Singh, the Indian minister for external relations, who had inquired what action was proposed concerning Sheikh Mujib, the secretary-general wrote that Mujibur's fate is "a matter of great concern to me. . . . I have been exerting my best efforts within my competence and authority to prevent an aggravation of the situation in East Pakistan. I shall continue to do so with . . . all the necessary discretion and lack of publicity."

CHAPTER 4

The Operation Takes Shape: August-November 1971

On 13 August—four and a half months after his first offer of assistance to the people of East Pakistan—the secretary-general convened a meeting of government representatives to discuss United Nations humanitarian assistance for displaced persons from East Pakistan in India and the United Nations relief operation in East Pakistan. It was the first quasi-formal step in the establishment of a relief operation in East Pakistan, as distinct from a purely coordinating effort, and appears to have been intended both to stimulate contributions and to secure a degree of at least informal intergovernmental endorsement of the venture or acquiescence in it. In 1972 and 1973, after the inauguration of the relief operation in Dacca, similar meetings provided an essential link between the secretariat and delegations and functioned as an informal and usually cooperative governing body for the operation.

Three overlapping categories of delegations were invited to the August meeting: major contributors to the regular budget of the United Nations, substantial contributors to the voluntary activities of the United Nations (including nonmember states), and potential contributors to the refugee operation and the operation in East Pakistan. Twenty-seven delegations attended: Argentina, Austria, Belgium, Brazil, Canada, Czechoslovakia, Denmark, the Federal Republic of Germany, Finland, France, Hungary, Iran, Italy, Japan, Libya, Mexico, Netherlands, Norway, Poland, Romania, Spain, Sweden, Switzerland, the USSR, the United Kingdom, the United States, and Yugoslavia.

An *aide-mémoire* to governments presented to the meeting provided a condensed progress report on the two operations.[1] It reiterated that they were "related, to the extent that the possibility of arresting and reversing the flow of refugees depends largely on the improvement of conditions in East Pakistan," and in answer to questions from the United States representative the secretary-general announced his intention of designating one person to be responsible at headquarters for the operations in India and in East Pakistan. In practice the two operations seem to have developed in parallel with no link between them beyond the political guidance furnished by the secretary-general and his senior colleagues.

So far as the program in East Pakistan was concerned, the *aide-mémoire* was optimistic. "The United Nations," it said, "has been actively engaged in assessing the requirements and establishing the administrative arrangements for the operation, and the secretary-general can now report that the operation is proceeding apace."

Significant pledges had been made by the United States, the United Kingdom, France, and Canada. "Nevertheless, only approximately $4 million in cash has been contributed to meet the initial requirement of $28.2 million, and the likelihood of a serious food shortage without such assistance forthcoming has not diminished." Besides the need for food grains, funds were urgently required for transport, medical supplies, clothing, shelter, and blankets.

Additional information on the progress of the operation had been given in a series of notes to correspondents earlier in the month.[2] A three-phase plan submitted by the secretary-general's representative in Dacca was, the notes said, being implemented. It was expected that all of the 38 international staff required for phase one, designed to set up the framework within which an effective humanitarian relief operation could be carried on, would be in East Pakistan by the end of August. Some of them were already there and some were on their way. The group included the staff of the office of the secretary-general's representative; an advisory team on agriculture, ports and water-transport management, health and general relief problems; an operations unit, including four area coordinators; and an administrative unit, including finance, transport, and communications personnel. The notes explained that recruitment of the administrative and supporting personnel had been entrusted to the field operations service, in close consultation with the office of personnel. Administrative

The Operation Takes Shape   45

control and responsibility for the relief operations rested with the field operations service.

The notes added that an inter-agency working group had been set up in Geneva to ensure coordination of the total effort from the United Nations system. The group was under the authority of Vittorio Winspeare Guicciardi, the director-general of the United Nations office at Geneva; it held weekly meetings and its work was closely coordinated with the similar group established by the high commissioner for refugees for assistance to East Pakistan and refugees in India.

The note of 11 August elaborated on the financial situation of the program. Of the $28,200,000 required to meet initial needs, it said, so far only $2,209,500[3] had been paid into the United Nations account, although various amounts in kind had been pledged by a number of countries. This sum was made up of $1,000,000 for operational expenses presented to the secretary-general by Secretary of State William Rogers on 9 August and $1,209,500 presented by the permanent representative of the United Kingdom the following day. The critical requirement was "for cash to meet logistical and administrative costs and to defray the expenses of urgent relief projects to be undertaken by the various agencies concerned."

The meeting of 13 August was chiefly concerned with the operation in East Pakistan. There were a few questions. Would contributions be used to pay for United Nations staff? They would not; salaries and normal allowances would be paid from the regular budget. A contribution had been received for administrative expenses, but most funds would be used for operational purposes. What procedures would be used to ensure that humanitarian assistance to East Pakistan would not be diverted? The secretary-general agreed that he must be in a position to assure all donors that supplies would go to the right people. He had, he said, so informed the government of Pakistan, which had provided the necessary assurances. He pointed out it would be physically impossible, of course, for the United Nations to provide direct supervision in every village, but the representative of the secretary-general and his staff should be able to report to the secretary-general that they were satisfied that all supplies were reaching the intended recipients. Freedom of movement for the UN staff in East Pakistan was an important aspect of the operation. So was the question of security of UN personnel. This, the secretary-general said, was becoming a serious problem and one that did not relate to the Pakistan government alone. The secretary-general's representative was discussing the security problem with the competent Pakistani authorities, and the secretary-general would in due course report on progress in this regard.

The representative of the USSR raised a question of principle. Could a program on the scale envisaged, he asked, be conducted by the secretariat in the absence of a decision by the competent organs? The secretariat could not, he argued, be regarded as a United Nations organ competent to take decisions binding on member states with regard to such a program. The secretary-general replied that he knew the Soviet position, and that the Soviet government knew his. The fact was, he said, that if no action was to be taken until there was a decision by a principal organ such as the Security Council, there would be no action for another ten years. He had no doubt about his competence to launch operations of the kind envisaged. Assistant Secretary-General Kittani reminded the meeting that the Economic and Social Council, a major organ competent in the matter, had discussed the operation and that its president had made a statement in support of the secretary-general's efforts.

The meeting ended with an expression of appreciation by the secretary-general for recent pledges by governments. Although there had been no great show of enthusiasm, some major contributors had made a first move, and the secretary-general had had some success in improvising arrangements in a dangerous and perplexing situation, for which the organization was totally unprepared. Despite the brave words of the *aide-mémoire*, much more would need to be done before the operation would proceed apace. For the time being, it seemed to many that it was at best limping forward.

The jigsaw puzzle of arrangements announced in the secretary-general's *note verbale* of 13 August and in the succession of

The Operation Takes Shape 47

notes to correspondents in early August took longer to put together than had been expected. Under the three-phase plan, UNEPRO was to have 38 internationally recruited staff members in Dacca by the end of August and 121 by the end of October. At the end of August there were 18 and only 52 by the middle of November. There were delays in recruitment. The office of personnel acted quickly, but it took time to discover properly qualified specialized staff, persuade them to accept appointments, issue contracts, and send them on their way. Where staff were being seconded from inside the secretariat, there were difficulties too. The kind of staff most required were likely to be in key positions, and departments could not always release and replace them at a moment's notice. The delay was exasperating but may have been less important than it appeared at the time. One of the early arrivals in Dacca has reported that there was "nothing to do in Dacca except raise and lower the flag" and make contingency plans.

In Geneva the inter-organization working group on humanitarian assistance to East Pakistan was in operation. It was modeled on the parallel body, the standing inter-agency consulting unit, set up to coordinate agency activities to assist the East Pakistan refugees in India, and consisted of representatives of the United Nations, WHO, UNDP, WFP, UNICEF, UNHCR, IBRD, FAO, the League of Red Cross Societies, and, from time to time, other voluntary organizations. It met regularly under the chairmanship of Erik Jensen, Winspeare's *chef de cabinet*, to review the situation, to consider projects, programs, and priorities, and to examine personnel matters. It was, to judge from the records of its meetings, a businesslike body and has been described by one agency participant as "an unusually rewarding experience in inter-agency cooperation." The group was, however, handicapped by a lack of business to transact and bedeviled, like all the other participants, by the fogginess that surrounded the operation and the uncertainties, the shifting and sometimes conflicting assessments of the rapidly deteriorating situation in East Pakistan. In a cable of 25 August, El-Tawil was informed that the group would draw up "a precise program with priorities on the basis of advice from Dacca." It never succeeded in doing so. The information was not available, and the possibility of precise planning—if it had ever existed—was soon swept away by the accelerating downward spiral of events in the subcontinent.

On 24 August the secretary-general informed the press of a further organizational change, the appointment of Paul-Marc Henry as assistant secretary-general in charge of the East Pakistan relief operation at headquarters.[4] The announcement explained that the need for a full-time senior official to direct the operation on behalf of the secretary-general had been keenly felt for some time. Hitherto the secretary-general himself, assisted by the under-secretary-general for special political affairs, Roberto Guyer, assistant secretary-general for inter-agency affairs, Ismat Kittani, and Brian Urquhart, the director of the office for special political affairs, had carried out this task. The need for a full-time senior officer had, the announcement stated, become more urgent with the substantial increase in United Nations and agency personnel who would be assisting in the organization, planning, and implementation of the relief operation, "thus enabling the secretary-general to assure donors and potential donors that all relief supplies reach the people of East Pakistan."

Paul-Marc Henry, a former assistant administrator of UNDP, was on loan from the French Foreign Service until 31 December 1971 and would be responsible "directly under the secretary-general, for the overall mobilization and expediting of international humanitarian assistance to East Pakistan." This would "involve the day-to-day running of the operation from headquarters, including the coordination of various United Nations secretariat units concerned and communications with the secretary-general's representative in East Pakistan and the inter-agency working group in Geneva." He would also be in charge of maintaining contacts with governments and other donors.

Henry's appointment marked the end of the first phase of the relief operation. He was the "dynamic administrator" whom Tripp and others, particularly in the delegations most directly concerned, believed necessary for the United Nations to move from a passive coordinating role to a directly operational function,

The Operation Takes Shape

one that would assure prospective donors that supplies and equipment were both needed and properly used.[5]

A man of quick and powerful intelligence and frightening energy—one of his collaborators described him as "a force of nature"—Henry was not content to run the operation from Headquarters. Within a few days of his appointment he left for East Pakistan and thereafter visited Dacca at least once a month. Apart from anything else, his visits gave the mission a sense of purpose and, at least while he was there, raised the dwindling morale of the staff. It was, one participant has said, as though the mission was given a whiff of oxygen. When Henry left, the oxygen went with him.

On 10 September, Henry, on his way back to New York from his first visit to East Pakistan, gave the Geneva inter-organization working group his impressions of the situation. "It was, if anything," he said, "worse than I had expected." The target of 2 million tons of food grain would be sufficient, he thought, but forecasting was impossible. He believed the greatest obstacle to effective relief action was the lack of information. It did not seem to be a case of information being withheld, but a genuine lack of knowledge. The condition of roads, bridges, river crossings, and other basic information was rarely available and never current. The highest priority was, he thought, moving out the supplies that were choking the port of Chittagong. The future role of the operation remained uncertain. The agreement originally reached with the government of Pakistan was vague and the government's interpretation of it not necessarily that of UNEPRO. For the present, the operation would, he considered, have to remain in Dacca, with subsidiary bases in Chittagong and Chalna—the two ports—"and mobile teams going to other places on occasion." It would be necessary "to await developments" before planning for a further phase.

Henry returned to New York to inform the secretary-general of his findings. He had a great deal to report. During his visit to Islamabad, he had found Pakistani officials "very sensitive" to criticism by the World Bank consortium, disappointed in the "poor performance" of the United Nations, and resentful of the organization's insistence on inspecting the use of relief supplies and equipment. As these officials saw it, the United Nations' attempt to introduce "observers" into East Pakistan "in the guise of relief specialists" contrasted sharply with "the preferential treatment given by the United Nations to India." In India supplies for the assistance of the refugees were simply handed over to the Indian authorities, with no international supervision of their use. In East Pakistan, for obvious reasons, donor countries insisted on international control over the employment of supplies.

Nevertheless, the authorities in Dacca, Henry reported, were prepared to accept phase two of the United Nations plan, which called for the use of mobile teams outside Dacca, although they doubted they could ensure the safety of United Nations staff away from the capital "so long as East Pakistan is threatened with increased guerilla activity supported openly by Indian authorities and originating from Indian soil."

So far as needs were concerned, Henry suggested that officials were "playing with figures," but he was inclined to accept the government of East Pakistan's estimate that 200,000 tons of food grain a month would have to be imported to avoid famine in the months before the country's main harvest, the *aman*, was reaped in November and December. There were three ominous caveats. The first concerned the activities of the insurgents. "Bangla Desh," he wrote, "moves at will and no relief effort can succeed without Bangla Desh acceptance." The second was the congestion in the ports, itself in large part a consequence of guerilla action. The situation was serious. The commodore in charge of the port of Chittagong had, he reported, said that no more food grain should be shipped to Chittagong until a distribution plan had been worked out. The third caveat related to the "lack of distribution," the result, it was suggested, of "lack of need, lack of demand or the unwillingness of the people to go to the ration shops."

Henry returned to Dacca almost immediately. In the meantime action was taken to remove one of the difficulties he had mentioned. In a letter dated 20 September to President Yahya Khan, the secretary-general proposed that the government of Pa-

The Operation Takes Shape   51

kistan and the United Nations should conclude an agreement setting out the conditions for the conduct of the operation. "Especially in view of the unusual nature of this operation," the letter said, "it is now necessary for its smooth functioning that we fill in the legal and other details which are normally required in an undertaking of this kind and which were omitted during the initial phase because of the speed with which the emergency had to be met." Two months later, after discussions at headquarters, agreement was reached on a statement of principles in an exchange of letters between the secretary-general and the permanent representative of Pakistan dated 15 and 16 November.[6]

Henry had touched on many of the difficulties that were hampering the progress of the relief operation. They were in large part the result of the circumstances in which UNEPRO had come into being. It had been launched helter-skelter to meet a threatening emergency, the dimensions of which could only be guessed at. As the secretary-general reminded President Yahya Khan in a letter of 20 September, the "operation was initiated because it seemed imperative to act with speed in order to forestall by a purely humanitarian action the possibility of famine and related disasters which might cost the lives of vast numbers of human beings in East Pakistan."[7]

The extent of the disaster was still uncertain, as was the extent to which assistance could be mobilized and effectively delivered. The possibility of famine, in particular, was debatable. In Bengal hunger and malnutrition are chronic, but some observers believed that the imminence of famine was exaggerated in the last months of 1971. El-Tawil, for example, in his reports to the secretary-general after his return to headquarters in September, suggested that the threat of famine—which had never been immediate—had receded. Grain was being imported at the rate forecast in the government of East Pakistan's food plan—200,000 tons a month—and although there might be local shortages, famine was, El-Tawil considered, a remote possibility. Other observers shared this view. On the other hand, experts from USAID were convinced that the danger was real. East Pakistan is a food-deficit area, and in 1969/70, the last normal year, had imported

1.5 million tons of food grain to supplement the 11.3 million tons available from local production. For 1971/72 the government estimated that import requirements would be doubled.[8] 1970 had been a bad crop year, and although the 1971 *boro* crop harvested in April and May had been good, the *aus*, harvested in July and August, was below average, and there was reason to believe that the main crop, the *aman*, harvested in November and December, would also be poor. One element was left out of the calculations. At least 10 percent of the province's population had fled to India. Until the refugees returned, estimates of food needs based on a population of 75 million would be at least 10 percent too high. The difference in import requirements would be over a million tons.

Whether or not there was an absolute shortage of food, the supply system was certainly on the verge of collapse. The food distribution arrangements established after the Bengal famine of 1943 used three main techniques to alleviate the food shortage and stabilize prices. The first was the system of "statutory rationing" maintained in the cities of Dacca, Chittagong, and Narayanganj. The entire population was covered and every ration-card holder was entitled to a ration. The second technique, "modified rationing," covered the rest of the province. Outside the cities, the government could not feed all the inhabitants, most of whom were farmers and relied on local production; instead it supplied food grain through modified rationing in distressed areas for distribution to people for whom the market price was too high. Lastly supplies were arranged for "all priority and essential consumers." In 1970/71, 1.3 million tons was issued under these arrangements through a network of dealers and 326 storage and distribution centers with a total storage capacity of 6.5 million tons.

In the latter part of 1971 this complicated system was under heavy strain. The government estimated that as many as 200 border and outlying *thanas* (administrative districts) with a population of roughly 35 million were suffering from "economic depression." In addition, between 10 million and 20 million people had fled from the towns to the countryside, imposing a further burden on local food supplies. The system itself was weakened by the

The Operation Takes Shape 53

breakdown of village administration in many places, the disappearance of many dealers and, most threatening of all, the dislocation of the transport system.

Restoring transport was the key to the success of the relief operation. There was a shortage of trucks. It was estimated that three-quarters of the province's 10,000 trucks had been taken to India by their owners or destroyed or requisitioned in the course of military operations. Many owners of the hundreds of country boats that plied the delta rivers had also taken their craft to India, and the operators of those remaining were reluctant to use them, from fear of insurgent action or because the returns were insufficient or uncertain. The railways, which normally carried 60 percent of the cargo from the ports, were repeatedly cut by insurgent action. The two main north-south routes run close to the border, and with the hundreds of bridges, culverts, and embankments necessary in the low-lying delta region were easy targets for saboteurs or even for shelling from the Indian side. The result was the virtual paralysis of the transport system and the accumulation of relief goods in the ports, principally Chittagong.

The problem had been recognized from the beginning. In its preliminary statement of needs the government had asked for 30 vessels and 500 trucks, and Kittani had reported that the Pakistani authorities attached high priority to the request in order to reduce the burden on other forms of transport "while the present tension prevails" and as part of a longer-term policy of making more use of water transport.

Donors were, however, slow to respond. In a letter of 26 July to the minister for foreign affairs of Pakistan, who had expressed disappointment at the delay in obtaining the requested food supplies and vessels, the secretary-general suggested that the main reason for the hesitation of major donors was the uncertainty of the situation in East Pakistan and their concern that the vessels might be used for purposes other than relief. Donors had cause to hesitate. In August El-Tawil found it necessary to suggest to the governor of East Pakistan that it would be "extremely helpful" if the government were to return "all their vehicles" to the United Nations agencies and "the 50 US-donated assault boats which are still being used by the Army" to the relief department. The governor said it would be done.

To make good the deficiencies in the transport system and guarantee the prompt, equitable distribution of food and other relief supplies, the United Nations had to do two things: it had to assure donor governments—and legislators and public opinion in the donor countries—that supplies and equipment would be used for relief purposes exclusively, and secure at least the acquiescence of the insurgents in the operation.

Neither task was easy. For political and practical reasons UNEPRO could not take over the transport system. Nor could it set up the parallel administration and distribution network necessary to guarantee that relief supplies reached the people for whom they were intended. In practice, relief shipments of food grains entered the established food supply system and were distributed through the normal channels.

Various mechanisms were considered. A suggestion that uniformed United Nations personnel should be posted on vessels carrying relief supplies and at distribution centers was rejected as impractical. Even if it had been acceptable to the martial law authorities, it would have required an army of monitors that it was beyond the operation's capacity to supply. A subsequent proposal that United Nations staff should make inspection trips on motor bicycles was rejected by Henry as being, among other things, unnecessarily dangerous.

In August USAID representatives in Dacca suggested that the United Nations flag should be flown on vessels financed by USAID and operated by the government of Pakistan. Headquarters confirmed El-Tawil's view that it would be improper to fly the United Nations flag or display a United Nations emblem on vessels not under United Nations control. Instead the office of legal affairs proposed that relief vessels and trucks should bear placards in English and Bengali reading, "Carrying humanitarian relief supplies provided under the auspices of the United Nations." A Pakistani official suggested that the word "provided" should be dropped. His suggestion was rejected. A Pakistani proposal to post armed guards on vessels was also rejected as improper.

The legal office's formulation was ingenious and was duly affixed to trucks and vessels. It can, however, have made no impression on the 80 percent of the local population unable to read. Nor was it likely to deter Pakistani soldiers or *razakhars*—the paramilitary force supporting the army—from requisitioning transport or to dissuade insurgents engaged on errands of sabotage. The only effective remedies open to the United Nations were vigilance, persuasion, and, when equipment or supplies were misused, protest.

The Pakistani civil authorities seem, on the whole, to have been cooperative. The insurgents were another matter. Throughout August there were signs of increased guerilla activity. On 13 August El-Tawil reported the explosion of a bomb at the Hotel Intercontinental in Dacca. On 26 August he informed headquarters that the British High Commission in Dacca was "concerned" about the safety of United Nations staff, in view of a reported threat by an Awami League spokesman that UN observers would be "treated as collaborators of West Pakistan if they were posted in the province without the permission of the elected representatives." The Pakistani authorities also were worried about security. El-Tawil was inclined to believe that they exaggerated the problem. He reported that John Kelly, the representative of the high commissioner for refugees in Dacca, considered that it was "safe to travel anywhere," and a member of the British High Commission staff believed that the security argument was being used to prevent the deployment of staff and avoid the detection of misuse of supplies and equipment.

The extreme insurgent position was sharply stated by a private American citizen, Professor Alice Thorner, who condemned UNEPRO as a device to bolster the shaky regime of the Pakistani generals and argued that international aid to reopen river and truck transport would negate the guerilla success in cutting transport lines and set back the chances of restoring peace.[9]

Professor Thorner's views were reproduced in *India News*, an action which understandably shocked the United Nations spokesman.[10] The statement totally misrepresented the humanitarian purpose of the mission which was, the United Nations spokesman explained, "to forestall a situation in which a very large number of human beings may perish from famine and other causes associated with the dislocation of their country." It did however highlight a dilemma that seems not to have been squarely faced. Asked by a UNEPRO staff member in September about the likelihood of famine, Father Timm, an American missionary with 19 years experience in East Pakistan, who later became the savior of UNEPRO, said there was no famine, but there was a civil war, and that was what the United Nations should be concerned about. Father Timm may well have been right, but his advice would have been difficult to follow. United Nations officials have limited freedom to act. Nevertheless, it is puzzling that the implications of carrying out a relief operation in a civil war situation were apparently not explored at an early stage. The existence of a civil war seems not to have been acknowledged. It is understandable that diplomatic discretion—and article 2, paragraph 7 of the Charter—should have prevented public references to its existence. It is hard, however, to see what there was to stop private discussion of its repercussions on the humanitarian mission in hand. The problems posed may well have been insoluble, but they might at least have been investigated. As it was, there seems to have been some insensitivity on the operational side to the delicacy of the situation and to the need to work with the Pakistan government without antagonizing its opponents. In October the acting chief of mission, Jacques Schoellkopf, cabled headquarters for information about a rumored crash-recruitment program for UNEPRO. USAID in Dacca had, he said, heard of a scheme to recruit United States citizens for emergency relief duties and was alarmed that it would jeopardize the international character of the operation and its acceptability to all parties. A handwritten note on the cable at headquarters explains that the scheme was "part of contingency plan— if famine breaks loose on a wide scale we will have to act more rapidly than ever before." The author of the note seems unaware of the political dangers that were apparent both to international staff and to national missions in Dacca.

Paul-Marc Henry continued his whirlwind visits to East Paki-

The Operation Takes Shape   57

stan and the operation began to spring to life. On 14 October, on his way through Geneva to New York, he was confident enough to tell the inter-organization working group that he expected UNEPRO to be in operation by November. Teams of UNEPRO staff had carried out a series of field surveys in 18 of the province's districts, and on the basis of their reports, Chief of Mission William McCaw and the head of the operations and planning division, Gualtiero Fulcheri, were preparing a detailed plan of action that would be discussed at headquarters later in the month.

Henry was not sanguine about the situation in East Pakistan. It had not improved. While reports of impending famine might be exaggerated, the crucial problem of distribution remained, and communications were, if anything, deteriorating. He believed, however, that the problems could be tackled. Supplies would be carried in vehicles and vessels clearly marked with the UN insignia, and it was hoped that it would be possible to distribute relief without interference or attack. Ultimately, he said, success would depend on the political-military situation.

On the contribution side, however, there was progress. By 12 October the secretary-general reported that governments had pledged a total of $83.6 million, in cash and in kind. He had received $3.8 million in cash contributions and some of the contributions in kind had been delivered. By 15 October, 16 coasters and 8 minibulkers—miniature versions of oceangoing bulk carriers with a capacity of about 3,000 tons—supplied by the United States under United Nations auspices were reported to be delivering food grains and relief supplies by coastal and inland water routes, and the first 100 trucks were moving the supplies inland.[11]

In a note of 22 October, Henry outlined the agreed plan of action. It called for a staff of 65 professionals, 45 general service and field service staff, and 84 local recruits. Fixed and mobile field teams would be deployed to establish a monitoring system and ensure that the best use was made of the equipment and supplies available. There was a note of optimism. He was pleased with the performance of field operations service and the contracts committee, which was, he said, "proving once more that the UN structure can be made to operate with speed and efficiency." There was also a cautionary note. As the operation became effective, it would, he pointed out, clash with the "obvious guerilla objective to stop the flow of humanitarian goods" to the interior and the outward movement of exports. When that happened, it would be necessary to "review the assumption that humanitarian objectives would be acknowledged by all parties."

Two incidents in the course of the month confirmed Henry's forebodings. On 22 October a bomb attack on the food department garage in Chittagong damaged vehicles used to carry relief supplies. In a note deploring the incident, the secretary-general pointed out that the "ultimate victims . . . are the people of East Pakistan whom alone this international relief operation is intended to help."[12] Four days later Henry informed the secretary-general that the chief secretary of the government of East Pakistan had opposed a scheme for the free distribution of food in Faridpur, because the food would be smuggled into India. Henry commented that the population was now so much and so openly on the insurgents' side that they would indeed "feed the rebels." There were obviously limits to both parties' understanding of the humanitarian purpose of the operation.

On 18 November Henry made a statement to the Third Committee of the General Assembly, which had agreed to discuss the humanitarian aspects of the situation in East Pakistan in connection with the report of the United Nations high commissioner for refugees.[13] He outlined the food supply and transport situation in some detail and explained how UNEPRO would supervise the use of supplies and equipment. Vessels would be chartered by the government departments concerned, but would operate under United Nations auspices and would be identified with UN markings and inscriptions. "Necessary instructions have been sent by the civil administration . . . to all departments concerned, including martial law authorities, so as to ensure that the exclusively humanitarian objectives and mission of these transport facilities should be repected at all levels and by all persons concerned, civil or military." UNEPRO and UNICEF staff would be given full facilities to supervise and would report any misuse of equipment to the civil authorities. The 1,000 trucks to be provided by

The Operation Takes Shape 59

UNEPRO would also have United Nations markings and would be subject to similar control. Problems of deployment and logistics would be discussed at a weekly meeting with the Chief Secretary, attended by the representatives of UNEPRO, UNICEF, FAO, WHO, WFP, UNHCR, and the League of Red Cross Societies. These arrangements, coupled with the network of field stations, would, he hoped, provide a mechanism to detect any shortcomings in the distribution network.

He also disclosed that plans were being discussed with the government of East Pakistan, the League of Red Cross Societies, and some voluntary agencies for the free distribution of relief supplies provided under the aegis of the United Nations. This would supplement the food-for-work program being considered by the government and would, as he pointed out in somewhat arcane terms, depend on "the capacity of the UNEPRO system and all participating agencies to have physical access to the categories of the population in urgent need of relief." "While due credit should be given to the exceptional effort made by the government of Pakistan to ensure that the basic conditions for the carrying out of the UNEPRO mission are fulfilled, there might," he emphasized, "be conditions which would make it impossible for the secretary-general to be in a position to assure the international community and donors in particular that all relief supplies reached their destination, the people of East Pakistan. If this proves to be the case, the secretary-general will have no alternative but to report to the donor countries."

The warning was presumably addressed to the government of Pakistan. He went on to caution the *Mukti Bahini*, the guerilla forces, and their supporters. UNEPRO had, he said, tried to avoid embroilment in the political situation in East Pakistan and hoped that all parties would understand its humanitarian objectives. "If, however, active and substantial opposition to UNEPRO were to develop from any quarter, a situation would inevitably arise in which it would become impossible to continue the humanitarian relief operation. . . . If hostile activities were to succeed in making the continuance of UNEPRO impossible, the ultimate victims will inevitably be the people of East Pakistan, whom alone and exclusively this international relief operation is designed to help."

The Committee devoted two more meetings to the discussion of the high commissioner's report and recommended two draft resolutions for adoption by the General Assembly. The first, sponsored by the Netherlands, New Zealand, and Sweden, endorsed the secretary-general's action in establishing the two humanitarian programs in the subcontinent and requested that he and the high commissioner continue their efforts. The second, sponsored by Tunisia, recommended that the president of the General Assembly should make a statement expressing the concern of the international community and urging support for the action taken by the secretary-general and the high commissioner.

Before the Third Committee's resolutions were considered by the General Assembly, Henry returned to East Pakistan by way of France to resume his ungrateful task. Before he did so, he held informal talks, with the secretary-general's permission, with the representatives of the provisional government of Bangladesh in New York. It was the first direct contact between a senior official of UNEPRO and the insurgents. It accomplished little immediately, but in December helped to ease the relationship between UNEPRO's successor and the new government of the country.

CHAPTER 5

The Secretary-General's Offer of Good Offices: October-November 1971

Organizationally the humanitarian relief operation in East Pakistan was moving forward. Politically the downhill slide continued.

There were no signs of reconciliation within Pakistan. At the beginning of September, President Yahya Khan appointed Dr. A. M. Malik, a Bangalee, as civilian governor of East Pakistan. As a move toward conciliation the appointment was futile. "It is," El-Tawil reported two days later, "very doubtful if his appointment will be considered by the Bangalee people as anything more than a superficial political gesture by Islamabad. It falls far short of what they consider is needed to bring about the return to normalcy and prepare for the transfer of powers." Later in September there was another gesture. The Pakistan elections commission announced that East Pakistan would go to the polls in November to fill the vacant seats in the provincial and national assemblies. In a broadcast to the nation on 12 October President Yahya Khan confirmed that the elections would be completed by 20 December and that the National Assembly would convene a week later, with the transfer of powers taking place soon thereafter.[1] An order issued a few days earlier had lifted the ban on political activity in East Pakistan without rescinding the bar against the Awami League, whose leader, Sheikh Mujib, was still on trial. Predictably the gesture was rejected by the Awami League and its supporters.

In his radio address, President Yahya Khan denounced, as his representatives had done in the debate in the General Assembly, India's efforts to disintegrate Pakistan in collusion with "certain secessionist elements." Shelling from across the border, the infiltration of saboteurs and frogmen were, he said, being used to dislocate the province and "to create famine conditions." There is no doubt, as the cables from Dacca attest, that guerilla action in East Pakistan was strengthening. The *Mukti Bahini*, the guerilla organization formed from the remnants of the East Bengal Rifles and the East Pakistan Regiment soon after the crackdown, were gathering recruits and receiving more and more open support from India. The Pakistan Army had been unable to control the rebellion during the monsoon and, as the monsoon receded and action might have become possible, it was faced with an increasingly effective guerilla movement inside East Pakistan and the Indian Army on the border. Both India and Pakistan had been calling up reserves since the middle of the year. It seemed only a matter of time before war broke out.

The secretary-general was deeply conscious of the organization's failure to grapple with the political aspects of the crisis. "Hitherto," he said at a press conference on 14 September, "the United Nations has been involved in only the humanitarian aspects of the problem, but the basic issues are political." He went on to point out, that "the restoration of a climate of confidence is not within the competence of the secretary-general."[2] As things stood, the creation of a climate of confidence seemed in any case a distant possibility. Even a temporary halt to ever-increasing levels of violence would have been an achievement.

The external obstacles to effective United Nations action were forbidding. There were also internal difficulties that must have seriously hampered the work of the senior officials responsible for dealing with the situation within the secretariat. U Thant was seriously ill, under heavy strain, and not expected to continue as secretary-general. A decision had still to come regarding the appointment of a successor, who would be faced with the consequences of the action taken. Dr. Ralph Bunche, who had been a pivotal figure in the handling of so many previous crises, was no longer with the secretariat. His absence was serious in itself, and the inexorable advance of his final illness must have been an added anxiety for the colleagues who were carrying on the work he had formerly done. To at least one outsider, the burden on the handful of officials at the center of the competing pressures, contradictory advice, conflicting information, and calls for action or inaction seemed impossibly heavy.

The Secretary-General's Offer of Good Offices 63

In October the secretary-general nevertheless decided to try again to effect comprehensive discussions between the heads of the India and Pakistan governments. On 20 October he asked Ambassador Sen and Ambassador Shahi to transmit to their capitals the text of letters he had addressed in identical terms to Prime Minister Indira Gandhi and President Yahya Khan. The letter began by recalling the secretary-general's memorandum of 20 July 1971 to the president of the Security Council, in which he had expressed his "concern at the possible consequences for international peace and security of the situation" in East Pakistan and the adjacent Indian states. Recent indications of a worsening situation on the borders of East Pakistan and reports of growing tension on the border between West Pakistan and India and on the cease-fire line in Jammu and Kashmir had, U Thant said, increased his fear that open hostilities might break out, "which would not only be disastrous to the two countries principally concerned, but might also constitute a major threat to the wider peace."

"I wish," the letter continued, "to emphasize that I have full confidence in the sincere desire of both governments to avoid a senseless and destructive war. I have noted the efforts which leaders on both sides have made, in spite of the severe pressures upon them, to discourage developments which might lead to open conflict. In the prevailing circumstances, however, where feelings run high and where both governments are under exceptional stress and strain, a small and unintentional incident could all too easily lead to more widespread conflict."

On the Jammu-Kashmir cease-fire line, the chief of the United Nations Military Observer Group was, U Thant pointed out, doing all he could to ease tensions, avert misunderstandings, prevent military escalation, and avoid confrontations that might lead to open hostilities. On the borders of East Pakistan and on the international frontier between India and West Pakistan there was, of course, no comparable United Nations mechanism.

"In this potentially very dangerous situation," the letter continued, "I feel that it is my duty as secretary-general to do all that I can to assist the governments immediately concerned in avoiding any development which might lead to disaster. I wish you to know, therefore, that my good offices are entirely at your disposal if you believe that they could be helpful at any time. Naturally the chief military observer of UNMOGIP will continue to do his utmost to assist in maintaining the peace in the area of his responsibility."

The letters were, of course, confidential. There were leaks and the text was released to the press on 27 October.[3] There had been considerable speculation in the press and elsewhere about possible United Nations action to bring about a solution, and there was still talk of attempts to station United Nations observers on the India-East Pakistan border. These were, the *New York Times* had reported earlier in the month, still "deadlocked after three months of intensive effort within and outside the United Nations."[4] It was also known that despite general expressions of concern, none of the great powers favored a Security Council meeting.

In one respect the timing of the letter was curious. Prime Minister Gandhi was scheduled to leave New Delhi for a three-week tour of foreign capitals, including Washington, on 24 October. She was unlikely to respond to the letter before she left, and the Indian armed forces were unlikely to move before she returned. It might well have been more profitable to have worked for a private meeting between the prime minister and the secretary-general during her visit to the United States and for the offer of good offices to have been made then.

Pakistan's reply was prompt and affirmative. In a letter dated 22 October, President Yahya Khan welcomed the secretary-general's offer of good offices and very much hoped that U Thant could pay an immediate visit to India and Pakistan to discuss ways and means of withdrawing forces. A public declaration by U Thant of his intention to visit India and Pakistan to seek a settlement of differences would, the president wrote, be most desirable. The letter said:

> It is a pity that at a press conference in New Delhi on 19 October 1971 the Indian prime minister has summarily rejected the proposal for withdrawal of forces of both countries from borders. The reason advanced for this is that Pakistan's

lines of communications to borders are shorter than those of India. I do not wish to enter into a controversy on this point and would suggest that withdrawals of manpower along with armor and artillery may take place all along the Indo-Pakistan international frontiers both in east and west, if not to peacetime stations, then at least to a mutually agreed safe distance on either side of the border to provide a sense of security on both sides. At the same time armed infiltration and shelling into our borders in East Pakistan should cease.

I further recommend that United Nations observers on both sides of the border should oversee the withdrawals and supervise the maintenance of peace. Only the recognized Border Security and Police Forces should then remain at border posts which they have traditionally occupied.[5]

Three weeks went by before the Indian reply was received. Its tenor can have come as no surprise. In his statement to the General Assembly in September during the general debate—the text of which Ambassador Sen rather pointedly transmitted to Under-Secretary-General Guyer on 22 October—the Indian Foreign Minister Sardar Swaran Singh had reiterated India's view that India was the victim of events in East Pakistan and that a political settlement between the military regime and the elected leaders was essential.[6] At her press conference in New Delhi on 19 October, Prime Minister Gandhi had made much the same point. "The first thing for the United Nations, if it wants to do anything, is to see that conditions are created within Bangladesh which will guarantee the return of the refugees in safety and dignity."[7]

At a press conference in Vienna on 30 October, she commented on the secretary-general's offer, which by that time had been published. The United Nations' and the secretary-general's actions and inactions on the whole issue of Bangladesh had, she said, been "so evenhanded" that neither the organization nor its secretary-general could do much by offering good offices. During her visit to Washington, Prime Minister Gandhi maintained the same position. The Indian people, she said at a White House banquet on 4 November, "cannot understand how it is that we who are the victims . . . should be equated with those whose actions have caused the tragedy."[8]

Prime Minister Gandhi did not visit the United Nations while she was in the United States. Ambassador Sen explained that she had been unable to call on the secretary-general during her visit to New York because the secretary-general was in the hospital. She would reply to the letter of 20 October soon after her return to India. Asked at a press conference in Washington why she had not visited the United Nations, Prime Minister Gandhi herself said "I didn't think it would serve much useful purpose." Until "the secretary-general, or whoever is taking an interest," succeeded in stopping the flow of refugees to India, she thought there was little the United Nations could do.[9]

Ambassador Sen delivered his prime minister's reply on 16 November.[10] It was tart, although milder than some of her extempore pronouncements, and not wholly negative. The letter recapitulated the Indian view of the crisis:

> The root of the problem is the fate of the 75 million people of East Bengal and their inalienable rights. This is what must be kept in mind, instead of the present attempt to save the military regime. To sidetrack this main problem and to convert it into an Indo-Pakistan dispute can only aggravate tensions.
>
> If the military regime in Pakistan persists in its policies, the situation in East Bengal is bound to deteriorate. Yet, there is no evidence of the wisdom or the desire necessary to seek a political solution of the problem. I believe that statesmen of good will all over the world are convinced that only such a solution could bring normalcy to that tormented region, stop the further influx of refugees and enable those now in India to return. You yourself have made several statements emphasizing the need for such a settlement. It is tragic that the Pakistan government has turned a deaf ear to all such appeals. Your offer of good offices could play a significant role in this situation.
>
> It is always a pleasure to meet you and to exchange views. Whatever efforts you can make to bring about a political set-

tlement in East Bengal which meets the declared wishes of the people there will be welcome, and if you are prepared to view the problem in perspective you will have our support in your initiatives.

I have stated my views frankly. It would not be fair to you not to do so, for I know how anxious you are to prevent the aggravation of the grim tragedy of East Bengal. I had hoped to discuss these matters with you in New York, but was very sorry to learn of your illness. I hope that you are well again.

The secretary-general's reply was handed to Ambassador Sen on 22 November. The secretary-general was, he wrote, grateful for the prime minister's "thoughtful and detailed exposition of her government's views" and in particular her statement that her government had no desire to provoke an armed conflict with Pakistan. He was, however, "puzzled" by the reference to "the present attempt to save the military regime" of Pakistan and by the statement that "to sidetrack this main problem and to convert it into an Indo-Pakistan dispute can only aggravate tensions." He was also, he said, puzzled by the suggestion that he would have the support of the Indian government if he was prepared to "view the problem in perspective." His letter went on to say:

In view of these statements, I feel obliged to make clear to you my intentions in offering my good offices. My letter of 20 October was deliberately written in the context of my memorandum of 20 July 1971 addressed to the president of the Security Council which took into account those aspects of the situation which you mention in your letter. In fact I had intended that this memorandum would serve as the terms of reference for the exercise of my good offices.

I had naturally intended to view this very serious situation in the broadest possible perspective and had hoped to have the opportunity to review it with the leaders of both governments. It was not my intention to sidetrack any of the main issues nor to confine the problem to any single particular issue, although naturally, as secretary-general, I cannot under the Charter ignore a potential threat to international peace and security such as now seems to exist in the subcontinent.

As you know, the exercise of good offices requires the assent and cooperation of all the parties concerned. Under the present circumstances, much to my regret there does not seem to be a basis for the exercise of the secretary-general's good offices in this infinitely serious and complicated problem.[11]

The offer of good offices was dead. The secretary-general's initiatives had been, at best, misunderstood. The offer might perhaps have been expressed more transparently. To a reader not prepared to read between the lines, especially one doubtful of the initiative's intentions, the letter of 20 October must have seemed simply a proposal to station observers on the Indian-East Pakistan border. It did not suggest that a military standstill would provide an opportunity for an attempt at political reconciliation inside East Pakistan; even the apparently perfunctory reference to the memorandum of 20 July spoke only of the threat to international peace and security.

The secretary-general chose not to test Prime Minister Gandhi's suggestion that his good offices might be useful in bringing about a political settlement. There was no doubt, however, about the way he personally saw the situation. As early as August he had told Secretary of State Rogers that the Indian attitude to the United Nations effort in East Pakistan would change only if Sheikh Mujibur Rahman and the Awami League returned to the province. Governments had, however, tried to bring about a reconciliation and failed. It was unlikely that the secretary-general, lacking the means of pressure available to governments, could succeed. He knew too that some governments, particularly that of the United States, did not accept Mrs. Gandhi's view of the situation. In late October Paul-Marc Henry reported from Paris that Henry Kissinger, the United States presidential adviser, had told him that India was at least partly to blame for the undoubted aggravation of the refugee situation. Kissinger was, Henry reported, inclined to believe that India had the power to reduce the activities of the guerillas coming from its territory, and he regarded

The Secretary-General's Offer of Good Offices 69

Prime Minister Gandhi's visit to Washington as the last attempt to prevent war. The attempt was clearly failing.

On 23 November the secretary-general received a personal message from President Yahya Khan. The president reported that the Indian armed forces had turned "from localized attacks to open and large-scale warfare on several fronts." The scale of these operations disproved India's claim that the incursions were being made by the *Mukti Bahini*, "a rebel force created, maintained, and sustained by India." In contrast to India, Pakistan had consistently expressed its willingness to accept United Nations assistance to resolve the crisis and had itself proposed a Security Council good offices committee to relieve the tension in the subcontinent. Despite India's recalcitrance, the president believed that the secretary-general's "personal intervention could still avert a catastrophe." He awaited, he said, the secretary-general's good counsel.[12]

In reply the secretary-general repeated his view that there did not seem to be a basis for the exercise of his good offices. He was anxious nonetheless to be of whatever assistance the parties might find useful and hoped that the United Nations could help avoid "a further escalation of violence into a senseless and destructive war." He continued:

"I note your statement that a personal initiative by me could still avert a catastrophe. While I am deeply anxious to do anything that I can to avert a further castrophe, I have been obliged to conclude that I have gone, for the moment, as far as my authority under the Charter permits me, usefully and meaningfully, to go in the present circumstances. As you mentioned in your letter of 23 November, I have brought this situation to the attention of the members of the Security Council, both in July, through my memorandum to the president of the Security Council, and in October, when I offered my good offices. I will, of course, remain in touch with the representatives of both Pakistan and India concerning ways in which the United Nations may prove able to assist both in attempting to preserve international peace and security and in working out a peaceful and lasting solution to the fundamental problems which underlie the present tragic situation.[13]

A second message from President Khan to the secretary-general was handed to Under-Secretary-General Roberto Guyer at 9 p.m. on 28 November. It requested the secretary-general "to consider stationing a force of United Nations observers on our side of the East Pakistan border immediately," to observe and report upon violations of Pakistan territory "in order to obviate a threat to peace and to arrest the deteriorating situation."[14]

The following day the secretary-general forwarded the message to the president of the Security Council, whom he had kept continuously informed of his correspondence with the two governments. He wrote:

> In the context of the present military conflict, the stationing of observers by the United Nations on the territory of a sovereign state, even at the request of that state, is obviously an action for which the authority of the Security Council should be obtained. I believe therefore that the members of the Security Council should be informed, in whatever manner you as president might deem desirable, of the request of President Yahya Khan for the stationing of United Nations observers.
>
> I also feel that, in the light of its primary responsibility under the Charter for the maintenance of international peace and security, the Security Council should give serious consideration to the situation prevailing in the subcontinent. In this connection I would wish to add that I have been obliged to conclude that in this matter I have gone, for the moment, as far as the secretary-general may usefully and meaningfully go in the present circumstances.[15]

There, for four days, the matter rested. On the Jammu-Kashmir line, the chief military observer reported that both Pakistan and India admitted breaches of the cease-fire agreement "for reasons . . . outside their military control," but were continuing to use the UNMOGIP machinery to prevent further escalation or an open confrontation.[16] On the East Pakistan border there was,

The Secretary-General's Offer of Good Offices 71

as the secretary-general had pointed out, no comparable machinery; in any case Jammu-Kashmir was a secondary front.

War seemed inevitable. Undoubtedly the Indian government would have preferred a peaceful solution, had one been available. There was no question, however, of the Indian government's need for an early solution, by whatever means. An unofficial Indian commentator later described the situation succinctly and plausibly:

> Because of the economic pressure of the refugees it was India that needed the war desperately to get the refugees back to their homes. With Indira Gandhi's foreign tour fetching her only tea and sympathy, the war clouds grew darker. The armed forces had been on the alert since August and by December their serviceability rate was reaching a point from which it would commence the dangerous downward curve. With the weather unsuitable for Chinese intervention and with Soviet support assured, it became India's game to provoke the Pakistanis to a showdown and, after numerous threats, on the evening of 3 December 1971, the military junta willingly obliged.[17]

Beyond the threat of an Indo-Pakistanti war there loomed the danger of a wider war that might involve the nuclear powers. In New York and in many capitals the possibility seemed frighteningly close. The Indian general staff presumably thought that the risk was one they could safely take. Fortunately, events would prove the Indian general staff correct.

CHAPTER 6

UNEPRO—The Attempted Evacuation: December 1971

On 28 November the secretary-general cabled Geneva asking the director-general of the United Nations office there to telephone Paul-Marc Henry urgently to inform him that a decision to continue or suspend UNEPRO could not be delayed. The secretary-general hoped that some substantial part of the operation might continue. Henry was snatching a few days' leave at Vaucluse on his return journey from headquarters to Bangkok, Singapore, and Dacca.

Since the middle of October a chain of incidents had undermined the optimistic assessment that UNEPRO would be fully functional by November, and made its continuance problematical. Guerilla activity and counteraction by the Pakistan Army were increasing. UNEPRO staff in Rajshahi reported 10 burning villages encircled by Pakistani troops. Two consular officials of the Federal Republic of Germany had been killed by a land mine, and a missionary, Father Evans, had been killed by *razakhars* in the Dacca area. There were riots and heavy loss of life in Chittagong and reported misuse of United Nations vehicles by the army and the *razakhars*. Vessels carrying relief supplies had been mined by the insurgents, and there was such congestion in the port of Chittagong that the shipment of further supplies would be futile. There had been talk of diverting supplies to Karachi. Headquarters informed Henry—who was then at Dacca—that the Canadian International Development Agency was worried, with reason, about diversion to Karachi, and suggested that he should investigate the possibilities of Singapore. He did so on 9 November before returning to New York to address the General Assembly.

On 22 November, headquarters instructed William McCaw, the chief of mission in Dacca, to regroup the staff and if possible evacuate less-essential personnel. Staff should, headquarters said,

UNEPRO—The Attempted Evacuation

be retained in Dacca for possible local relief action and the protection of the civilian population "together with possible operation neutral." Operation neutral evidently was a scheme to provide essential supplies for insurgent-held and other areas outside Pakistan government control using airlifts, airdrops, and UNEPRO vehicles. It does not seem to have been worked out in any detail. Headquarters was, the cable said, trying to activate an outside base for operation neutral as soon as possible.[1]

The following day McCaw reported from Dacca that the minibulkers *Minilion* and *Minilens* had been mined at Narayanganj and that the minibulkers might withdraw. Six United Nations trucks had been seized by the army. He had instructed the port officer at Chittagong to immobilize the 162 trucks that had been unloaded but not yet distributed to the food department, and suggested that the *Pioneer Moon*, which was lying in the anchorage with another 153 trucks, should sail for Singapore without unloading. He recommended also that there should be no further United Nations travel to East Pakistan.

On 24 November headquarters confirmed that the New York-based owners of the minibulkers were withdrawing the vessels to "safe waters." The ships would be available only for "service they can safely perform."

The same day, field service operations instructed Geneva that the movement of personnel and shipments to East Pakistan should be stopped. From New York, Henry confirmed the message and asked Winspeare in Geneva to advise donor countries that supplies should be diverted to Singapore. "UNEPRO will," he said, "continue to operate and assist in humanitarian assistance to the extent feasible." He himself was about to leave New York for the operations area. In the meantime headquarters was requesting donor governments "to divert all shipments for UNEPRO to Singapore," the secretary-general having "regretfully decided to instruct his representative as a precautionary measure to curtail the operations of UNEPRO wherever necessary for the time being," in view of "military-type action." At the same time the secretary-general asked McCaw, his representative in Dacca, for a "frank personal assessment of the situation as it affects the continued operation of UNEPRO." That day the United Nations spokesman informed correspondents that the secretary-general was "gravely concerned about the situation relating to East Pakistan."

In Chittagong the port officer, Charles Kiser of UNICEF, carried out McCaw's instructions, and with his colleagues spent the night of 23 November removing the rotors from the 162 trucks on the dockside, ignoring the threats of Lieutenant Commander Siddiqui, the Pakistani officer in charge of the port. The following morning, Kiser and his colleagues left in the *Minilatria* for the outer anchorage with the rotors, pursued by a motorboat manned by armed Pakistanis demanding their return. Kiser decided that he could not hear the Pakistani officer's shouted orders above the noise of *Minilatria*'s engines. The United Nations group eventually reached the *Pioneer Moon* in the anchorage and at 1400 hours (2 p.m.) on 24 November sailed for Singapore.

From Dacca McCaw reported on 25 November that staff had been regrouped and that arrangements had been made to evacuate 44 of the 90 staff to Bangkok. Headquarters seems to have been perturbed by the size of the evacuation. In cables on 25 and 26 November, headquarters noted that "departures of UNEPRO staff including several security officers are continuing" and suggested that "UNEPRO should continue, and be seen to continue its work to the maximum extent possible in the present circumstances." A cable the following day called for every effort to maintain the UNEPRO presence "so far as possible."

The same day, 27 November, McCaw cabled the frank assessment that had been requested four days earlier. He reported that there was a "progressive and accelerating deterioration of the government's ability to operate effectively throughout the province.... It is unrealistic to think that [relief] supplies and equipment . . . will not be seized ultimately for military use when the need arises." He pointed out that as UNEPRO's transport effort was "a means of improving the transport capabilities of the government while the rebel forces are attempting to cripple such capabilities . . . it is not surprising that the rebel forces and supporters of the Bangladesh movement could consider those en-

UNEPRO—The Attempted Evacuation

gaged in UNEPRO as collaborators." In the circumstances, apart from the work being done by the four WHO public-health doctors and the UNICEF child-feeding projects in the Dacca area, there was little left for UNEPRO to do beyond "tidying up administrative affairs and maintaining radio contact between Dacca, New York and Geneva." There were, he suggested, three possible courses of action: total withdrawal, the reduction of UNEPRO to a skeleton staff, until effective operations could be resumed, or a substantial continuance of UNEPRO activities. He believed that the second option was the best.

Henry arrived in Dacca from Bangkok on 2 December. The flight on which he was a passenger was the last to make the run. From then on, until the end of the war some two weeks later, Dacca was isolated.

Since leaving New York on 24 November, he had visited Bangkok, where he had met the staff evacuated from Dacca, and Singapore. He reported from Bangkok that "the assumptions" on which UNEPRO had been based—that its humanitarian purpose would be recognized by all parties to the conflict—were "no longer valid." He proposed the establishment of "neutral zones" to protect the population and suggested that UNEPRO should be tacitly discontinued and replaced by an undesignated UN relief office temporarily based in Singapore. Neither idea commended itself to headquarters. There were doubts about neutral zones, and on 2 December the secretary-general cabled that "the Singapore staging area is an integral part of UNEPRO . . . part of the operation" that the Third Committee had asked him to continue. Any modifications were, he said, "for me to make."

From Dacca Henry cabled that the chief secretary and commissioners for food, transport, and relief, whom he had met on 3 December, urged the immediate resumption of the minibulker operation. If it were not resumed, the government would be unable to distribute the statutory rations "within a period of seven to ten days. . . . If this occurs there will be a total breakdown as the city and the area are depending exclusively on government supplies. . . . This situation results from the total isolation of the city." There was no possibility of resuming the minibulker operation.

UNEPRO—The Attempted Evacuation

The owners had ordered the minibulkers to withdraw to Singapore. The Chittagong port authorities were slow in granting port clearance. Captain Sikoutris, the minibulker port captain, decided to sail without authorization. It was only after the war that he discovered clearance had been refused because the Chittagong port authorities were not sure of the position of the mine fields that had been laid outside the harbor. The minibulkers sailed over the mine field without incident. However, they did not escape the Indian air and sea blockade unscathed. Two ships—*Minilabor* and *Minilady*—were disabled by aircraft, and the master of *Minilabor*, Captain Karatzas, was killed. The two damaged vessels and a third, *Miniload*, standing by, were seized by the Indian Navy and taken to Calcutta. The secretary-general protested in the strongest terms, and after diplomatic pressure by the Greek government the vessels were released. *Minilion*, which had been mined, was abandoned at Narayanganj.

Henry also proposed the immediate evacuation of the remaining UNEPRO staff. The secretary-general concurred, "if you consider the measure necessary," and once again suggested that Henry's "neutralization idea" was unrealistic. He also urged Henry to return to New York where his "assessment and recommendation" were urgently needed.

Henry was unable to return to headquarters until after the war. The story of the evacuation attempt is a catalogue of frustrations. At the beginning of the war UNEPRO had two Pilatus Porters, light aircraft capable of carrying 13 people without baggage to Akyab airstrip across the border in Burma. One was destroyed and the other seriously damaged in the first day's air attacks on Dacca airport. On 4 December the Canadian government provided a C-130 for the evacuation. The aircraft was delivering supplies to Canadian missions overseas and was in Bangkok, a 2½-hour flight from Dacca. Efforts in New York, New Delhi, Islamabad, and Dacca to obtain an eight-hour cease-fire in the Dacca area and the Bangkok-Dacca air corridor for 5 December failed, because the Indian authorities could not make the arrangements in time.

The attempt was postponed to the following day when the Indian authorities agreed to a two-hour cease-fire from 10:30 local time. In the meantime Henry, with the approval of the secretary-general, had agreed, on the request of various consulates in Dacca, to help evacuate their officials and nationals. Ten minutes flying time out of Dacca, the C-130 was told that the field was under attack and that it could not land. It returned to base. On the ground a bomb exploded 25 meters from the first group of evacuees, mostly women and children. They had gone to the airport without awaiting clearance from the United Nations staff in charge of the evacuation.

On 7 December the C-130 made a second attempt. It was to be followed by a United Nations chartered Boeing 707, if conditions were suitable. A four-hour cease-fire had been arranged. In the Rangoon area the captain was informed by Dacca tower that the runway was not available. He circled Rangoon for 85 minutes and was then given permission to fly over Dacca. Over the Bay of Bengal, he sighted an aircraft carrier which "began to smoke." He noticed an antiaircraft burst below him, heard explosions which he concluded "were directed at the aircraft," broadcast the international distress signal, and returned to Bangkok.

Henry was understandably disappointed. After the first abortive attempt, he cabled "I respectfully submit that the Security Council should be informed of the present situation." After the second attempt, the secretary-general did so. He issued a report covering the whole transaction.[2] Two days later the resident representative of UNDP in New Delhi reported that senior officials of the Indian government were indignant at the failure of headquarters to absolve India from blame in interfering with the evacuation. Earlier the Indian authorities had informed headquarters, through the resident representative, that the C-130 was off course, and that the carrier *Vikrant* had launched two aircraft to identify it, but had taken no further action when the C-130 was seen to be Canadian. The government of India's spokesman was particularly annoyed by the suggestion in the secretary-general's report that a "cursory examination" revealed no damage to the C-130. How, an air officer asked, could ground crews servicing aircraft rely on cursory examinations? He might also have asked why the captain of an aircraft that was fully airworthy and in no immediate danger should have made a distress signal instead of simply announcing that he was returning to base. The incident is murky. Except in a dire emergency, one would not expect a carrier-operating aircraft to make smoke or to resort to antiaircraft fire, all of which the captain of the C-130 reported to have happened. As so often in human affairs, there were doubtless faults on all sides.

The evacuation attempts continued. For the staff in Dacca, trapped in a beleaguered city, expecting a battle of Dacca and a possible uprising in which the insurgents were unlikely to show them much sympathy, the delay must have been agonizing. For the officials in New York responsible for the mission's safety, with little information to go on and much of that conflicting, caught up in political discussions in and outside the Security Council and the General Assembly, and trying desperately to maintain communications—often at second hand—with the governments and authorities involved, the situation was not, except from the standpoint of personal safety, much easier. On 11 December headquarters informed Henry that the secretary-general had met with 22 representatives of countries interested in the evacuation. No useful ideas had emerged. The British government was negotiating to send three RAF C-130s from Calcutta to Dacca to complete the evacuation. Headquarters was doubtful both of the propriety and the feasibility of the operation. Dacca airport was unserviceable as a result of air attacks, and on 11 December Henry reported that General Farman Ali, the military assistant to Governor Malik, confirmed that "no, repeat no, clearance will be given by Pakistani authorities to any aircraft originating from Calcutta airfield or Indian airfield and/or returning there. . . . This decision is final."

It was not final. On 12 December the three RAF C-130s landed at Dacca and in four flights evacuated 387 persons, including two United Nations staff members, one WHO doctor, two UNICEF officials, and the crews of the United Nations chartered Pilatus Porters. A fifth flight was planned but was not carried out. Henry was disappointed and surprised that no United Nations aircraft had participated in the evacuation. Headquarters explained that the Canadian C-130 "was no longer available on 12 Decem-

UNEPRO—The Attempted Evacuation

ber for evacuation and in any case the British plan, if carried out fully, would have been adequate." Henry was not mollified. If a fifth flight had been made, only the hard-core group of United Nations staff, seven volunteers, would have been left behind. "The fact remains that this opportunity did not occur due to lack of action on the part of the United Nations plane. I am noting. I am not protesting."

CHAPTER 7

The End of UNEPRO: December 1971

On 4 December the Security Council met "to consider the recent deteriorating situation which has led to armed clashes between India and Pakistan." A meeting had been urgently requested by the representatives of Argentina, Belgium, Burundi, Japan, Nicaragua, Somalia, the United States, and the United Kingdom, later supported by Tunisia.

Throughout the crisis, the secretary-general had kept the president of the Council informed of his efforts under the broad terms of article 99 of the Charter, and on 3 December he had published a selection of his correspondence with the governments of India and Pakistan and with the president of the Security Council.[1] On 4 December he reported receiving two further communications, an oral message from the prime minister of India and a written message from the president of Pakistan.[2] Each message informed the secretary-general of spreading hostilities between the two countries and charged the other party with aggression. The document was supplemented by a series of reports from the chief military observer of the United Nations Military Observer Group in India and Pakistan regarding the situation on the Jammu-Kashmir cease-fire line.[3]

It was not the Security Council's finest hour. The debate followed a predictable pattern.[4] Two of the Council's permanent members, the United States and China, were, to use a term later popularized in the American press, "tilting" toward Pakistan. One, the USSR, was on India's side. The remaining two, France and the United Kingdom, were leaning, though more discreetly, toward India.

A United States draft resolution[5] calling for the cessation of hostilities, the withdrawal of forces, the stationing of observers on the Indo-Pakistan border, an affirmative response to the secretary-general's offer of good offices, and efforts to create a climate conducive to the voluntary return of the refugees received 11 votes in favor, but was vetoed by the USSR. A Soviet draft resolution[6] calling for a political settlement in East Pakistan and the cessation of all acts of violence by Pakistani forces in the province received 2 favorable votes, the adverse vote of China, and 12 abstentions. A third draft[7] sponsored by Argentina, Belgium, Burundi, Italy, Japan, Nicaragua, Sierra Leone, and Somalia calling for an immediate cease-fire and the withdrawal of troops coupled with efforts to bring about "speedily and in accordance with the Charter conditions necessary for the voluntary return of the refugees," had 11 votes in favor and was defeated by the negative vote of the USSR.

The debate ended on 6 December with the adoption of a resolution[8] sponsored by Argentina, Burundi, Japan, Nicaragua, Sierra Leone, and Somalia, which simply noted the lack of unanimity among the permanent members and referred the question to the General Assembly in accordance with the "uniting for peace" procedure established by General Assembly resolution 377A (v) of 3 November 1950. Eleven delegations voted in favor. Four—France, Poland, the USSR, and the United Kingdom—abstained. France and the United Kingdom had abstained in each of the four votes taken.

There were no surprises in the General Assembly discussion on the matter the following day. After a two-meeting debate in which sixty delegations took part, the Assembly adopted resolution 2793 (XXVI) by 104 votes to 11 with 10 abstentions. The text, sponsored by Algeria, Argentina, Brazil, Burundi, Cameroon, Chad, Colombia, Costa Rica, Ecuador, Ghana, Guatemala, Haiti, Honduras, Indonesia, Italy, the Ivory Coast, Japan, Jordan, Liberia, the Libyan Arab Republic, Morocco, the Netherlands, Nicaragua, Panama, Paraguay, Sierra Leone, Somalia, Spain, the Sudan, Tunisia, Uruguay, Yemen, Zaire, and Zambia, called for an immediate cease-fire and withdrawal of forces, efforts to bring about the return of the refugees, assistance to the refugees, and efforts to safeguard the civilian population.[9]

The debate reflected governmental sentiment, particularly in the third world, and confirmed U Thant's earlier predictions about the conflict between the principles of self-determination and of territorial integrity and the overriding importance attached by governments to the Charter injunction against interference in the domestic affairs of states. At least a third of the speakers, all from developing countries, emphasized the principle of noninterference in domestic affairs. Political settlement was talked about, but there was disagreement on how, and when, it should be achieved.

Before the adoption of resolution 2793 (XXVI) on 7 December, the secretary-general informed the Assembly that he had instructed his representative in Dacca to examine urgently, in cooperation with the ICRC, what practical measures could be taken to protect the civilian population. He was, he said, in close touch with the ICRC, which, in its traditional humanitarian role, would do its best to implement the Geneva Conventions of 1949.[10] The following day, he informed the permanent representatives of India and Pakistan of the action he was taking and requested their governments' cooperation. At that stage three "neutral zones" were planned: UNEPRO headquarters, the Intercontinental Hotel, and the Holy Family Hospital.

The matter had been a subject of discussion between Dacca, Geneva, and New York for some days. On 5 December Henry, who was then contemplating the total evacuation of UNEPRO staff to Bangkok and Singapore, reported that he had been discussing the possibility of having the League of Red Cross Societies take over UNEPRO's assets during its "temporary absence." He thought there would be legal difficulties that should be discussed with Henrik Beer of the League of Red Cross Societies. The following day he proposed an alternative: a volunteer hard-core team of six field service officers under Jacques Schoellkopf should stay behind to help the ICRC fulfill its obligations under the Geneva Convention. By 8 December, however, there were signs of a rift between the local ICRC officials and Henry. He was, he said, faced with a situation in which the ICRC could offer nothing except "the use of their emblem," and the local ICRC representative took too "strict a view of the 1949 convention, which makes no room for UN intervention." He was irked also by a suggestion that ICRC should be responsible for the air evacuation.

The End of UNEPRO 83

From Geneva Winspeare reported that the president of ICRC favored a joint humanitarian effort without too much regard for "legal niceties" and would instruct his representative in Dacca accordingly. At the same time, he had stressed that ICRC delegates "could not be seen as being under Henry's orders" since ICRC, as a last resort if other actions failed, must retain a degree of autonomy. The ICRC had, the cable reported, already approached all the parties concerned about neutralized zones before, and independently of, the secretary-general's note to the permanent representatives of India and Pakistan. Headquarters confirmed to Henry that the secretary-general would meet with Ambassador Shahi and Ambassador Sen to propose "neutralized zones under UN/Red Cross protection." These would be "a cooperative venture" with the Red Cross. Nevertheless Henry's authority was "paramount and unlimited."

On 9 December Henry warned headquarters "to stand by for further communications on general proposals for neutralization." That morning Governor Malik, General Farman, and the chief secretary had expressed interest in the possibility of declaring Dacca an open city. Later in the day the proposal came. Dacca would be an open city. No armed forces would operate in it, and all citizens would be disarmed. The United Nations would guarantee the necessary agreement between the Pakistan Army, the Indian Army, and the "rebel forces" until other arrangements could be made by the parties concerned. The East Pakistan authorities including the military command accepted the proposal, and Islamabad's approval was being sought.

The secretary-general thought the proposal, whether made by him or the government of Pakistan, would probably be unacceptable to India, "since it gravely affects the status of Dacca which is the main military and political objective of the war." He urged Henry to do no more "until I send more detailed comments and instructions." The details came later in the day. An open city is "completely undefended from within and without" and can be occupied "without combat." It would be unrealistic to expect India or the de facto Bangladesh authorities to accept a proposal of the kind made and pointless therefore to consider the suggestion of the United Nations observers. In a third cable the secretary-general said:

> I fully realize urgent and horrific possibilities of Dacca situation. This was the reason for my appeal in the General Assembly and the suggestion of UN/Red Cross presence and neutralized zones. I shall use your ideas in my conversations tomorrow with Prime Minister Bhutto of Pakistan and Foreign Secretary Kaul of India. . . . Frankly I am not confident of results, but I agree with you that we must try. . . . Meanwhile I extend to you and your beleaguered colleagues my deep appreciation for your courage and for what you are trying to do in the name of human decency.

On 10 December there was a startling new development. Henry transmitted to New York what purported to be "a definite proposal for a peaceful transfer of power" in East Pakistan. Earlier that day he had been summoned to Government House and had met General Farman Ali and Chief Secretary Muazzaffer Hussein. General Farman Ali handed him a note and asked him to transmit it to the secretary-general for communication to the Security Council. The general said the note had the approval of the president. Henry complied and transmitted the message to the secretary-general with an explanation of the circumstances in which he had received it and the comment that "we are now dealing with a matter of hours concerning the avoidance of the final assault on Dacca. . . . Only a Security Council resolution can be binding on both parties concerning cease-fire and peaceful evacuation of the city of Dacca and the territory of East Pakistan by the Pakistani Army." The first part of the message could, as Henry commented, probably be dismissed as political face-saving. The second amounted to a proposal for United Nations supervision of a voluntary surrender by the Pakistan Army. It said:

> I therefore call upon the United Nations to arrange for a peaceful transfer of power and request: (1) an immediate cease fire; (2) repatriation with honor of the armed forces of Pakistan to West Pakistan; (3) repatriation of all West Pakistan personnel

desirous of returning to West Pakistan; (4) the safety of all persons settled in East Pakistan since 1947; (5) guarantee of no reprisals against any person in East Pakistan. . . . This is a definite proposal for a peaceful transfer of power. The question of the surrender of the armed forces will not be considered, and if this proposal is not accepted the armed forces will continue to fight to the last man.

Later in the day Henry reported that General Farman Ali had warned him another message was on its way. A few hours later it came. Islamabad had decided that all parts of the political preamble to the message were "reserved by the Center." The second part should have called for a "guarantee of safety" for the army and West Pakistan personnel, not their repatriation. General Farman regretted having misled the secretary-general and apologized to Henry for "any inconvenience caused to him."

Headquarters had told Henry that the message "had been submitted to the General Assembly and Security Council with a request for urgent consideration." The message had in fact been reproduced as a Security Council document but had not been officially distributed. In a later cable, headquarters instructed Henry to "have no further connection with General Farman's démarche which has been officially withdrawn by the government of Pakistan through its permanent representative. . . . In present complex situation please abstain, repeat abstain, from any initiative other than strictly humanitarian." The secretary-general reinforced the instruction the following day. "Highly confused state of political situation and vital necessity of preserving purely humanitarian nature of your operation makes it more important than ever that you should avoid completely any activities with political connotations. Your dealings with all authorities should be based exclusively on humanitarian matters."

Henry had no further dealings with General Farman Ali. John Kelly, the UNHCR representative in Dacca, who had been appointed by Henry as liaison officer with the Pakistani authorities, was involved in a further attempt to draft a cease-fire proposal. Governor Malik resigned on 14 December and took refuge in the neutral zone in the Intercontinental Hotel. The next day he told Kelly he had been instructed by President Yahya Khan to stop the war and asked him to arrange a meeting with General Niazi, the Pakistani commanding officer. Instead, on Kelly's suggestion, General Farman came to the Intercontinental Hotel and drafted a proposal for a transfer of administration. Islamabad rejected it on 15 December. The next morning, after India had demanded the Pakistani forces' surrender, Kelly went in search of General Farman. He found him at the military cantonment. General Farman dictated a message of acceptance and told him that he had authority to accept the Indian surrender demand. Kelly is reported to have transmitted it by walkie-talkie to UNEPRO headquarters from which it was forwarded to New Delhi by UN radio ten minutes before the surrender deadline.[11] General Aurora, commander in chief of the Indian and Bangladeshi forces, has told a different story. In an interview on 10 February 1973, he said that General Niazi, the Pakistani commander, realized on 12 December that he was fighting a losing battle, sought the President's approval to negotiate a cease-fire, and on 14 December handed a surrender message to the United States consulate in Dacca for transmission to New Delhi. The message was delayed in transmission and reached New Delhi the following day.[12]

The facts of the surrender that never was, as Henry has called it, and the circumstances surrounding the transmission of the eventual surrender message to New Delhi are still obscure. One can only speculate about General Farman Ali's motives and the degree of authority he had from Islamabad. In the course of his meeting with Henry in the almost deserted Government House, General Farman Ali claimed he had full authority, and Chief Secretary Muazzaffer Hussein, who was present, did not dissent. The governor, Dr. Malik, who later joined the meeting, suggested merely that some points remained to be clarified. In a private interview later in the day, after the message had been transmitted, Governor Malik, looking "skeptical and depressed," confirmed that there had been an exchange of messages with Islamabad and said that the president had graver reservations than Farman Ali had suggested. General Farman Ali, a few moments

The End of UNEPRO

later, repeated on his honor that he had passed the message on the personal instructions of the president of Pakistan.

The exasperation evident in headquarters' reaction to the Dacca cables, transmitting and then withdrawing General Farman Ali's message, is understandable. The message was immediately disowned by the Pakistan government, and its arrival in the middle of tense and emotional discussions must have been seen by many delegations as evidence that the secretary-general's representative in Dacca was meddling in a complex and dangerous situation in which the United States and China were ranged against the other permanent members of the Security Council. The proposal would have undercut the position of the government of Pakistan and cannot have been wholly palatable to its opponents. It is hard, however, to see how Henry could have refused to transmit the message through the UNEPRO communications link to New York. Whether the proposal was simply General Farman Ali's, or had stronger authority, it was clearly important enough to be transmitted to the secretary-general without delay, and in the isolation of Dacca, with no way of ascertaining Islamabad's intentions, the claim that it had presidential backing must have seemed plausible. The rumors that a United States carrier task force was cruising in the Bay of Bengal, the talk of superpower intervention, and the prospect of a bitter and destructive battle to capture Dacca must have made it almost irresistible to regard the message as authentic.

It is understandable too that the Secretary-General should have urged Henry to limit himself to humanitarian initiatives and to refrain from political activities. The borderline between humanitarian and political action is, however, dubious and disputed, and, in the East Pakistan situation, was more uncertain than in many others. A high United Nations official in Dacca could not hope to insulate himself completely from actions with political implications and was bound to support—if only as a channel of communications—initiatives that seemed to promise shortening the war and avoiding loss of life.

For much of the time Henry must have had only the haziest idea of what was being done at headquarters or indeed outside

Dacca. Headquarters had only episodic and sometimes irritating and easily misunderstood glimpses of the problems facing Henry and the solutions he was contemplating. The radio-cable link between Dacca and New York was useful—and better than the channels available to most of the other actors in the crisis—but it was slow and ponderous. A direct telephone or telex circuit, if one could have been provided, would have eliminated many misunderstandings. Instant communications would not have been a complete answer and would not likely have affected the course of events, but there might have been greater peace of mind both at headquarters and in the field.

In New York the Security Council started a second round of meetings on 12 December. The meeting was requested by Ambassador George Bush, the permanent representative of the United States. "One of the parties, Pakistan, has accepted the resolution [of the General Assembly calling for a cease-fire]," he wrote in his letter requesting the meeting, "the other party, India, has not yet done so. The United States believes that the Security Council has an obligation to end this threat to world peace on a most urgent basis."[13] The same day the secretary-general circulated India's response to the General Assembly resolution, the text of which he had cabled directly to the government on 7 December.[14] The reply recapitulated the Indian government's views. "As far as the armed forces of India are concerned," the reply said, "there can be a cease-fire and withdrawal of India's forces to its own territory, if the rulers of West Pakistan withdraw their own forces from Bangladesh and reach a peaceful settlement with those who were until recently their fellow citizens, but now owe allegiance to the government of Bangla Desh, which has been duly constituted by the representatives freely chosen in elections held in December 1970."[15] India earnestly hoped that in the light of the facts the United Nations would once again consider the realities of the situation, so that the basic causes of the conflict would be removed and peace restored. "Given an assurance of a desire to examine these basic causes with objectivity, India will not be found wanting in offering its utmost cooperation."

The Indian minister for external affairs, Sardar Swaran Singh,

The End of UNEPRO

and the deputy prime minister and foreign minister of Pakistan, Zulfikar Ali Bhutto, participated in the meetings.[16] They were passionate, protracted and, not much more productive than the earlier round of discussions. The lines were drawn in very much the same pattern as they had been during the previous series of meetings. A United States draft resolution restating the provisions of General Assembly resolution 2793 (XXVI) was not adopted owing to the negative vote of the USSR. Eleven delegations voted in favor, Poland and the USSR voted against, and the United Kingdom and France abstained. On 16 December the debate was overtaken by events. Sardar Swaran Singh read a statement by Prime Minister Indira Gandhi announcing that as the Pakistan armed forces had surrendered in Bangladesh and Bangladesh was free, there was no point in continuing the conflict, and India had ordered its armed forces to cease fire on the western front at 2000 hours (8 p.m.) Indian time on 17 December. Both the USSR and the United States, with Japan, put forward draft resolutions, neither of which stood any chance of adoption. At the 1621st meeting on 21 December the president introduced and put to the vote a draft resolution sponsored by Argentina, Burundi, Japan, Nicaragua, Sierra Leone, and Somalia. The text was the outcome of intensive consultations with the parties concerned and combined the generally acceptable features of the many drafts that had been submitted. The draft was adopted. Thirteen delegations voted in favor and none against. Poland and the USSR abstained. Under the principal provisions of the resolution, the Council demanded a durable cease-fire and cessation of all hostilities until all armed forces had withdrawn to their respective territories and to positions that fully respected the Kashmir cease-fire line; called for international assistance in the relief of suffering and the rehabilitation of refugees and their return in safety and dignity to their homes, and for full cooperation with the secretary-general to that effect; and authorized the secretary-general to appoint if necessary a special representative to lend his good offices for the solution of humanitarian problems.

No delegation was entirely happy with the resolution or the way in which the Council had handled the situation. The most positive comment came from the representative of the United Kingdom, who expressed satisfaction that the Council had been able to adopt a resolution that looked primarily to the future. The closing statements by the two parties, and their differing interpretations of the provisions adopted, suggested that the future would be, if not as dangerous as the past, at least as difficult.

The following day the secretary-general circulated information received from the chief military observer of UNMOGIP.[17] The UNMOGIP machinery had worked remarkably well and had survived the crisis. An unpublished exchange of messages forwarded to headquarters on 13 December illustrates both the difficulties with which the machinery contended and the unexcited, almost eighteenth-century, professionalism that marked its work.

General Manekshaw, the Indian commander in chief, wrote: "I fully appreciate the problem your observers are facing and I sympathize with them. However the existing situation is neither of my making nor choosing. I reiterate that I cannot risk the security of my people and my territory by giving an assurance which I know Pakistan will not honor and can in fact take advantage of. I am sure you will understand. With my warm personal regards and many thanks for awarding such a big CFV [cease-fire violation] against Pakistan."

The chief military observer's reply was equally frank, courteous, and imperturbable: "I deeply regret that even though you appreciate and sympathize with the problems we are facing you are unable to help. I must emphasize that even if to some my attitude may seem surprising, farcical or even odd, it is my duty to have requested this cease-fire while of course not wanting to burden you with it. I therefore hope that in the near future, you will be disposed to reconsider your decision. In the meantime, my best regards, and thanks for the consideration you have given my request."

The military were setting an example that the diplomats might well have followed. In the hurly-burly of conference diplomacy, under the television lights and with the press at their elbows, they had little chance of doing so.

In Dacca Henry and his colleagues waited for the battle of

The End of UNEPRO

Dacca to begin and the expected rising of the *Mukti Bahini* in the city. On 10 December he informed the Secretary-General that if the air evacuation failed he would regroup his staff in Notre Dame College.

On 11 December the move was made. It brought most of the staff together in one place—a few continued to live in the Intercontinental Hotel—reduced movement through Dacca and made it easier to provide protection. It had one other great advantage.

Father Timm, the principal of the college, was well known for his sympathies with the *Mukti Bahini*. He had expressed them freely and had tried without much success to convince the insurgents and their covert supporters that the United Nations operation was intended as a neutral humanitarian effort. To function, the UNEPRO staff had had to work with the authorities in East Pakistan, and, in the eyes of at least some of the rebels, were stamped as collaborators. The fact that Pakistani soldiers and *razakhars* had been seen using United Nations and UNICEF vehicles reinforced their suspicions. Father Timm's protection was valuable in itself and helped to clear the United Nations of the taint of "collaboration."

In reporting the move, Henry told headquarters that the college would display the United Nations flag and the Red Cross. It was, he thought, too late to negotiate a "neutral zone" in the sense of the Red Cross Convention. From headquarters efforts were made to secure ICRC protection, and on 15 December Winspeare reported from Geneva that ICRC would instruct its delegate in New Delhi that the college should be recognized as a neutral zone. ICRC had not known that UNEPRO had found a haven in the college. Earlier, headquarters had informed Henry that the Indian government—and by implication the Indian-recognized government of Bangladesh—did not object to a "continued United Nations presence" in Dacca.

The morale of the staff marooned in the college remained high. There was little to do. The UNEPRO office in Dhanmondi and the radio room remained open during the day. At five in the evening, during the hours of curfew and blackout, it was closed. Messages could then be received from Bangkok in the college, but nothing could be transmitted until the radio room was reopened. The group of 36 was, Henry told headquarters, "too large for a hard-core presence and for its possible activities, which are nil." It could only watch and wait.

The cease-fire was signed during the afternoon of 16 December. The streets were filled with cheering crowds. There were fusillades of shots, cries of "Jai Bangla" (long live Bengal), trucks dashing through the streets full of Bangalees waving Bangladesh flags, and bloodshed as guerillas mopped up pockets of resistance and disposed of "collaborators." "It was," a United Nations observer said, "Paris at the Liberation—including the sharpshooters on the rooftops." The Bangalees who had taken refuge in the college left. Their places were taken by Biharis. The UNEPRO staff gave them rice.

The following morning Henry received two cables from headquarters. There was good news. The minibulkers had been released from Calcutta and the minibulker charter with the government of Pakistan had been terminated. There were also questions. Headquarters wanted a quick estimate of needs. Would extra personnel be needed for a short-term assessment? What were the relief needs of the returning refugees? What was the state of the railroad from Calcutta to Jessore? What was the need for rehabilitation work in the near future?

Henry was outraged, and understandably so. The questionnaire was the kind of communication that reinforces the line officers' traditionally jaundiced view of the capability of the staff. One of the questions was absurd. Jessore is more than 90 miles from Dacca. If anyone could say what the state of the railroad was, it was the resident representative of UNDP in New Delhi. The other questions asked for information that Henry would undoubtedly seek to assemble as soon as conditions permitted. For the time being he was not in a position to do so. It was not the first time headquarters had asked questions that irritated the people in the field. At an earlier stage headquarters had, for example, cabled for demographic information, some of which was unobtainable and some of which could be found in any good library. In newly liberated Dacca, the string of questions was peculiarly irritating. "Your 672 and 673," Henry cabled in reply, "seem to indicate that you believe that situation has returned to normal. . . . In fact it is getting graver by the minute. . . . Please abstain from any communication which is not directly relevant to security of personnel."

Conditions were far from normal. The Indian Army was, he reported, thinking of taking over UNEPRO's radio equipment. He was taking precautions, but urged the Secretary-General to "make the Indians feel their clear responsibility towards us and not hide behind purely political concepts." It was his understanding that the Indian Army did not consider itself responsible for the maintenance of law and order, as it did not wish to be regarded as an army of occupation.

For the time being Dacca was in a state of anarchy. Few Indian troops were visible. Mobs roamed the streets. *Mukti Bahini* were threatening to blow up the Intercontinental Hotel if Governor Malik and the other Pakistani officials there were not surrendered to them. At the last moment the situation was saved. The Red Cross persuaded the guerillas to withdraw the ultimatum and Indian troops arrived to guard the hotel.

Headquarters and, through the ICRC, Geneva had been working to arrange for the protection of the staff in Dacca. On 17 December headquarters informed Henry that Indian Army protection had been promised and asked whether he still insisted on complete evacuation. He replied that he did. "The only soldiers we see are irregulars from Bangladesh trying to get our vehicles and gasoline." He thought "a limited United Nations presence" would make no sense. "I am not denying the vast needs of this country for relief and humanitarian assistance. On the contrary I think we need a much larger operation based on a sound working agreement with well-defined responsibilities on each side. This cannot possibly be negotiated now with disorganized military groups or the Indian Army, which does not consider itself responsible for any civilian matters."

Headquarters concurred but was cheered by a cable later the same day, which proposed that a small group of volunteers headed by Robert Walker of UNICEF should stay behind as a relief and liaison office. The situation was, Henry reported, slightly improved. The Indian Army was more in evidence and the "excellent relations" of Father Timm with the *Mukti Bahini* and the practical humanitarian assistance being given by United Nations staff were slowly creating "a better climate of respect and understanding." Headquarters—which considered complete withdrawal politically unwise—replied that the proposal was "most sound." Henry read the superlative as a comparative and was offended. Only someone on the spot, in constant touch with all the ups and downs of the local situation, could, he said, judge the soundness of a proposal. For the moment there were more downs than ups. The Red Cross estimated that thousands of civilians had been killed in the previous two days. Mass graves of intellectuals slaughtered by the Pakistani Army had been discovered, and there was rising anger against the Biharis and West Pakistanis.

On 22 December the secretary-general received a more optimistic assessment. In a long cable, written to take advantage of "the waiting period granted by the lack of transport," Henry provided the secretary-general with an appreciation of the situation and his views concerning the future of the relief operation. Thanks, he said, to the energetic and systematic intervention of the Indian Army, law and order was being restored. Civil servants, other than West Pakistanis, were returning to work and services were being resumed. The operation could, he thought, resume within one or two weeks, if asked to do so by the local authorities. For the time being, he accepted the view of the chief secretary of the new government that the United Nations should limit itself to assessment, analysis, and limited practical assistance in the sectors where it could be most immediately useful.

In the previous few days there had been several developments. Through the resident representative of UNDP in New Delhi, New York had been continuing its efforts to protect the mission. One evening there was a tap on Henry's door. He opened it to find an Indian officer, dapper, alone, and armed only with a swagger stick. It was General Singh. What, General Singh wanted to know, were these tales New Delhi had received from New York that the army had lost control in Dacca? His people in New Delhi were furious with him. He invited Henry to go for a

The End of UNEPRO 95

walk to see how things were. Henry and the general went for a walk, with the general's jeep and driver following fifty yards behind. They returned unscathed.

It was the beginning of a better relationship. The day before Henry cabled, General Singh took Robert Walker with him on a helicopter visit to Chittagong to see the state of the harbor and the condition of the United Nations supplies there. Walker had achieved another success. With Father Timm and Peter Wheeler, of WFP, he had gone out "to look for the government." He found it, and Henry had a first meeting with Chief Secretary Ruhul Quddus of the new government. Accounts of the meeting are conflicting, but it seems not to have been particularly cordial. Ruhul Quddus and others were still suspicious of the United Nations and conscious of the ambiguities of the operation. However, they were beginning to realize, Henry has suggested, that although the United Nations had been mute during the previous months, it had not been deaf or blind.

There was one last setback. Headquarters had, after complicated negotiations involving the United Kingdom mission in New York, New Delhi, Nepal, and Bangkok, succeeded in chartering a Short Skyvan to evacuate Henry and his colleagues. The United Nations staff who were helping to man the control tower at Dacca airport cleared the Skyvan to land.[18] There was a long interval, then a voice asking whether there were two airfields at Dacca. There were, one of them unused. The Skyvan was on the unserviceable field, tail in the air, with a broken nose wheel. It was the last straw. From headquarters Guyer and Urquhart could only assure Henry that they shared his feelings exactly.

In the end, Henry and his colleagues left Dacca in an Indian aircraft and Henry returned to New York. By that time, UNEPRO was officially dead. On 20 December the secretary-general had renamed the operation UNROD, the United Nations Relief Operation in Dacca.

UNEPRO had foundered in a sea of political troubles. The first chief of mission of UNROD, Toni Hagen, later wrote that UNEPRO had been ill-conceived from the beginning, and that the war had saved the United Nations from a major scandal.

The judgment is picturesque and at first sight not unreasonable. It is, however, based on a half-truth and grossly simplifies a complicated situation. UNEPRO broke down, as Henry predicted it would, because the political assumptions on which it was based were falsified by events. The United Nations effort to bring humanitarian assistance to the people of East Pakistan could work only if it was accepted by both parties to the civil war as neutral and nondiscriminatory. By November it was clear that that condition was not satisfied and the decision to divert supplies to Singapore for all practical purposes brought UNEPRO to an end. Some participants in the operation, Hagen most prominently, and some observers in Dacca believe that the condition could never have been satisfied and that UNEPRO was bound from the beginning to fail. Some of them argue that the operation should not have been launched in the first place, at any rate in its initial form in August 1971.

These arguments have, in the clear and comfortable light of hindsight, a degree of plausibility. In the summer of 1971 they would have been a good deal less convincing. The secretariat is not an autonomous body. It was propelled into UNEPRO by the pressure of governments and of public opinion. The operation was an improvised response to an imperfectly defined emergency and was not so much ill-conceived as continuously replanned as it went along. In retrospect, it is puzzling that Kittani's mission to Pakistan in June 1971 was not coupled with a serious, independent effort to assess the needs for humanitarian assistance and to define the conditions in which they could be met with some prospect of success. At the time it must, however, have seemed more important to take advantage of Pakistan's willingness to accept the United Nations as a channel for international assistance and to assume that the difficulties and obscurities would be removed as the operation developed. In any case, the secretariat was not at that stage in a position to provide more than a focal point for the coordination of relief activities. It lacked the capacity to organize an operation that exceeded the fields of competence of any United Nations programs and agencies. In the case of the refugees from East Pakistan in India, the high commissioner for refugees provided an effective focal point for the mobilization of international

The End of UNEPRO

supplies. In the vastly more complex situation in East Pakistan itself, machinery had to be built up in the field and at headquarters. By October 1971 the machinery was largely in place as a result of the efforts of Henry and his colleagues, and would have been able to function if the course of events had been different. The effort was frustrated by the realities of the political situation, but it was one that had to be made and that could not be abandoned until the faint remaining hopes of a peaceful resolution of the crisis were finally swept away.

UNEPRO had, in any case, laid the foundations for the future and demonstrated, as the operations in the Congo, the Middle East, and elsewhere had done, the capacity of United Nations staff to rise to an emergency. The staff in Dacca had, U Thant told them, performed beyond the call of duty. What was more, he added, through their courage and persistence, they had ensured that United Nations humanitarian operations in the area could continue and be built up again quickly.

CHAPTER 8

UNROD—The Early Days: December 1971-February 1972

On 20 December the secretary-general informed Henry in Dacca that the successor operation to UNEPRO would be known as UNROD—the United Nations Relief Operation in Dacca. The following day he issued a report to the General Assembly and the Security Council on the implementation of General Assembly resolution 2790 (XXVI) and Security Council resolution 307 (1971).[1]

The first resolution had been unanimously adopted by the Assembly on 6 December on the proposal of the Third Committee. It endorsed the secretary-general's designation of the high commissioner for refugees as the focal point to coordinate assistance to East Pakistan refugees in India and his initiative in establishing UNEPRO, and requested the secretary-general and the high commissioner "to continue their efforts to coordinate international assistance and to ensure that it is used to the maximum advantage to relieve the suffering of the refugees in India and of the people of East Pakistan." The Security Council resolution, adopted on 21 December, called upon all concerned to take all measures necessary for the preservation of human life and the observance of the Geneva Conventions of 1949. It further called for international assistance to relieve suffering and rehabilitate the refugees and return them to their homes; and authorized the secretary-general to appoint a special representative if necessary to lend his good offices for the solution of humanitarian problems. The two resolutions provided the first firm legislative authority for the two humanitarian operations launched by the secretary-general.

In a statement read to the General Assembly on his behalf immediately after the adoption of resolution 2790, the secretary-general had already told member states of his decision to suspend

UNROD—The Early Days 99

UNEPRO and to resume operations as soon as conditions permitted.[2] The report of 21 December, which had been prepared after consultation with the secretary-general elect, Kurt Waldheim, confirmed U Thant's announcement to the General Assembly. It was more realistic than the earlier statement to the General Assembly. In that statement the secretary-general told the Assembly that UNEPRO had been "making good progress" until the events of the previous week, and claimed that it had developed "the capacity to provide approximately 200,000 tons of food commodities monthly." The basis for the claim is far from clear. It was months before UNROD was able to supply food on this scale. The report states more modestly that supplies including "over 35,000 tons of wheat shipped by Canada" had been stockpiled in Singapore, that other supplies were "available or on the way," and that they were "very small in proportion to the great and as yet unassessed needs of the situation." Nearly $95 million had, the report said, been pledged by 16 donors, but of this amount $76.6 million had been committed for specific items, such as food and vehicles, and the balance available for operational needs would be exhausted within a few weeks. Moreover, as the report pointed out, the earlier projections of requirements had been based on a purely relief operation. As soon as a more precise assessment of needs was available, the secretary-general would, he said, make further and more specific appeals for international assistance.

In Bangladesh the process of organizing UNROD, which Henry had initiated before he left for headquarters, was continuing. As soon as possible after the war was over and Dacca began to emerge from its nine-month nightmare, the nucleus of staff who had remained in the city under Robert Walker of UNICEF returned to their hotels and offices and began to resume the operation. It was a period of improvisation in which the staff turned their hand to anything, unloading aircraft, helping to man the control tower at Dacca airport, and assisting in the evacuation of hospitals and orphanages. The banks were closed. Johan Boe, the acting administrative officer, carried the operation's cash in a zippered kit bag.

By the end of the month, the nucleus was reinforced by staff returning from Bangkok and Singapore. On 27 December Toni Hagen, who had earlier that month been designated as officer in charge in Dacca, entered Bangladesh clandestinely in a Red Cross aircraft from New Delhi. Gualtiero Fulcheri, his deputy, who arrived legitimately in a United Nations Skyvan from Calcutta on 1 January, later legalized Hagen's entry for him after the fact.

Hagen's entry was characteristic. He was not an international civil servant's civil servant, and was not a man to be fettered by rules and regulations. A Swiss geologist of some distinction, he had impressed colleagues who had worked with him in technical assistance projects in the field, and was vigorous and experienced in relief work. He was also, as events were to prove, unorthodox, outspoken to the point of tactlessness, and given to rapid judgments. He sometimes reversed these, but tended to recall his own role as having been right. Headquarters had doubts about appointing him as chief of mission in Dacca, but these were overridden by the excellent relationship he developed with the Bangladesh authorities, particularly with Sheikh Mujibur. There was in any event no other obvious candidate to head the mission, and Hagen had the advantage of being on the spot and familiar with the situation. He was well liked by his staff, most of whom believed, and continue to believe, that he was the right man for the job at that stage in the operation.

Hagen met the prime minister of the provisional government, Tajuddin Ahmed, on 30 December. It was a stormy meeting. Tajuddin Ahmed "complained bitterly" about UNEPRO's activities, Hagen reported. Hagen thought this was "a very healthy letting off of steam." Headquarters was not so sure. It later told him that reservations about past UN activities, from any quarter whatsoever, were not acceptable, were unfounded, and were not a subject of discussion. However vehement his complaints, the prime minister gave Hagen his approval, and on 2 January Siddiqur Rahman, secretary of the ministry of relief and rehabilitation, delivered the first list of aid requirements. "The total requirement will," he wrote, "be forwarded to you within a week or so. I hope you will be able to arrange for delivery of some of these items within a very short time."

UNROD—The Early Days 101

On 4 January Hagen cabled his preliminary assessment of needs. It was sent uncoded, and, as he said, differed considerably from the one given by the government. Any government is keen, he commented, to make the best out of a disaster. In Dacca he thought the government was making an admirable effort, and he agreed with the prime minister that the emergency operation should be as short as possible—he thought three months would be enough—and that the main effort should be to help the nation stand on its own feet by providing the necessary material resources and expertise. On the basis of his experience in Peru and Yemen, he was convinced that "the capability of rural subsistence farmers to bounce back after a disaster is much greater than do-gooders from industrialized countries could imagine." He was in favor of supplying some 200,000 tons of food grain in the first quarter of 1972, but believed that "it would be wrong to swamp the country with cereal food aid at this stage."

Hagen's estimate of food grain needs was wrong. By March, he himself was clamoring publicly for increased grain imports. He did, however, touch on a point crucial to the relief operation that was never successfully tackled. As an argument against huge food imports, he reported that "already, due to the considerable price difference of food between Bangladesh and India, uncontrolled food export from Bangladesh to India across the border has started." This was true, and, according to reliable reports, it continued. Some observers in Dacca have argued that the outflow of rice to India could have been reduced by establishing a suitable price structure in Bangladesh or by providing material incentives—transistor radios have been suggested—to induce farmers to sell their grain to the government procurement agencies. Whatever the theoretical feasibility of schemes of this kind, there was, as subsequent events demonstrated, no practical possibility of putting them into effect. It would not have been easy for an established administration to make the necessary adjustments, and in the difficult circumstances of newly independent Bangladesh the government could not be expected to undertake the task.

In New York, Paul-Marc Henry, Roberto Guyer, and Brian Urquhart, the senior officials principally concerned, were working to piece together a new operation. On 7 January they informed Hagen they intended to lay the groundwork for a future rehabilitation program, if such a program was acceptable to the governments that had supported UNEPRO and to the main powers directly concerned. In the meantime they urged him to use what resources he had and to make no commitments of any kind. The task of assembling support for the relief program in Bangladesh was not easy. Governments were in no hurry to recognize the new government. Some, most obviously the government of Pakistan, might be expected to oppose any action that would involve the treatment of East Pakistan as a separate entity. Henry's description of the new effort as "operation neutral," an attempt to help the Bangalees survive while avoiding political entanglement, was picturesque, but not immediately persuasive.[3] At the same time, the operation had to win support of the other main powers directly concerned. Two of these, India and the USSR, had had doubts about UNEPRO and were unlikely to be satisfied with a new operation that did not at least tacitly recognize the existence of the new nation.

By 12 January sufficient progress had been made to convene an informal meeting on UNROD at United Nations headquarters. It was attended by the representatives of fifteen governments that had contributed to UNEPRO. From an unofficial record, it seems the meeting was inconclusive. Henry gave an account of the resources available and the needs, drawing on the Bangladesh government's assessment rather than Hagen's. He also confirmed that a single appeal for funds would be made by the secretary-general "as soon as the facts were known." There appears to have been general agreement that there should be one major United Nations operation in the area, and that appeals for funds and assessments of needs should come from a single source. One representative asked whether donors could be given an account of what had been done "to date." Henry said he would be glad to do so.

In the meantime the secretary-general announced his decision to appoint Vittorio Winspeare Guicciardi, under-secretary-general and director-general of the United Nations at Geneva, as his special representative to undertake the humanitarian good

UNROD—The Early Days

offices mission contemplated in Security Council resolution 307 (1971).[4] Initially the secretary-general thought that the possibility of United Nations action to help solve humanitarian problems was limited. When the United States representative expressed his government's concern over the fate of the two Bihari communities in Mohammadpur and Mirpur, who were reported to be blockaded by the *Mukti Bahini* and in danger of extermination or death by starvation or disease, U Thant's first reaction had been to instruct Winspeare to contact the ICRC as the body primarily responsible for the kind of humanitarian protection the situation required. The involvement of UNROD would, he thought, "unquestionably jeopardize" its relations with the local authorities in Bangladesh. UNROD might supply food for the minority groups, but should not become involved in the political-humanitarian problems of their protection. It soon became clear that the difficulties went beyond the traditional responsibilities of the Red Cross and that in the minds of some governments directly concerned, United Nations, if not UNROD, involvement was essential.

Winspeare flew to the area on 27 December and visited New Delhi, Dacca, and Islamabad. The account of his mission circulated by the secretary-general on 17 January[5] made it clear that the problem of the Biharis—the Urdu-speaking minority of Indian Moslems who had settled in East Pakistan after partition and were supposed to have sided with the government of Pakistan during the civil war—could not, in the minds of the governments most closely concerned, be dissociated from the question of the Pakistani prisoners of war, the return of the Bangalees, in particular civil servants, in West Pakistan, and the fate of Governor Malik and thirty-three senior East Pakistan officials threatened with trial in Bangladesh. The report recorded one promising development; Sheikh Mujibur Rahman had been released on 8 January and had left Rawalpindi for London on his way to Dacca.

Moreover Winspeare had been given to understand that the Pakistani cabinet had approved in principle the free movement of Bangalee officials and others should they wish to leave the West. He had also been asked by the Pakistani authorities to transmit to

New Delhi their continuing concern for the non-Bangalee minorities in the East and their hope for a conciliatory approach to problems of common concern.

In New Delhi, Dacca, and Islamabad Winspeare had, the report noted, received full assistance from government officials at all levels, and the nature and scope of his mission had been generally well understood. Without the willingness of the relevant authorities concerned to use the good offices of the special representative, the mission would, the secretary-general pointed out, have been ineffective. Although reconciliation seemed a distant goal, the rigidities of the past appeared to be lessening. Nevertheless, the Pakistani authorities had asked the special representative to convey their concern to New Delhi, not to Dacca. Months would pass before there was a possibility of direct talks between Dacca and Islamabad.

In Bangladesh, Hagen and his colleagues had begun to assess the country's needs. Two-man teams, including UNICEF staff, undertook a program of field visits and by the end of January had visited each of the nation's nineteen districts.

The picture that emerged from their reports—the first is dated 2 January—was bleak.[6] Over large areas of the country, normal life had practically ceased and was being laboriously resumed. The cyclone of 1970 and the nine months of internal conflict and war since the crackdown of 25 March 1971 had left visible scars everywhere: damaged bridges, culverts, and ferries; wrecked buses, trucks, locomotives, rolling stock, and tracks; sunken and damaged vessels in the ports and waterways; ruined houses, factories, and schools. Economic life had been nearly halted, leaving millions without work or means of subsistence. In many places fields were untilled, and everywhere fuel, feed, fertilizers, raw materials for industry, tools, and cash were lacking. A food crisis was imminent. The yield of the country's main harvest, the *aman*, reaped in November and December, had been rumored to be "unusually bountiful." In fact it was 20 percent below the 1970 figure, and government food grain stocks, normally at their highest in January after the *aman*, had dropped almost 40 percent since October 1971, when stocks had been considered danger-

UNROD—The Early Days 105

ously low, even for what is normally a lean period before the new crop is harvested. Rice prices were rising and large segments of the population, especially the landless laborers with no rice reserves of their own, faced starvation.

At the same time a massive, spontaneous resettlement was under way. The ten million refugees who had fled to India and Burma began returning to their homes and fields. They came at first in a trickle, then in a growing flood, "drawn," as one United Nations observer said, "as though by a magnet to their hearths," largely bypassing the reception centers set up for them. Millions of others were returning to their homes from the places in the country where they had sought refuge.

Grim as the situation was, observers argued that the spirit of the people was a brighter side to the medal. Despite the damage and the shortages, there was activity everywhere. One observer commented on the "incredible resilience of an underdeveloped country like this one, its capacity for taking a short step back from disaster to normality in a few weeks." "The general impression," he wrote, "is one of regained confidence and activism, of greater personal security and of whatever belief in the future one can have in these conditions. . . . Something must have changed quite radically in a short time and the psychological, if not the material, conditions for reconstruction are there." But, as Hagen pointed out, even the most resilient destitutes can only survive if they are given a minimum of standby assistance to start with. UNROD's immediate task was to provide that assistance.

Fortunately the supplies and equipment delivered under United Nations auspices before December 1971 provided the basis for a prompt response. Some losses had been suffered during the fighting, the most tragic being the death of Captain Karatzas, master of the minibulker *Minilabor*. Four tugs had been lost. One minibulker was under repair at Narayanganj. Two light aircraft had been destroyed at Dacca airport. Thirty-four jeeps and several trucks had been destroyed, some stocks of blankets burned, and some office equipment lost. The trucks immobilized at Chittagong were safe, and the supplies that had been diverted to Singapore were ready to be moved as soon as transport was available.

On 12 January Sheikh Mujibur Rahman returned from his imprisonment in Pakistan to a tumultuous welcome in Dacca and began reshaping the government. Three days later he received Hagen. The meeting was cordial and a series of working-level meetings were initiated between the government departments concerned and senior UNROD officials. In a working paper prepared for the meeting with the prime minister, Hagen outlined the situation as he saw it. He said the restoration and reconstruction of transport facilities must have absolute priority. Shipments of relief goods would have to be coordinated and kept to a level the ports could handle. Chittagong, he estimated, could handle 190,000 tons a month with United Nations assistance. Chalna, which was blocked by wrecked vessels, could deal with an additional 69,000, once it was operating again. He recommended the appointment of a high-level coordinator for relief and rehabilitation and efforts to rehabilitate local production to avoid the need for imports.

The first working-level meeting was held two days later. Pierre Sales, the director of the UNROD office in New York, attended it and reported that agreement was quickly reached on a series of working groups to review the food supply situation, the distribution system, shelter requirements, and emergency salvage operations. He also reported that Hagen thought Henry's visit, timed for later in the week, was "propitious." Previously Hagen had thought that Henry should wait "until the dust had settled" and had doubts about obtaining authorization for his visit. Headquarters had rejected the notion that authorization was necessary. The situation was now improved. The prime minister had assured Hagen that problems involving United Nations communications and clearance of arriving personnel would be speedily resolved.

Henry arrived, unauthorized, and met the prime minister on 20 January. Rab Chaudhuri, the government's chief coordinator of relief, was also present. In his encouraging report, Henry confirmed that the prime minister gave "his unreserved support and trust" to the relief operation and was "clearly aware of the legal framework in which we have to operate." Sheikh Mujib would not, he said, create legal difficulties by injecting the question of

UNROD—The Early Days

international recognition. Immediate needs were being assessed sector by sector, and the prime minister had endorsed sending a high-level assessment mission under UN leadership, but with IBRD and IMF participation, to consider longer-term rehabilitation and reconstruction work. Henry proposed to discuss the matter with Robert McNamara, president of the World Bank, when he met him in New Delhi later in the month.

Henry was equally encouraging about Hagen, about whom headquarters continued to have doubts. The relationship Hagen had established with the prime minister would, Henry said, have to be taken into account "in whatever decision might be made concerning the composition of the mission and the relationship between headquarters and the field."

In a later cable Henry outlined his preliminary conclusions. UNROD was acceptable as "the agency responsible for the overall planning and administration of the relief program," on the understanding that it would work through established government channels and that its role would be mainly logistic. UNROD could use its transport and communications facilities freely, and staff could be posted wherever required. They would have free access to government services, and the government's chief coordinator of relief would be accommodated in the UNROD offices. Finally, UNROD would be the government's main channel of communication with the United Nations membership and would present consolidated statements of needs in such fields as transport, food supplies, and shelter material.

UNROD's start appeared to be propitious. Relations with the government were excellent. The work of assessing needs and priorities was in hand, and the available resources were being quickly mobilized. By mid-January, the freighter *Spitfire* had unloaded 15,000 tons of high-protein food and the cargo had been almost entirely distributed. The trucks that had been delivered earlier or immobilized in Chittagong were back on the road moving food grains from the silos to the central supply depots. The small fleet of minibulkers had been transferred to United Nations charter and was being remobilized. By the end of January nine minibulkers were in service. Tugs and barges were arriving. Two

Pilatus Porter light aircraft and one Short Skyvan were brought in, and by late January were operating the first scheduled air service in Bangladesh. The supplies—about 40,000 tons of food grain, 184 vehicles, and other items—that had been stored in the Singapore staging area were being ferried across the Bay of Bengal to Chittagong.

By early February the assessment was sufficiently advanced for the secretary-general to launch an appeal to governments, intergovernmental and nongovernmental organizations, and private sources for further contributions to the United Nations Relief Operation in Dacca.[7] The requirements were formidable: to meet only the most immediate needs and to avert the threat of large-scale misery and hunger, the secretary-general estimated that Bangladesh—for diplomatic reasons it was still referred to officially as "the affected area"[8]—would need external assistance, through the United Nations and other channels, in excess of $620 million in 1972. To meet that need, the organization had in hand pledges in cash totaling $18.1 million and pledges in kind amounting to $76.5 million. An additional $565 million was needed.

Of the $620 million requested, 90 percent or $530 million was for food imports, at the rate of 200,000 tons a month, to alleviate the shortage and eventually replenish run-down stocks. Of the remainder, $14.4 million was reserved for emergency transport needs—purchasing trucks, chartering vessels and aircraft, starting salvage operations, and providing navigational aids and handling equipment; $2.3 million for a vehicle-maintenance program; $30 million for child feeding; $6.5 million for fertilizers and insecticides; $21.1 million to provide simple shelter for up to one million people—if possible before the onset of the monsoon; $6 million for water supply; $5.8 million to rehabilitate education and health institutions; $1.4 million to rebuild the country's shattered telecommunications network; $1.4 million for raw cotton and tools for artisans to permit the resumption of economic activity; and $2.7 million for general operational requirements.

The estimate was provisional. The report stated that UNROD had not tried to inventory the total relief and rehabilitation re-

UNROD—The Early Days 109

quirements. The authorities in Dacca had, the report explained, defined overall sectoral needs, and these had been refined to ensure that UNROD concentrated on the most critical areas and to keep estimates manageable.

In fact, in the six weeks since independence, the government had not had time to do more than establish a shopping list. Some of its estimates were clearly inflated. For example, there was an estimated need for 10 million shelter units. This would have meant that over 90 percent of the population was without housing, which was visibly not the case. Other needs were almost certainly underestimated, and there was only the sketchiest indication of priorities.

The government's predicament was well described later in the year by the planning commission. The commission had, it said, started systematic work only in February, with the staff it had inherited "from the erstwhile planning department, which was badly inadequate in number and short of competent hands at strategic points." One of its first tasks was to provide a framework of priorities for the government's nonrevenue expenditures and to indicate how these expenditures could be financed. "This involved on the one hand a frantic search for ways of quickly mobilizing domestic resources from out of the little that the wartorn economy had, and negotiating for external assistance and its speedy disbursement to supplement the meager domestic resources; on the other hand, the demands for relief, rehabilitation and reconstruction, all of them agonizingly urgent, had to be drastically cut in view of the overall paucity of funds."[9]

The government's difficulties are easy to understand. It is harder to see why the United Nations, standing somewhat back from the immediate crises and equipped with greater analytic resources, could not have set firmer priorities of its own. The report recognized that priority attention would have to be paid to the transport system and salvage operations in the country's two major ports, but in practice UNROD, despite the head start it had been given by UNEPRO, appears still to have been grappling with emergencies as they arose. There was no clear plan of action, no firm decision as to what could and should be tackled at once and what could or must be deferred until later. The consequence of this failure soon became apparent, in the discomfitures of March.

Whatever the deficiencies of the estimate of needs, the international community's response was encouraging. The appeal was backed up by a meeting between the secretary-general and thirty permanent representatives of governments on 18 February, and by late April the secretary-general reported pledges to UNROD totaling $143,387,000.[10] Of this amount, $48,757,500 had been pledged by governments in cash and $94,630,000 by governments and the World Food Program in kind, chiefly in the form of foodstuffs, including rice, wheat, and vegetable oils. These new contributions supplemented a carry-over of $45,776,352 from the earlier United Nations operation in the area.

In addition, after the return of all refugees in March, the government of India proposed, with the assent of the high commissioner for refugees, that supplies already delivered to India or in the process of delivery under the refugee program should be transferred to Bangladesh. The transfer included shelter material, clothing, milk powder, medicines, and more than 1,200 vehicles valued at over $20 million, as well as a sum of $6.3 million, which was transferred to the government of Bangladesh in the original currencies, with the consent of the donor governments, for assistance in areas where there were large concentrations of refugees. UNICEF also allocated the equivalent of $38,400,000 for its relief activities within the framework of UNROD.

Including reported bilateral pledges or contributions to the Bangladesh government of $290 million, and $76,250,000 contributed by voluntary agencies, the total from all sources—multilateral, bilateral, and voluntary—pledged or contributed in 1972 for the relief of the people of Bangladesh stood at approximately $570 million. The total was impressive, but as the secretary-general pointed out, the emergency was by no means over, and considerable effort was still needed to meet even the minimum relief goals for the people.

In the meantime Under-Secretary-General Winspeare had again visted New Delhi, Islamabad, and Dacca in the exercise of his good offices mission under Security Council resolution 307

UNROD—The Early Days

(1971). The secretary-general's decision to ask Winspeare to visit the subcontinent once again had, he explained in a message to Sheikh Mujibur, been prompted by the "increasingly disturbing news" about the dangerous and deteriorating position of some minority groups. The mission had been reactivated for several reasons, among them a message from President Bhutto on 7 February expressing deep concern about the threat to the lives and safety of the Bihari communities isolated in the townships of Mirpur and Mohammedpur near Dacca.

The report, like its predecessor, gives a full and, within understandable limits, frank account of the mission. The conclusion was that the minorities problem would ultimately require the transfer of populations between east and west, possibly with United Nations and Red Cross assistance. "Mr. Winspeare feels," the report said, "that the most constructive, and possibly the only, prospect for a solution to the many humanitarian problems of the subcontinent would certainly seem to lie in achieving direct contacts between the principals involved at the earliest occasion. Without such contacts it is unlikely that humane answers can be quickly found to the humanitarian problems of prisoners of war, non-Bangalees in the east and the other minorities affected."[11] The secretary-general was ready, he said, to provide whatever assistance he could in whatever form the parties thought desirable, and he hoped that direct talks could begin soon.

The secretary-general had also asked Winspeare to look into the problem of displaced persons in Punjab and Sind. In January the permanent representative of Pakistan to the United Nations had asked the secretary-general for help in providing relief for two million Pakistani nationals who were homeless as a result of military action on the border areas of the two provinces; during his first mission, Winspeare had received an identical request from the government in Islamabad. On his second visit he discussed the matter with many of those responsible for relief action in Pakistan, including United Nations system officials and the Red Cross delegate. The representatives of the international organizations and voluntary agencies agreed that emergency assistance was needed for a large number of people and supported the idea of an appeal to the international community to supplement the efforts of the League of Red Cross Societies. The report suggested that the United Nations system could be expected to help significantly by contributing from its own resources and more particularly channeling assistance from donor governments. However, it was generally agreed that there was no call for special machinery or an operation distinct from the normal functioning of the organizations concerned.[12]

The report was silent on two points. It gave the reader no inkling of the danger to which Winspeare and his assistant, Erik Jensen, had been exposed while visiting the Bihari community in Mirpur or the resourcefulness with which they, and the unarmed Bangalee officer accompanying them, had extricated themselves from the situation.[13] It also made no mention of a curious incident concerning the delivery of the secretary-general's letter to Sheikh Mujibur. The prime minister was nettled because UNROD had delivered the letter in an envelope addressed to the prime minister, Dacca. Winspeare reported that Sheikh Mujib treated the matter very lightly but was clearly sensitive about the recognition of his government. He pointed out he was the prime minister of Bangladesh not of Dacca. In a letter thanking the prime minister for the assistance he had given Winspeare, the secretary-general explained the formal problems he had to consider in dealing with questions of recognition and informed him that in Winspeare's report and subsequent documents the name Bangladesh would be used with an explanatory footnote.[14] Relations between the government of Bangladesh and the United Nations had come some way since January when headquarters, disturbed by reports from Dacca of Bangladeshi sensitivities, had told the chief of mission that the local authorities must understand that, for reasons outside the secretariat's control, formal recognition had not yet taken place. "In this situation, which is difficult both for them and us, it is absolutely essential, if they wish assistance through United Nations as we understand they do, for them not to raise unnecessary formalities and not to ask the United Nations to accept procedures with which the secretary-general cannot at present legally comply."

CHAPTER 9

UNROD—The End of the Beginning: March-April 1972

In Bangladesh—and at headquarters—the operation was in trouble. The high hopes of January were being disappointed. Staff were being recruited, equipment—minibulkers, tugs, barges and trucks—was being mobilized, contributions were beginning to build up, but the visible effects in Bangladesh were few and discouraging. The period of emergency relief was obviously going to extend far beyond the three months Hagen originally foresaw.

Even the efforts to keep UNROD clear of the minority problem and political entanglements were being frustrated. At the highest levels of government there were no objections to UNROD's providing food for the Red Cross to distribute to the minority communities, although the prime minister made the condition that minorities could not claim special privileges. Lower officials openly resented the supplying of food to the Biharis, and on 27 February a demonstration outside the UNROD offices in Dhanmondi protested this favored treatment and demanded United Nations action to effect the return of the Bangalees from Pakistan. With some difficulty, Hagen persuaded the demonstrators and the attendant cameramen and reporters to disperse. Meanwhile the Red Cross was complaining of lack of cooperation from UNROD in feeding the Bihari enclaves.

On 18 February Hagen issued the third in a series of UNROD information papers.[1] The papers were a unique feature of the operation. At this period they were usually signed and were intended "to help international organizations, governments and voluntary agencies to identify rehabilitation projects" and to offer suggestions as to the direction in which "relief and rehabilitation efforts should proceed." A note explained that the papers were not cleared by "United Nations headquarters who, therefore, may not necessarily agree with the views expressed." They were the kind of publication that a good international civil servant would automatically expect to cause trouble. In fact, they seem to have been reasonably well received and may even have done some good. The service was continued, rather more circumspectly, by Hagen's successor, Victor Umbricht.

Information paper no. 3 presented some "blunt facts on relief and rehabilitation in Bangladesh." The summary speaks for itself: "(a) The situation in Bangladesh is desperate; (b) Practically no food grains are in the pipeline; (c) Entirely insufficient measures have been taken so far to restore the transport system; (d) Blankets won't do; (e) Baby food won't do; (f) Midwifery kits won't do; (g) Charity won't do; (h) Cash is required for employment and reconstruction; (i) Plain cash." The arguments were idiosyncratic, overstated, and in some cases wrongheaded, but there was more than a grain of truth in the thesis propounded. The accepted system of priorities, insofar as there had been one, was undoubtedly falling apart.

Blankets were, according to Hagen, a case in point. The international community, he said, had approved overnight the expenditure of $6 million for blankets, but had still not found the $700,000 needed to repair the Ghorosal fertilizer plant, the $6 million the salvage operations in Chalna and Chittagong would cost, or the $3 million required to restore the vital Hardinge and Meghna railway bridges.

The blanket story was more complicated than information paper no. 3 suggested. On 12 January Hagen reported to headquarters that the first UNROD voluntary agency coordination meeting had been held and had decided that the most immediate need was one million blankets to be delivered "within one week," in time for the cold season at the end of January. The working paper, discussed with the prime minister on 15 January, listed this as the top human priority. Headquarters went to work with a will and was chagrined to receive a cable on 28 January asking that all further shipments be canceled. McCaw and Tripp, who had been organizing the blanket-buying, declined. They complained that they had made "an all-out effort," involving UNICEF, UNHCR, the United Kingdom, Sweden, the Netherlands, the Federal Re-

UNROD—The End of the Beginning

public of Germany, Japan, and the United States. There would, they said, be a "credibility gap" if they canceled the airlift and the diversions of ships they had arranged. In any case, the blankets would, they argued, provide "protection for all types of weather, privacy and clothing year round." The flow was not stopped. The blankets continued to arrive and were warehoused at UNROD expense. There was no alternative: if they had been distributed the recipients would have sold them for food. They were eventually distributed in time for the 1973 cold spell.

Hagen's suggestion that the money spent on blankets could have been used to finance salvage operations at Chittagong and Chalna is simplistic. The implication that something was radically amiss in the implementation of UNROD's scheme of priorities is correct. The salvage operation was discussed in January at the working-level meetings with the government in Dacca and was accepted as a high priority project. Rab Chaudhuri, the chief of the government's relief coordination division, later told a meeting of voluntary agencies that Paul-Marc Henry had promised on 24 February that the salvage operations would be started soon. The minister of communications believed they were scheduled to start on 15 March. Discussions were initiated with SELCO, a Singapore salvage company, which was reported to be ready to begin work within two weeks. The process of inviting tenders and letting a contract, however, dragged on. It was 7 March before bids were solicited and mid-March before the bids were opened. By then it was too late. During his visit to Moscow the prime minister had accepted the Soviet offer to undertake the salvage operations and a new "credibility gap" had opened up in Dacca.

In strictly practical, if not in political, terms it obviously did not matter whether the salvage operations were undertaken by UNROD or by the USSR. The important thing was that the ports and waterways should be cleared. What really mattered was the loss of time. In the early months of 1972 the wrecked and damaged vessels at Chittagong and Chalna could have been moved fairly easily in a relatively inexpensive and straightforward salvage operation. The longer they stayed in the water the more difficult the operation became. The rivers in Bangladesh are swift-flowing and carry the heaviest sediment load in the world. Scouring and silting were rapidly making the wrecks immovable by normal salvage techniques. Vessels that were still afloat were in danger of capsizing. Others were being dug deeper into the river bottom and were filling with silt. The government of Bangladesh had every reason to press for an early start to the operation so that work could be well advanced before the onset of the monsoon, when operations would have to be suspended until the weather improved. There was every reason, too, to be disappointed in how long the United Nations had taken to start the project.

Headquarters was inclined to blame UNROD in Dacca for the time it took to organize a contract. In a letter of 13 March, Pierre Sales, who had become anchor man of the operation in New York, told Hagen ". . . you will be pleased to know that we are forging frantically ahead in selecting a company to undertake the emergency salvage operation." Commenting on the criticism of the delay "in getting things off the ground," "you should," he said, "bear in mind that we were unable to proceed any faster until we received the list of the vessels to be removed and your late cable identifying the 13 vessels involved. Finally the funds did not become available until 10 days ago."

Hagen had little reason to be pleased with the news. He believed that Sales had taken a complete list of all the wrecks to New York on 3 February and since the prime minister's return from Moscow on 6 March he had been pressed every day for news from New York about the salvage operation. On 9 March he had been informed that the prime minister, having received no reply from New York, had decided he must confirm his acceptance of the Soviet offer to undertake the salvage operation. Five days later he had "a frank discussion" with the prime minister on the implications of having a major naval power in the heart of Bangladesh waters, and reported that the prime minister was willing to accept the UN offer if no reply came that evening from the USSR. At lunch time the prime minister telephoned to say that a reply had come and that Soviet salvage vessels were en route to Bangladesh. The following day, on instructions from New York, Hagen sug-

UNROD—The End of the Beginning 117

gested there might be room for both United Nations and Soviet salvage operations. The reply was negative: the prime minister confirmed having signed an agreement with the USSR for both ports, Chittagong and Chalna. He also confirmed that there was no room for simultaneous salvage operations by the USSR and by UNROD. The prime minister had accordingly requested the United Nations to abandon further preparations for any salvage operations.

In Dacca there was no doubt, in government circles at any rate, that the United Nations had fumbled and that headquarters was to blame. In mid-February the minister for communications, Mansoor Ali, reminded Hagen that the government had been asking the United Nations from the beginning to tackle the salvage operation "on a priority basis," and that no tangible progress had been made. He asked Hagen "to kindly project the matter in its correct perspective to the United Nations headquarters . . . so that the task can be taken up on an emergency footing." At a coordination meeting for voluntary agencies on 8 March, Rab Chaudhuri was more outspoken. According to the minutes of the meeting, he said:

> As to UNROD, the government was currently evaluating its compatibility in relation to national needs. When Paul-Marc Henry last saw the prime minister he had spoken about the secretary-general's appeal for large-scale help, but it was better not to talk of $600 million until they were available. Henry had promised an early reply to the question whether UN would take on port salvage operations, but the reply, long overdue, was still awaited. Hagen was their good friend in Dacca but seemed powerless to shake up the bureaucracy in New York. The prime minister had asked Chaudhuri how long this was going to continue.

The situation was more complicated than Chaudhuri supposed. Headquarters could not simply endorse the salvage operation. It had to find funds to finance the undertaking and to convince donor governments that it was a necessary part of the relief operation. According to United Nations regulations, it had also, as it reminded Hagen in cables of 3 and 11 February, to invite international bids for the contract and for that purpose needed much more detailed information than Dacca had supplied. The mission in Dacca seems not to have fully understood the headquarters predicament, just as headquarters appears not to have fully grasped the urgency, for political and practical reasons, of getting the salvage operation under way as rapidly as possible. There were also differences of opinion. Early in February headquarters informed Dacca that the purchase and transport office in New York had checked company capability and could not agree to invite SELCO alone to undertake the operation. Later in the month Henry cabled from Dacca that a decision should be taken as quickly as possible on the SELCO proposals. SELCO was, he said, the only firm in a position "physically and technically" to start the work within a few weeks.

Henry may have been wrong, although his marine adviser, Captain Pfeifer, had been in touch with the company and thought that it was qualified to do the work. Headquarters was, however, reluctant to accept Captain Pfeifer's unsupported judgment. The captain was an experienced naval officer, but not a salvage specialist. It would have been reasonable for headquarters to have called in a salvage expert to make a professional survey of the ports, assess the capability of the contractors available, including their ability to mobilize equipment quickly in Bangladesh waters, and prepare a plan of action. According to reliable sources, Captain Searle, the United States salvage expert who planned the later Chalna clearance, offered his services but received no response. It is surprising, in any case, that no one sought the advice of the late General Raymond Wheeler, the organizer of the United Nations Suez Canal clearance operation. In fact, it seems the headquarters officials involved completely underestimated the urgency of starting the salvage operation and allowed the contract negotiations to take their normal course through the ordinary channels of purchase and supply. For his part, Hagen seems to have been less than cooperative and to have behaved more as an independent authority than as a representative of the secretary-general. The problem was compounded by difficulties of communication, the divi-

UNROD—The End of the Beginning

sion of responsibility between UNROD and the administrative services concerned with the contract negotiations, and the impending change in the top management of the operation.

The situation could have been saved by an "all-out effort" like that devoted to the provision of blankets. If the responsible officials in New York had been less burdened with detail and had had time to develop a clearer scheme of priorities, they might have made such an effort. They might also have challenged Hagen's preposterous request for a million blankets to be delivered within a week. What UNROD needed in New York was not simply a purchasing agency or fund-raising unit but a staff in the military sense.

At headquarters, Secretary-General Kurt Waldheim and his senior colleagues were working to make good these deficiencies. The first step was to obtain a clear picture of Bangladesh's relief and rehabilitation needs. The secretary-general's February appeal listed emergency requirements for the balance of 1972. It was based on the government's shopping list and the assessment made by Paul-Marc Henry and the UNROD staff in Dacca, and it was not intended to be an inventory of total relief and rehabilitation requirements. For this purpose, as Paul-Marc Henry had informed Prime Minister Mujib in January, the secretary-general planned to send a high-level survey team to Bangladesh as soon as arrangements could be completed. Henry had discussed the proposal with the President of the World Bank, Robert McNamara, who had visited Bangladesh at Secretary-General Waldheim's request in late February, and the bank was eager to assist the United Nations in assessing relief needs by providing the services of staff with extensive experience in the area. In the latter half of February the arrangments were completed. The government of Bangladesh gave its approval, and Dr. Erna Sailer, the Austrian Ambassador to India, agreed to head the mission. The World Bank provided nine specialists for the team and the International Monetary Fund three. FAO, UNESCO, and UNDP each provided a specialist from headquarters, and UNICEF and WHO made available the services of their representatives in Dacca. On 3 March the mission assembled in New Delhi and arrived in Dacca two days later. It was the first decisive step in the consolidation of the operation.

In Dacca the troubles continued. The food crisis in Bangladesh was deepening. Government grain stocks were down to 350,000 tons at the beginning of February and were being run down faster than they were being replenished by arrivals from India and overseas. In January the offtake was 83 thousand tons, in February 132 thousand tons, and in March 183 thousand tons. During the same months, food grain arrivals were 28 thousand, 61 thousand, and 98 thousand tons. Hagen hammered at the point in his information paper. On 10 March the *New York Times*[2] printed a dispatch from Dacca that quoted a United Nations relief official who had discounted threats of starvation since June 1971 as saying that the threat of widespread hunger or starvation was imminent. According to the dispatch, Hagen complained that the ports were choked with relief supplies and said that he had set the government a deadline to clear them. The same day Hagen cabled the director-general of FAO forecasting food riots if action were not taken urgently to deal with the food crisis.

Headquarters was disturbed. It was more disturbed a week later when an Associated Press dispatch from Dacca reported Hagen as saying Bangladesh was "heading for disaster" because of the food shortage and the lack of response to the United Nations appeal for cash contributions and again asserting there would be food riots "a few weeks from now." Headquarters asked whether the AP report was correct. Hagen's response was a simple yes. He had made the statement at a press conference given by Ambassador Sailer, who was in Dacca as leader of the high-level expert team appointed by the secretary-general to assess relief and rehabilitation needs. Ambassador Sailer's statements had been diplomatic, accurate, neither unduly optimistic nor unreasonably alarming. Hagen found them anodyne and made his comments as the conference was breaking up.

It is tempting to dismiss Hagen's outburst as tactless, alarmist, and likely to provoke the food riots he—and presumably the government—feared. From his viewpoint, it was a necessary call to action, a deliberate attempt to overcome the dilatoriness head-

UNROD—The End of the Beginning

quarters had displayed in the salvage contract negotiations, and to stir the consciences of donor governments. His comments had some foundation. For the first four months of 1972 Bangladesh survived on a knife-edge. By mid-April government stocks, which supply 12 to 13 percent of comsumption needs, were down to 190,000 tons, less than a month's supply at the current rate of withdrawal. It was the end of May before imports of food grains drew ahead of the offtake from government stocks.

Hagen stood by his prognosis. It was corroborated by the Sailer mission. Before leaving Dacca, Ambassador Sailer cabled the secretary-general and told him:

> My colleagues on the high-level consultative mission have expressed great concern about supply shortages in certain critical areas. They advise me these should be corrected as soon as possible in order to avoid serious food shortages and further damage to the economy. In view of the early June monsoon and the strength of my colleagues' representations which are reinforced by UNROD, I feel it is my duty to report these recommendations covering the most critical needs to you now without awaiting submission of our complete report in mid-April. The total amount is large (approximately US$100 million of which one half is for food items), but the situation is very serious.

Some observers believe that Hagen's bombshell produced results. It is certainly a fact that at a press conference in New Delhi a few days later, Prime Minister Indira Gandhi denounced United Nations predictions and said that India would ship 500,000 tons to Bangladesh before the end of June.[3] It is, on the whole, improbable that India's action was prompted by Hagen's statement. If it was, the same result could have been achieved more discreetly and with less embarrassment. Approaches could have been made to the Indian High Commission in Dacca. Ambassador Sailer, as Austrian envoy in New Delhi, could have been asked to raise the matter directly with the Indian government.

In the event, Bangladesh was saved from the knife-edge by India. The food deficit could not be filled by shipments from overseas. The stocks in the Singapore staging area were small and soon exhausted. Food pledged in response to the secretary-general's February appeal could not reach Bangladesh before the end of May. Obtaining the grain, arranging shipment, and loading took an average of two to three weeks. The sailing time from North American ports—the source of most of the grain pledged multilaterally—was 45 to 55 days. In the best of circumstances, there was bound, therefore, to be a delay of 60 to 70 days between the announcement of a contribution and the arrival of the grain at Chittagong or Chalna.

India was the only source of supply which could shorten the long lead time and move grain into the deficit areas while imposing the smallest demands on the country's limping transport system. In March, the Indian government announced it would increase its pledge of 750,000 tons of food grain in 1972 to 900,000 tons and would ship 500,000 tons by midyear. By the end of May, India had moved 490,000 tons of grain into Bangladesh, 265,000 tons by road and rail, and the remainder by sea. By the end of June the total had reached 600,000 tons, almost twice the amount received from all other sources.

The food shortage was alleviated. In other sectors, too, progress was being made. It was slow and inconspicuous, but it was real. It was not enough, however, to satisfy either the government of Bangladesh or the international press. The government was openly critical. According to Hagen, the representative of the Prime Minister told a meeting of voluntary agencies at UNROD headquarters in March that dozens of survey missions and delegations turned up with big promises, but nothing tangible followed. The government, he said, would not receive any more study groups, assessment missions, appraisal missions, goodwill delegations, and the like. A correspondent in Dacca was more acidulous. "The United Nations relief effort, the largest ever attempted, has not really gotten off the ground," he reported. "One big reason is lack of money, but there are others: appalling bureaucratic delays in both the government and the United Nations headquarters in New York; corruption; the failure of the United Nations, the government and the myriad foreign private relief agencies to coordinate their programs. Confusion and infighting are rife. The

UNROD—The End of the Beginning 123

prime minister has asked how long this mess is going to continue, a government official told a meeting of relief agencies earlier this month.... With everything gone sour, at least so far, everyone is blaming everyone else—and there is some truth in all the charges."[4]

The charges were unduly sweeping. Ambassador George Bush, the permanent representative of the United States to the United Nations, rejected them in a public statement, and a United Nations spokesman countered some of the criticisms. "We are not," he said, "miracle people."[5] The spokesman could have been less defensive. He had explained the breakdown of the salvage plan. He could also, and with greater justification, have explained why food grains donated through UNROD were slow in reaching Bangladesh and the way in which the immediate crisis was being surmounted by stepped-up deliveries from India. If the information had been made available to him, he could also have pointed to the solid, although scattered, progress being made in various sectors, as UNROD continued the process of building up its capabilities and began, as best it could, to meet the most pressing relief needs.

In the transport sector, for example, a team of Royal Engineers from the United Kingdom,[6] operating under UNROD auspices and with UNROD logistical assistance, was working to erect bailey bridges before the monsoon. By the end of April, 189 of the 276 damaged bridges and culverts were open to traffic. Road conditions were still poor and vehicles in short supply, but headway was being made. The rail network was, on the other hand, still not fully operating. Some vital links had not been repaired, the speed of trains was restricted, and the capacity of the system was far below the prewar level.

In these circumstances UNROD's fleet of minibulkers, tankers, and tugs was crucial. During February and March the minibulkers were the lifeline of the Dacca area. The railway north from Chittagong was cut at Feni, and without the minibulkers, the movement of food grains from the silo at the port would have been virtually impossible, creating a severe food shortage in the capital. At first, food movements were low—averaging under

4,000 tons per minibulker per month—but with improved organization the tonnage increased.

An UNROD transportation task force was set up in Dacca to control the movement of vessels, and plans were made to charter additional ships, including some to serve as floating warehouses at the port of Chittagong. Preparations were also made for an emergency airlift to cope with the increased transport difficulties that were expected when the monsoon season began.

UNROD was also looking ahead to the problem of lightering cargos from large oceangoing vessels in the outer anchorage at Chittagong. The depth of water over the bar at the entrance to the port is small, and large vessels can only enter after part of their cargo has been unloaded in the outer anchorage. No private or governmental lightering organization was available, and until one could be organized, some minibulkers would have to be diverted to lightering. UNROD brought in 24 vacuvators—machines to suck grain from the holds of ships—and 24 bagging machines to speed the unloading and onward movement of grain.

As more international staff became available, UNROD established a network of field stations, initially at Chittagong, Jessore, Dinajpur, Sylhet, and Khulna. The field stations, normally manned by one or two international staff, a field service officer, and one or two locally recruited staff, continued the work of assessment that had begun in January. Their reports to Dacca provided the UNROD office there—and through it the government, prospective donors, the specialized agencies, and the voluntary agencies—with a continuous picture of relief needs and the success of the efforts made to meet them. The field stations were in radio communication with UNROD in Dacca, and Hagen claimed, with some justice, that the information they supplied was better than that available to the government through its own channels. Through their contacts with the local authorities and by firsthand observation, they provided a steady and invaluable flow of information on the state of roads and railways, ferries, grain stocks, food grain prices, crop prospects, medical supplies and health conditions.

At Chittagong the station also reported on ship arrivals, the un-

UNROD—The End of the Beginning   125

loading of shipments, and the onward movement of supplies. The Chittagong field station soon assumed other functions, and became the lynchpin of the port operations, organizing lightering and stevedore operations, keeping the minibulkers on the move, and maintaining the flow of supplies from the incoming ships to points of need in the interior. Fortunately the officers concerned exemplified field service's happy knack of producing the right man for the job. Paul Wiis, for instance, the Danish field service officer who became de facto UNROD port manager, harbormaster, shipping agent, and chief stevedore at Chittagong, had been in the merchant navy and had worked on port movements with the United Nations peacekeeping forces in the Middle East. The other field stations played a part in the onward movement of supplies. For example, field station officers ensured the prompt delivery of the bailey bridging equipment that arrived in April and had to be moved upcountry in time for erection before the monsoon.

The field stations acquired other functions. Much of their time—some of the field station teams thought too much—was spent in greeting and escorting visitors, from Ambassador Sailer to specialized agency representatives and *Life* magazine reporters. The visitors arrived, one officer said, "at the drop of a hat and are greeted as if their arrival was expected for months."

They also played a part in the rural works projects supported by UNROD and started in cooperation with officials of the ministry of local government, rural development, and cooperatives. These were the outgrowth of an ambitious and innovative agreement UNROD had concluded with the government of Bangladesh. Under the agreement, food grains and other food commodities imported through UNROD and supplied by friendly countries were to be sold in the open market through the food ministry's distribution channels, and the local currency obtained was to support rural works programs to build up the organizational and physical infrastructure and promote agricultural development.[7] Information on the results is hard to obtain.

In addition, the field stations set up and supervised two special projects in the districts of Sylhet and Rajshahi. The Sylhet project, carried out in conjunction with the Bangladesh Rehabilitation Assistance Committee, helped over 200 families engaged in the production of fishing nets. In Rajshahi, UNROD helped rehabilitate 2,000 families engaged in rearing silkworms to provide raw material for the local silk factory. Disinfectants, spray guns, and a cash grant were provided to repair the damaged and infested rearing houses. Although the amounts spent on these projects were small, they initiated useful action at a time when more-ambitious schemes were still in preparation. There were unofficial projects also; for example, a field station officer at Dinajpur used his previous experience in poultry farming to help the Christian Organization for Relief and Rehabilitation rebuild its prewar project.

These, although inadequate to the needs of Bangladesh, were substantial achievements. They were the product of energetic, imaginative, often heroic improvisation, and they had been offset by equally substantial failures. The blanket affair and the collapse of the salvage contract negotiations proved that something was radically amiss both at headquarters and in Bangladesh. The hand-to-mouth, buccaneering management that had carried the operation through the closing months of 1971 and the early months of 1972 had, given the circumstances and the resources available, performed prodigies. The supporting services—field operations service, purchase and transportation, the frequently maligned contracts committee, and the office of personnel services—had demonstrated, as they had done on previous occasions, that the United Nations machine, creaking, cumbrous and eccentric as it may seem, could be made to work quickly and effectively. The task now was to consolidate the operation and enable UNROD to tackle the long haul ahead.

The secretary-general and his immediate collaborators had long been looking for a suitable successor to Paul-Marc Henry, who had been seconded to the United Nations from French government service until the end of December 1971. He had agreed to remain with the operation until 29 February 1972, but was anxious to return to France where he was to take up a key appointment in the Organization for Economic Cooperation and

UNROD—The End of the Beginning 127

Development. On 23 March the secretary-general announced the appointment of Sir Robert Jackson as under-secretary-general in charge of the operation. Jackson was an acknowledged expert in relief and logistics. During the Second World War he had served as chief staff officer to the commander in chief, Malta, and as director-general of the Allied Middle East Supply Center, where he had been concerned, among other things, with providing assistance to the government of Bengal during the 1943 famine. Subsequently as senior deputy director-general of UNRRA he had controlled UNRRA's operations in Europe, the USSR, and China. He had been active in the United Nations from the beginning. In 1948 he had served as assistant secretary-general in charge of coordination under the first UN secretary-general, Trygve Lie, and two decades later directed the celebrated, and in some quarters controversial, study of the capacity of the United Nations development system. During the intervening years he had undertaken a variety of important assignments in the United Kingdom, his native Australia, India, Pakistan, Ghana, and Liberia, and was known to command the confidence of governments, particularly those most intimately concerned with the operation.

Over the next two weeks the process of consolidation gathered momentum. Jackson had visited headquarters at the secretary-general's request in the week preceding the announcement of his appointment, and in the course of discussions with the secretary-general and his senior advisers decisions had been taken on a set of measures to begin organizing the operation better, to improve its cohesiveness and make it an acceptable, efficient instrument for the delivery of assistance. These decisions were quickly put into effect.

By the beginning of April Jackson was in Dacca, where he reviewed the situation with Prime Minister Sheikh Mujib, members of the government, and the UNROD staff. There were some encouraging signs. The firm pledges of assistance already received from governments in response to the secretary-general's February appeal met some of the emergency requirements listed in Ambassador Sailer's preliminary cabled report, and other contributions were in the offing. The most critical problem would be, Jackson told the government, to improve the internal transportation system and effectively organize the distribution of supplies. UNROD could not afford to ask donor governments to send more supplies than could be successfully handled. Skillful planning and firm management would therefore be needed to ensure that the increasing volume of supplies did not exceed the capacity of the country's transportation system or of its two main ports, Chittagong and Chalna.

From Dacca Jackson flew to London to report to the secretary-general and to attend the meeting of ACC. His report was cautiously optimistic. He was not disposed to underestimate the difficulties, but was confident that with improved organization at headquarters and in the field they could be overcome. He had also, he reported, concluded who was the best available candidate to head the operation in Dacca following Hagen, whose public criticisms of the United Nations were generally thought to have created an untenable situation. The secretary-general accepted his recommendation and on 14 April announced that through the good offices of the Swiss government he had obtained the services of Dr. Victor H. Umbricht as chief of mission in Dacca to succeed Hagen. Umbricht was a member of the board of Ciba-Geigy, Basel, and had served in the Swiss Foreign Service, with the International Bank, and with the United Nations operation in the Congo. He was a member of the International Committee of the Red Cross and of various United Nations panels on development problems. Like his predecessor, he was vigorous, strong-minded and utterly dedicated to the humanitarian purposes of the mission. Unlike Hagen, he had had extensive diplomatic and managerial experience.

During the discussions in New York, Secretary-General Waldheim had welcomed Jackson's suggestion that the operation in Bangladesh be organized as an integrated effort undertaken by the United Nations system as a whole, and when the ACC met on 10 April he personally appealed to his colleagues, the executive heads of the specialized agencies and programs, for their support in ensuring the effective coordination of all the activities of

UNROD—The End of the Beginning 129

United Nations organizations in Bangladesh. He suggested that all the organizations and agencies concerned should not only work together but, as far as humanly possible, speak with one voice, in field operations, in setting priorities, and in fund raising and appeals. The response of the heads of the organizations represented in ACC was, the secretary-general reported to the General Assembly and Security Council, immediate and positive.[8] The one-voice principle was accepted and was a major contribution to the success of the operation.

With these developments the operation had, as the secretary-general said in announcing the appointments of Jackson and Umbricht,[9] entered a new phase. Paul-Marc Henry had successfully brought the operation through the crises of late 1971 and early 1972. The bridgehead was established. The world was aware of the great and urgent needs of Bangladesh. The task now was to ensure effective delivery of assistance. Jackson returned to headquarters to lay down the overall strategy for governing the operation—a strategy conditioned by the fact that the monsoon was only six or seven weeks away—and the main tactical actions needed to implement that strategy.

CHAPTER 10

The Consolidation of the Operation

In mid-April the secretary-general received and transmitted to governments the report of the high-level assessment mission headed by Ambassador Sailer, which he had sent to Dacca the previous month.[1] In the month that had elapsed since the mission left Dacca progress had been made. From Dacca Ambassador Sailer had cabled a list of critical shortages that needed urgent correction to avoid suffering and further damage to the economy. In the formal report the mission recorded the action being taken by bilateral donors and UNROD to meet the most pressing needs. The results, although insufficient, were impressive evidence of UNROD's increasing efficacy as a mobilizer and coordinator of aid.

The mission's broad objectives had been to advise the secretary-general on relief and rehabilitation requirements over the next twelve months and to provide some indication of technical assistance needs and of interim studies that might be needed pending the normalization of development aid programs. Its two-volume report generally confirmed the accuracy of the preliminary assessment on which the secretary-general's February appeal for funds had been based. It recommended a program of immediate and longer-run rehabilitation and estimated that a minimum of $648 million in assistance—exclusive of food aid—would be needed to sustain the recovery program in a number of sectors: agriculture and rural reconstruction, transport, telecommunications, health, education, power, industry, housing, community water supplies, technical assistance, and credit expansion to the private sector, trade, and industry. The mission also offered a number of policy recommendations and urged strengthened coordination of relief and rehabilitation assistance. It pointed out that if each donor government, intergovernmental agency, and voluntary agency interested in helping Bangladesh

The Consolidation of the Operation 131

tried separately to assess needs and match them to resources, confusion was inevitable. The difficulties would increase as reconstruction and development requirements began to overlap with relief needs; donors would be reassured, the report suggested, if a reconstruction fund were established and the government strengthened its own aid coordination mechanism. Such a coordinating agency might benefit from technical assistance from international organizations familiar with preparing and executing reconstruction projects.

As Ambassador Sailer's earlier cable to the secretary-general had made clear, the greatest effort was required in the food sector, to meet immediate needs and to build up a viable supply position. The mission considered that until the *aman* crop was harvested in November the government would have to meet relief and rationing requirements at an estimated rate of 200,000 tons a month. The estimate assumed a target of 15 ounces a head a day and was intended to cover the basic needs of 23 percent of the entire population, the balance being provided from local production.

As UNROD itself had done, the mission identified transport as the most serious bottleneck in the economy. Speedy improvisation would be needed, it said, to handle increased imports, notably by emergency measures to make greater use of the country's natural waterways. In the longer term, the road and railway system and inland water transport would have to be rehabilitated and reconstructed. This would have to be coupled with strengthening the management of all transport, emphasizing improved coordination to ensure fuller utilization of all resources. The mission recommended that the government appoint a transport controller to direct the transport system as a whole.

Rural reconstruction and rehabilitation were also, in the mission's view, urgent in order to restore agricultural production to prewar levels and to begin working on rural unemployment and underemployment. Social stability was threatened, the report stressed, by the combination of high unemployment and the breakdown of food production as a result of the loss of tools and draft animals and the lack of seeds, fertilizers, and pesticides. Jute and rice production commanded high priorities, the report said, as did the reactivation of labor-intensive rural works programs planned and executed at the local level.

In accordance with its terms of reference, the mission did not suggest a longer-term development strategy. To have done so would have been premature, since the government had not had time to establish longer-run priorities or to set up a development program that would meet the needs of the new nation. The mission recognized that relief, rehabilitation, and development were inextricably bound together. For the time being, however, it suggested that the world community should set itself the limited goal of making sure the 1972 relief program met immediate needs and would allow for the prompt resumption of normal development as soon as circumstances permitted.

Ambassador Sailer's report provided the first authoritative international assessment of Bangladesh's immediate needs and of the resources necessary to meet them. It brought forward little or no new information on the country's problems and offered no new insights into ways they might be tackled. The report could not reasonably be expected to do so. It was compiled hastily after a two-week visit to the area and was inevitably a compendium of what was already known and a catalogue of immediately available remedies. Nevertheless, the report was, as the secretary-general said, of much value to all concerned in understanding the nature and scope of the problem and in undertaking the measures needed to cope with it. In particular it provided a framework for UNROD's future work and, with some adjustments, a yardstick for measuring the progress made in mobilizing resources. Ambassador Sailer's leadership and the participation of the World Bank and the IMF also gave the assessment a stamp of authority, which the earlier review of needs by UNROD itself would otherwise have lacked. The fact that Ambassador Sailer was her country's representative in New Delhi must have helped to convince doubters, if any remained, that UNROD was in fact neutral and had no bias toward Pakistan. Her personal reputation and her long association with United Nations development work were evidence of the solidity of the organization's commitment to the relief project.

The Consolidation of the Operation   133

For all its merits the mission's report created some difficulties for the managers of the operation. On 28 May Umbricht, in a message commenting on the economic and political situation, said that some members of the government were irritated "with UNROD for not implementing various important parts" of the Sailer report. They noted, he said, that the report frequently cited UNROD as a source of finance and wondered whether UNROD was "prepared and in a position to perform." Jackson replied that while greatly appreciating the quality of the work carried out by Ambassador Sailer and her colleagues, he shared Umbricht's sensitivity about the effects of the report. "The inherent difficulty of appointing survey missions is," he commented, "that the content of the report itself invariably tends to become regarded as a commitment in contrast to being a recommendation. This is exactly what has happened with the Sailer report and we are now faced with an unfavorable political situation affecting UNROD directly yet arising from circumstances outside its control." All that UNROD could do, he suggested, was to assist as best it could in areas where it was invited to do so. If it could help maintain a steady supply line of essential foodstuffs and reinforce the transportation and distribution systems, it would, he pointed out, make a vital contribution in a basic and most sensitive political area.

The confusion of recommendations and commitments was not a new problem and was not one created by the Sailer report. Statements of needs are easily interpreted by potential recipients as implied promises to deliver. In 1971, the government of Pakistan had repeatedly complained of UNEPRO's inability to meet its needs. In the early months of 1972, Paul-Marc Henry and Hagen had, several times, been brusquely confronted with what the Bangladesh government regarded as unfulfilled promises. The cost estimates of recommended requirements in the Sailer report were almost sure to be taken by the government, which faced growing unrest as a result of food shortages, rising prices, and the lack of economic progress, as a list of commitments that had not been honored.

In retrospect some foreign observers in Dacca and elsewhere

were inclined to fault the Sailer report and to argue that it did not go far enough. It has been suggested, for example, that the mission might have insisted more forcefully on its recommendations concerning the provision of foreign advisers and the equalization of prices between Bangladesh and India to avoid the growth of an unofficial market and the leakage of supplies to India. A few were more ambitious. The report was, they believed, a traditional approach to an unprecedented situation and might have been more productive had the mission given more attention to some of the broader problems of constructing a new nation and maintaining the momentum of independence. The criticisms are debatable. What Bangladesh needed was not advice but assistance and time to work out its own problems in its own way. The Sailer mission was concerned with assessing assistance needs and rightly concentrated on that task. It is hard, given the political circumstances and the constraints of time, to imagine that any other approach could have achieved more than the Sailer mission, created fewer difficulties, or produced a greater or more useful impact on the government officials and others in donor countries to whom the report was primarily addressed.

The Sailer mission's emphasis on the coordination of relief activities was in line with the secretary-general's thinking. In reporting the appointments of Sir Robert Jackson as under-secretary-general in overall charge of the relief operation and of Victor Umbricht as UNROD chief of mission in Bangladesh, he stressed that one of their most important tasks, cooperating with the government of Bangladesh, would be to organize the growing range of UNROD activities to ensure close, harmonious coordination within the United Nations system and between UNROD and the programs arranged bilaterally by governments and by the voluntary agencies, to the extent that the governments and agencies were willing to make this possible.[2]

Within the United Nations system itself the necessary framework for coordination was provided by the ACC's acceptance of the secretary-general's suggestion that the specialized agencies and programs active in Bangladesh should work together and speak with one voice. Applying the one-voice principle, as it came to be called, in this kind of operation was innovative, and highly successful. The principle itself was not new. It was implicit in the view of the functions of the UNDP resident representatives taken in the Jackson study of the capacity of the United Nations development system,[3] but it had not hitherto been effectively applied in a broader context.

From its beginnings in UNEPRO, the relief operation had, of course, been seen as a combined effort by the United Nations system as a whole. Reporting to the secretary-general in June 1971, Assistant Secretary-General Kittani, for example, suggested that the effort to work out arrangements for a coordinated emergency assistance through several agencies of the system, under the auspices and leadership of the United Nations could be described as "the first imaginative move of its kind." The means of coordination used, however, were traditional and initially, at any rate, did not contemplate centralized fund-raising. The principal task of the inter-agency groups in Dacca and Geneva was to harmonize the work of the various agencies and programs in the field and to share the available funds among them. The arrangements eventually established might have worked in a more nearly normal situation. The successful effort under the leadership of the high commissioner for refugees to assist the government of India in meeting the needs of the refugees from East Pakistan was coordinated through a substantially similar mechanism. The high commissioner's operation was, however, different in kind, as well as in scale, and was in any case centered on a well-established program with recognized competence in refugee matters. UNROD, which, like UNEPRO, was shouldering direct operational responsibilities in a new situation requiring the joint efforts of a variety of organizations and programs, called for a more innovative approach in which the United Nations could provide effective, efficient, and continuous leadership.

The one-voice principle carried the process of coordination an important step further. Policy making and fund raising were centralized at United Nations headquarters, and agency staff in Bangladesh worked as members of the UNROD team under the leadership of the chief of mission. The chief of mission represented the system in his dealings with the government of Bangladesh, and agency operations were, with some few exceptions, an integral part of the UNROD effort. The principle worked well. The activities of the specialized agencies and programs in Bangladesh were for all practical purposes merged with those of UNROD. UNICEF—while carrying on its normal programs to the extent that these were compatible with the relief operation's needs and priorities—participated fully in the operation from the beginning, as did FAO, WFP, and WHO. Other agencies—ITU, ICAO, ILO, and UNESCO—provided expert assistance when it was required. The representative of IMF in Bangladesh served as an adviser to UNROD throughout the operation. The representatives of the World Bank also participated continuously in UNROD's work, although the bank maintained a separate office in Dacca since its primary concern was with reconstruction and the resumption of development rather than with relief.

The secretary-general's actions to ensure coordination paralleled and complemented those of the Bangladesh government. The prime minister had already set on foot similar arrangements to ensure that all relief activities were conducted in an integrated manner within the government and effectively coordinated with the operations being conducted by UNROD or under its auspices. The planning commission and the coordination division for external assistance and rehabilitation of the prime minister's secretariat provided mechanisms through which the desired coordination could be achieved. UNROD's relations with both the planning commission and the coordination division were close and went far to ensure that coordination and cooperation were effective at the working and administrative levels as well as at the policy level.

UNROD was concerned with providing relief, helping the government meet the immediate needs of the people for food, shelter, clean water, and protection against disease, and restoring the shattered infrastructure. It was nonetheless necessary to look ahead to the time when the phase of relief and emergency rehabilitation could be completed and the process of reconstruction and development could begin.

The Consolidation of the Operation 137

A realistic target had therefore to be set for the end of the relief phase so that the authorities—national and international—responsible for reconstruction and development could plan their work effectively. This was not easy. The situation was fluid and there were, as the Secretary-General recognized, many imponderables that made forecasting uncertain. Sudden emergencies—the hazards of weather, crop failures—could upset the most carefully planned timetables. Nevertheless, the secretary-general, in agreement with the government of Bangladesh, suggested that the relief phase should be concentrated in the period ending 31 March 1973.[4] If all went well, it was reasonable to suppose that by then the food shortage would have declined to normal proportions and that the need for emergency assistance in the transport and other sectors would have been reduced to a level permitting a shift in emphasis from relief to reconstruction and development. The target was realistic but not rigid. The door had to be left open to the possibility of prolonging the operation beyond 31 March 1973 if circumstances required it.

During the first phase, UNROD, working with the assistance of the various United Nations agencies and programs, would bear primary responsibility, the secretary-general explained, for coordination and operations undertaken by the United Nations system. Later, as the relief phase increasingly contained elements of reconstruction, the normal agencies and programs of the United Nations system would take over according to the usual pattern of United Nations assistance. The two phases could not, of course, be sharply differentiated, and some reconstruction work had to be started during the relief phase. For this reason, UNROD, with the assistance of the specialized agencies and programs working under its umbrella, would, the secretary-general said, attempt to dovetail plans and projects for reconstruction with its ongoing relief program.

The steps taken by the secretary-general to strengthen the management of the operation at headquarters and in the field and to improve coordination were coupled with an effort to define an effective strategy. It was the first time the exercise had been attempted. Hitherto there had been organigrams, schemes for the deployment of staff, assessments of needs, and statements of priorities—which were swallowed in further lists of proliferating needs—but no clear plan that set out what the operation could hope to do and the means by which it would seek to do it. In the rapidly shifting situation in the latter half of 1971 there had been no hope of evolving a rational plan of this kind. In the months leading up to the December war, Henry and his colleagues were like desperate men trying frantically to scramble up a rapidly accelerating down escalator; after the war, in the first weeks of 1972, they had been preoccupied with the immediate problems of establishing relations with the new government, regrouping supplies, and making a start with the most urgent tasks of relief. Hagen had glimpsed some of the priorities but had not had the time or, it may be suspected, the cast of mind needed to translate his insight into a workable plan. In any case, planning presupposed a confident relationship between headquarters and the field, which Hagen's conduct in Dacca was rapidly destroying.

Jackson's objective was to define a clear-cut strategy to control the UNROD program as a whole and to convince donor governments that UNROD was being managed so effectively both internally and externally that further financial support was justified. The strategy was based on six "fundamental factors": the secretary-general's determination to do everything in his power to alleviate suffering in Bangladesh; the state of international relations, in which there would be serious political difficulty in generating further financial support, the bulk of which would have to come from governments, unless the government of Bangladesh and UNROD could conclusively demonstrate that failure to meet certain essential needs would inevitably lead to disaster; the need to demonstrate that the government and UNROD were working to a basic, well-thought-out plan based on minimum essential requirements to prevent disaster; the possibility that India might not be able to provide relief indefinitely on the scale it was doing; the imponderable effects of the approaching monsoon; and the planned termination of UNROD on 31 March 1973.

Because of these factors and the imminence of the monsoon, which would heavily restrict the movement of supplies, the relief

The Consolidation of the Operation   139

program adopted was austere. For practical reasons it had to be limited to supplies and equipment necessary to preserve life—essential foodstuffs, transport equipment, medical supplies, corrugated iron, and other materials to meet emergency shelter requirements—and the seeds, fertilizers, pesticides, and mechanical equipment needed to make food production possible later in the year. For the time being, measures of reconstruction had to be confined to those elements of the infrastructure—transport, storage, and distribution—that were essential to the conduct of the relief effort.

The strategy was, in a sense, a retreat from the program of immediate and longer-term rehabilitation foreseen by the Sailer mission. However, it was clear, unambiguous, and effective and enabled UNROD to provide the support the Bangladesh government needed with the minimum of misunderstanding and without floundering in ever-lengthening lists of impractical commitments.

The strategy was based on the identification of requirements. UNROD's preliminary assessment in the first weeks of the operation and Ambassador Sailer's report gave aggregates of relief requirements, but these needed constant updating. Monitoring relief requirements and the resources available to meet them, therefore, became a continuous UNROD service.

Phasing relief supplies was vital. For supplies from overseas a long lead time was inevitable. It could be shortened by using air transport, but this was expensive and for bulk cargoes impossible. Internal factors had also to be taken into account. In the short term, Indian generosity and the efficiency of Indian railways provided an answer to the deficiencies of the country's transport system. In the longer run the inflow of supplies had to be correlated with the availability of transport and cargo-handling capacity and with shifting needs within the country.

The new policy was defined in a letter of 5 June from Umbricht to Rab Chaudhuri, the secretary of the government's coordination division for external assistance for relief and rehabilitation. The letter was intended, he said, "to clarify a number of issues regarding the role, the achievements and the aspirations of UNROD, not only as an operating agency implementing the relief program which was initiated by the secretary-general last February, but also as a catalyst to induce donor countries to give maximum support to the priority needs of the people and government of Bangladesh in the face of the immense tasks this new nation is confronting." UNROD's role was, he said: to help ensure sufficient supplies of food grains to meet the nation's consumption requirements; to help build up stocks of food grain to some 600,000 tons by the end of 1972; to provide coordinated logistical support for the transportation and distribution of food; to participate in emergency rehabilitation projects that increased the effectiveness of the relief operation; to keep donor countries continuously informed of the country's relief needs and to issue appeals through the United Nations secretary-general for pledges to finance these needs either bilaterally or multilaterally.

As Jackson put it, the new policy called for a "sympathetic and hard-headed relief operation with no trimmings." UNROD would be primarily concerned with facilitating the coordination of logistical plans and would not be involved in further financial responsibilities apart from those resulting from assistance in the internal distribution of food grains using the ships under UNROD control. Jackson suggested that food-grain needs should be met through bilateral agreements between the government of Bangladesh and the principal suppliers, with the secretary-general providing support for the government's requests. Any proposed new expenditures by UNROD would be limited to items considered essential in the relief phase and, where possible, needs would be met locally or through bilateral sources. UNROD—which had only $13 million of uncommitted funds—would function as a treasury of last resort.

Umbricht had some doubts about the proposed strategy, which, he thought, might "emasculate" UNROD. In a cable to headquarters, he explained that the prime minister and government would want UNROD to perform certain functions in preference to bilateral donors, since the latter's efforts were inclined to carry overtones. UNROD, he said, is "the only organization here able to advise the government objectively on policy matters and to ensure a balanced and coordinated endeavor." The differences between Umbricht and headquarters were differences of emphasis and viewpoint and, in part at least, based on misunderstanding. "I curse, repeat curse, lack of telephonic communications," Jackson replied, "which would let us demolish these misunderstandings in a matter of minutes." It was a curse he was to repeat often in the course of the operation.

The misunderstandings were quickly removed, and at headquarters and in the field UNROD concentrated its efforts on mobilizing the greatest possible flow of resources—multilateral, bilateral, and voluntary—to assist Bangladesh, and on ensuring the best possible use could be made of them. Bilateral assistance had been important from the start and became increasingly so. India and the USSR, among major contributors, were already providing assistance on a bilateral basis, and the United States, which had recognized the government of Bangladesh in April, was now in a position to do so. In this situation, the new strategy that sought to match supplies and needs, to determine the content of the relief program, and to identify danger points in the period of the operation proved invaluable.

CHAPTER 11

The Right Road: May-September 1972

From May onward, grain shipments from overseas began to arrive at the country's main ports, Chalna and Chittagong, in larger volume, supplementing the increasing overland flow from India. On 17 May the *Montpellier-Victory* arrived in the outer anchorage at Chittagong with 48,000 tons of bulk wheat from the United States. It was the largest single UNROD shipment to date and brought to 125,000 tons the total amount of food delivered through UNROD.[1] The period of waiting was over and with more than 400,000 tons of grain still in the pipeline, the crisis seemed to have been surmounted.

There was no ground for complacency. Soon after Umbricht's arrival in Dacca, headquarters requested him to make a new assessment of food import needs in consultation with the planning commission and the ministries of food and agriculture. The results were disquieting. Government stocks were shrinking rapidly as more people depended for survival on the food grains provided from official stocks through the statutory- and modified-rationing and relief-distribution mechanisms. Although stocks at Dacca and in the upcountry storage depots were good, the silos at Chittagong and Chalna were emptying fast. If the rate of offtake continued, government stocks would be down to 200,000 tons by the end of May, barely sufficient for one month's rationing and relief needs. To meet immediate needs and build reserves to a reasonably safe level, the country would have to import one million tons of grain between June and November.

The estimate of import needs was based on a food grain balance which UNROD had prepared and discussed with the planning commission and the ministries concerned. It was, like all estimates of food needs in Bangladesh, riddled with uncertainties. The country's food grain import needs were established by calculating the total tonnage required to feed the population at an assumed rate of consumption—15 ounces a head a day—and subtracting this figure from the total estimated domestic production. None of the figures was reliable. The last census in East Pakistan was taken in January 1961. Estimates of the 1972 population ranged from 72 million to 77 million. A figure of 75 million was accepted for planning purposes. Estimates of domestic production were equally uncertain. The planning commission thought that the *boro* and *aus* crops would be catastrophically low. The ministry of agriculture and the UNROD food adviser believed they were unlikely to be less than 90 percent of normal. There was a further uncertainty; rice was undoubtedly finding its way across the border into India, but estimates of the amount taken out of the country ranged from 100,000 to 400,000 tons.

From the standpoint of long-range policy, the uncertainties were important and would need to be accounted for in planning a national food import program once the emergency was over. From UNROD's point of view, they were offset by the fact that the government stocks required to feed the 10 percent of the population dependent on official supplies were so depleted that mass starvation was possible and they could only be replenished by heavy imports.

In light of these needs, the secretary-general launched an urgent appeal on 31 May to a selected group of potential donor countries for a million more tons of grain in addition to the supplies already donated or pledged. Speaking to a meeting of potential donor countries, he said the grain "would help to sustain the lives of 75 million people until the new harvest is available at the end of the year." He added: "The effects of the destruction and dislocation brought about in Bangladesh by war and the cyclone that preceded it are only now becoming fully apparent." In human terms the suffering was on a vast scale. "In material terms the extent of destruction seems," he said, "to be endless. What we do know with certainty is that the economy has been flattened, that probably half the working population—12 million men and women—are without work; that food production has been badly dislocated; that enormous damage has been done to the entire infrastructure." He went on to say that he had consulted the authorities in Dacca and as a result was satisfied the additional imports could be handled with reasonable efficiency. The facilities would, of course, be under heavy strain. For that reason, he specifically asked donor governments to consult with the government of Bangladesh and the chief of the mission in Dacca, as well as with Sir Robert Jackson and his staff in New York, before making shipping arrangements, so that detailed schedules could be worked out. He suggested also that governments unable to supply grain could help by financing shipping costs and providing the cash needed to support UNROD's essential operations, including the use of the minibulkers, barges, and other craft on charter.[2]

The movement of grain on this scale would have been impossible without UNROD's logistic assistance. The railways were still not fully operational. Road transport had been improved since the beginning of the year with the repair of bridges and ferries but would be hampered during the monsoon. The capacity of the country's two sea ports, which had been reduced by wartime damage and sunken vessels in the channels, was still substantially impaired. At Chittagong, Soviet salvage vessels had begun clearance operations, but the work was complex and far from complete. To cope with the inflow of food grain, the UNROD minibulker fleet was strengthened, from 17 vessels in April to 25 at the end of June, and the transportation task force set up in March increased its efforts to control and coordinate the movement of relief supplies. It was in radio touch with most of the fifty vessels under UNROD control and with the loading and unloading points and was making progress in hastening the process of lightering and unloading. There were difficulties. Umbricht complained that the task force was not always informed of the arrival of grain shipments from bilateral sources, but in general the system was working well. From June to November the minibulkers alone carried over 100,000 tons of cargo a month and, despite the handicaps, the incoming grain was successfully moved from the ships to the silos and storage depots.

In August the distribution network was further strengthened. On 5 August the *Manhattan*, the largest vessel in the United States merchant marine, arrived off Chittagong with 66,063 tons of wheat and remained there as a floating silo for the next four

The Right Road

months. She was financed by USAID—at a cost of $19,000 a day—and was not the ideal vessel for the job. Umbricht and his colleagues made it clear they would have preferred smaller vessels or perhaps inflatable warehouses. Jackson was aware of the disadvantages and also of Washington's interest in the project. "*Manhattan* is," he cabled Umbricht, "of critical importance and has already become a political issue in Washington. It is essential that she should be used successfully and we must all break our backs to ensure that this happens for political reasons as well as practical." In the end the operation was successful and the *Manhattan*, according to Umbricht, "proved her value beyond expectations."

The *Manhattan* operation started badly. Within hours after the UNROD party boarded—the coordinator of the operation and 320 stevedores and mechanics—the *Manhattan*'s bosun was swept over the side by a breaking line and drowned. It was the first of a series of misadventures. Because of her draught, the *Manhattan* was anchored 56 miles from Chittagong, 14 miles from the nearest land. In the heavy monsoon swell, she rolled up to 10 degrees, and the hazards of coming alongside were increased by the ice belt—a 1,500-ton projecting-steel structure—that had been fitted above the waterline to ward off ice during the *Manhattan*'s attempt to carry oil through the Northwest Passage. The lightering vessels—antique, poorly equipped, and inefficiently manned liberty ships—had great difficulty remaining alongside. "It was," UNROD coordinator Richard Murray reported, "quite a sight: pipes pulling away and breaking, vessels pulling apart and nothing much that could be done except try to save the ship and pray that no laborer gets hurt by snapping lines while they try desperately to pull in the pipes." The minibulkers managed rather better, but some of the incoming grain ships had difficulties. One, the *Eagle Voyager*, broke away when the tide got between her and the *Manhattan* and drifted with a wire line entangled in her rudder. The minibulker *Mini Lid* brought a diver from Chittagong to free the rudder, and a week later when the seas calmed, the *Eagle Voyager* tried again. Once again she broke away and this time damaged her superstructure. The *Eagle Voyager* finally discharged her cargo in the outer anchorage.

The operation was nevertheless a success. The *Manhattan*'s

crew—which included six masters, the captain, the port captain and four mates qualified as masters—was seamanlike and cooperative. The UNROD team worked day and night and by the end of the operation had unloaded and discharged 109,597 tons of wheat. In all, 28 ships were lightered alongside the *Manhattan*, reducing the burden on the overcrowded port facilities.

There were other problems. The vacuvators used to suck grain from the holds of the ships were old and broke down frequently. There were labor difficulties too. The mechanics were inefficient and the stevedores who had been brought on board for 10-day periods became restive when bad weather prevented their return to Chittagong. On the whole, though, morale was high and the work was done. It must have seemed appropriate to all concerned, however, that the operation ended on Thanksgiving Day, 23 November.

The operation was expensive. Apart from the charter costs—said by a USAID official to have exceeded $4 million—which were borne by the United States government, there were other penalties. The *Manhattan* was eight hours steaming time from Chittagong. Had smaller vessels been available as floating silos in the outer anchorage, sailing time would have been reduced, more incoming grain vessels could have been handled, and the lightering vessels and minibulkers could have moved grain faster to Chittagong, Chalna, and Narayanganj. Nevertheless, in tactical terms the exercise was justified. The grain was kept moving. The ports did not become clogged, and supplies arrived where they were needed.

By mid-1972 UNROD was on the right road. The press reported United Nations officials were "cautiously optimistic."[3] Food supplies were on the way. The secretary-general's May appeal, backed by insistent direct approaches to individual governments, in person, by telephone, and in writing, was producing results. On 11 June Umbricht informed Prime Minister Sheikh Mujib that the response was satisfactory.[4] The transport equipment needed to move the food supplies—minibulkers, lightering vessels, trucks, and aircraft—was in place or on the way, and UNROD had brought in four chartered tankers with the diesel fuel to keep the transport moving.

The Right Road

There was another big gain. The Bangladesh government's disenchantment with the relief operation was being overcome. Umbricht and, during his visits to Bangladesh, Sir Robert Jackson, had established a new, frank and friendly relationship with the prime minister that was percolating to the lower levels of government and was strengthened by the visible evidence of the relief effort's effectiveness. In July the president of Bangladesh, Abu Syed Chowdhury, chose to make his first flight from Dacca in the United Nations Skyvan. He told Umbricht it was a symbol "of the direction we are going to take."

There was no reason to believe the worst was over. As the government's first annual plan, published later in the month, limply said, "the economic problems of Bangladesh are many."[5] Jackson described them as an "avalanche." Those that could be tackled were being tackled, and many of them would require years of effort. For the moment, UNROD's immediate concern was the coming monsoon and the new problems that would create.

The first crisis came in June. The monsoon started early and flash floods in the Sylhet and Pabna districts took a heavy toll of lives and left thousands marooned. Umbricht and the ICRC provided a helicopter for the district commissioner and UNROD immediately mobilized all the craft available to rush relief goods to the disaster area. Between 26 June and mid-August three Hercules aircraft chartered for UNROD by USAID and the United Kingdom government flew over 400 sorties and delivered more than 7,500 tons of food grain. A DC-6 placed at UNROD's disposal by the Swiss government and the ICRC flew in over 700 tons in more than 70 sorties. UNROD's small air fleet was equally active. The Skyvan successfully delivered boats, 10 tons of hand pumps, medical supplies, and spare parts for repairing damaged tubewells in the area. The eight-passenger Pilatus Porter aircraft and two helicopters made available by ICRC were used to ferry UNROD and other relief agency staff to the striken areas and to carry out reconnaissance flights with officials of the Bangladesh government.

By July it was clear from reports reaching the government of Bangladesh and the chief of mission in Dacca that another crisis was imminent in the country's five northwestern districts. Once again the weather was frustrating the government's rehabilitation plans. The monsoon rains had begun early, but in late June and early July the rainfall was far below normal. The harvest was in jeopardy and local food stocks were dropping to a critically low level. Joint surveys undertaken by the government and senior UNROD officials showed that at least 65,000 tons of grain would have to be brought into the northwestern districts between mid-July and early December. The government had initially thought that 84,000 tons would be needed but agreed to the lower figure. Ample grain was in the silos at Chittagong and Chalna, but it could not be used to replenish the supply depots in the northwest on the required scale in the time available. The tonnage needed could not be moved from the south by road. Even if the trucks and fuel had been there, movement would be difficult and in some places impossible during the monsoon. Rail transport was also out of the question as the Hardinge Bridge, the vital rail link across the Ganges, was still not open to traffic.

In late June the subject dominated the weekly senior staff meetings, which Umbricht had instituted and which provided a regular opportunity for the senior members of the UNROD team, including the agency representatives and experts, to pool their information and experience. The first and obvious source of additional grain was India. Supplying the district from the south would be difficult. Colonel Earley, UNROD's senior transport adviser, thought there was no practical way of moving 65,000 tons a month from the ports to the north bank of the Ganges. Supplies from the south would, if possible, have to be supplemented by shipping more grain by road and rail from India. That raised difficulties. India is not a grain-rich country and had already been especially generous by any standard.

Umbricht flew to New Delhi and a memorandum outlining the crisis was submitted to the Indian cabinet on 11 July. The following day, the political affairs committee decided to send an immediate additional shipment of 50,000 tons. The decision was prompt and generous and had, Umbricht reported to headquarters, been "facilitated by personal friendship." It had also been assisted by the efforts Jackson and Umbricht had made, since their

The Right Road

appointments, to repair relations between the government of India and UNROD. These had been strained by Hagen's outburst in March and his reported reluctance to provide UNROD facilities to unload Indian vessels. Other visits followed and the government of India agreed to move an additional 150,000 tons into the northwest by road and rail in August, September, and October. There was some talk of diverting grain shipped to Bangladesh to replace the Indian donation, but this was not done.

It was decided also that as much grain as possible should be moved upcountry by river, using the biggest vessels feasible. Umbricht authorized an experimental run using the minibulkers, and on 26 July the *Mini Log* sailed from Narayanganj to Paksey on the north bank of the Ganges immediately below the Hardinge Bridge with 1,500 tons of bagged grain. She grounded twice but completed the voyage. At Paksey, four 15-ton pontoon motorboats flown from the south by UNROD were waiting to receive her. The cargo was successfully discharged at the improvised port and moved by truck to the interior. In the following months, 11,090 tons were moved upcountry by this route.

The *Mini Log* was the largest vessel ever to sail so far up the Ganges and the first of any size to do so since 1954. The voyage was the most spectacular of the minibulkers' many achievements in Bangladesh. The record does not show who first thought of sending minibulkers to the area. It was presumably a USAID official, but whoever it was deserves commemoration. The minibulkers saved Dacca from starvation in the immediate postwar months and continued to be the mainstay of the relief operation.

Originally designed for work on the Mississippi, the minibulkers are miniature versions of the big bulk carriers that transport most of the world's grain and oil supplies across the oceans. They are maneuverable and with their flat keelless bottoms ideal for use in shallow waters. Unlike conventional inland water craft, they are capable of work in the open sea and can make the bay crossing from Chittagong to Narayanganj and Chalna in almost any weather. In a report to the chief of mission, a naval architect, L. C. Penning, said that if he were to design a ship for the Bangladesh trade, it would be basically "not very much different, maybe somewhat smaller as to draft." The minibulkers' strongest point was, he added, that they were there, and that their crews—mostly Greek with Bangalee deckhands—knew the job.

There was some criticism of the minibulkers. The time-charter was expensive and the operating cost was relatively high. Because of the shallow water in which they operated, the minibulkers could not carry full cargoes—2,000 tons instead of the possible 3,000—but they were still more efficient than conventional coasters. The main reason, however, for the relatively high ton-mile cost was slow turnaround time. Loading and unloading took longer than they should have. There were labor troubles and there was no money to pay stevedores to work at night. Movement was also slowed by the absence of night navigational aids in Bangladesh inland waters. Light buoys were supplied by a bilateral donor, but remained on the quay side at Chittagong.

In a further effort to relieve the shortage in the northwest, UNROD organized an airlift to the northwestern districts, to be supplemented by an airdrop. This kind of operation had been contemplated for many months. Relief officials, like generals, seem drawn to aviation, and, like generals, they appear to believe that if only enough objects can be dropped from the air, problems will disappear, and like generals they are often disappointed. An airlift to liberated areas had been discussed in the closing months of 1971, and UNEPRO, with its two light aircraft, had been equipped with an air adviser.

In April 1972 R. P. O'Quinn, the head of the Foundation for Airborne Relief (FAR), a California-based nonprofit organization, visited Bangladesh with plans for an airdrop of relief goods using a new technique devised by Air America in Laos. USAID agreed to finance the operation—at a reported cost of $1.5 million dollars—and FAR arrived in Bangladesh with two helicopters and two amphibians. A C-130 was to be used for the drop. There was, as the official assessment says, a learning phase in which the bagging technique was perfected. The rice was placed in a plastic bag with an outer covering of burlap. The bags were test-dropped from helicopters at heights of 1,000 to 20 feet, "greatest damage being experienced," the assessment reports, "with drops above

The Right Road 151

300 feet." The laws of nature were clearly operative in Bangladesh.

Between 13 August and 9 September the C-130 flew 18 sorties to the Dinajpur district and dropped 169 tons of rice. The number of bags that burst is not recorded. The operation is reported to have been successful and, in fact, rice prices fell. Hoarders and speculators were said to have been discouraged. There was also, an UNROD assessment claimed, a psychological impact. "The value of the food dropped was not all that great. But it was far surpassed by the lift that it gave to local morale."

Unofficial comments are less enthusiastic. The tonnage dropped was small and could have been delivered less expensively by other means. Dinajpur was not an isolated pocket where starvation could only be averted by airdropping food. During the same period 1,100 tons were flown in by a conventional airlift, suggesting that the drop was unnecessary. Moreover, rice prices, it is argued, would have fallen in any case as the *boro* surplus came on the market in early August. "With respect to arguments of psychological advantage," an unpublished report by UNROD's economic unit hints darkly, "one suspects their empirical base."

There was another line of criticism. Asked about the drop, a British expert who happened to be present in the area said, "Well, it was not the way we did it in the Airborne Regiment." The operation was amateur. Jackson had suggested that one or another of the politically acceptable national air forces should be asked to undertake any airlift or airdrop operation that might be needed. Umbricht believed that for political reasons this was impossible.

FAR left Bangladesh later in the year. The operation had one lasting consequence. Field service operations became one of the world's largest holders of heavy gauge plastic bags of an unusual size. It was able eventually, by the exercise of commercial dexterity, to liquidate its stocks. In Dacca, some bags were still visible in 1973, holding grain in shops in the old town, shining and incongruous among the local burlap sacks.

Whatever the deficiencies of the airdrop and however questionable its cost benefits, UNROD's contribution to the operation was efficient and ingenious. Plastic bags were provided, labor was found—and trained—to fill them, and arrangements were made to receive and store the rice airlifted or airdropped. At Chittagong, inflatable warehouses were set up at the airfield for storing and bagging the grain. The warehouses arrived in Bangladesh without the promised technician and with no compressor to inflate them. Someone remembered that the cholera vaccine laboratory in Dacca used a vacuum chamber in its manufacturing processes. A technician was borrowed, a compressor was improvised and the warehouses were inflated. It was the second successful improvisation of its kind. Earlier the crew of a jet transport carrying sea trucks[6] from England could not find an air compressor at Chittagong airfield. The nearest equipment was at Dacca. It struck the UNROD port officer that the vacuvators used to draw grain from ships could be made to blow as well as suck. He brought two vacuvators to the airfield, rigged a pipe to connect them to the aircraft, and the problem was solved.

UNROD's effort to grapple with the monsoon crisis was successful. Improvisation played a part, but the success was mainly the result of planning, diplomacy, and the skillful deployment of the equipment and staff available. Two additional lightering vessels were chartered so that stocks could be built up at Chalna in anticipation of the reopening of the Hardinge Bridge and the rail route from Chalna to the northwest. The bridge was reopened at the end of October and the movement of grain by rail from the south was resumed.

The immediate crisis had been surmounted. After the arrival of grain overland from India and the supplies moved in by UNROD, the shortage in the northwest had been eased. UNROD could begin to accelerate the movement of other relief goods—edible oil, high-protein food for the UNICEF child feeding program, roofing, medicines, and educational equipment that had been held at the ports while absolute priority was given to grain shipments.

In the meantime, UNROD had taken on a new task. In early August Umbricht informed headquarters that the government would welcome an offer to help clear the port of Chalna. The Soviet salvage crews' work at Chittagong was making progress, but

The Right Road

it was unlikely that the Chittagong clearance could be completed before 1973. Valuable time had been lost at the beginning of the year and conditions were unexpectedly difficult. The captain in charge of the Soviet operation told a Dacca newspaper, "Everything has to be done in the dark. The water is so turbid that visibility is practically nil. Work is restricted to a brief interval between the high and low water when there is no current."[7]

On 23 August Marcel d'Astugues, the deputy chief of mission, reported from Dacca that the Soviet Embassy confirmed the USSR salvage vessels would not undertake the Chalna clearance. This time the United Nations was ready. Jackson had consulted his friend, the late General Wheeler, who had directed the successful Suez Canal clearance, and on his recommendation had obtained the services of Captain Searle, a retired United States Navy officer and a salvage expert of international reputation. By the end of the month, Captain Searle was on his way to Bangladesh to make a survey and confer with the government.

Captain Searle completed his reconnaissance quickly, and on 8 September the government formally requested the United Nations to undertake the clearance operation. On 14 September Jackson told a meeting of donor governments in New York that he had consulted the secretary-general and that it was his intention—unless the meeting advised him to the contrary—to clear as much of Chalna as possible. He explained there were two reasons why the United Nations should undertake the clearance—the time factor and the fact that no government had as much information as the United Nations on the problem. The United Nations was, he thought, the only organization capable of performing the task before the onset of the 1973 monsoon. Some representatives attending the meeting had misgivings. As they saw it, the salvage operation was primarily directed toward rehabilitation and might divert funds and energies from UNROD's main task as a relief organization. They did not press their point. The borderline between relief and rehabilitation is hazy and from the standpoint both of immediate relief and longer-term reconstruction it was clearly desirable that the port be reopened to normal operations as soon as possible.

Five days later, twenty-two salvage firms in fifteen countries were invited to bid and six responded. Despite the speed with which Captain Searle had completed his survey, none of the bidders asked for additional information or questioned the accuracy of the data he had provided—a tribute to his professional expertise. Three weeks of intensive analysis and negotiation followed, and on 24 October a contract was signed with a consortium headed by Smit Tak International Salvage Company of the Netherlands, Fukuda Salvage Company of Japan, Ulrich Harms of the Federal Republic of Germany, and Michael J. Batty Associates of Singapore. The contract, one of the most complex ever entered into by the United Nations, had been negotiated in record time. As soon as it was signed, divers were sent to Bangladesh to begin demolition work and the contractors began to move heavy lifting equipment from Japan, Germany, and the Netherlands. The target—to complete the essential clearance work by 15 May 1973—was ambitious but the plan was sound, and if the initial momentum could be maintained there was every reason to believe that, given good fortune and fair weather, the operation would be completed on schedule.

UNROD had come a long way since the first months of 1972. In mid-September Umbricht sent a jubilant cable to headquarters. The relationship between the government and UNROD had, he reported, reached "a degree of closeness and trust which augurs well for future cooperation." Cooperation with the various United Nations agencies and the foreign missions was most satisfactory. "What a wonderful morning," he said, "everything is coming my way." There were still problems, as there always would be, but UNROD was a going concern.

CHAPTER 12

UNROD—The Last Six Months: October 1972-March 1973

For UNROD and the government of Bangladesh, 1972 ended in disappointment. UNROD and, with its assistance, the government of Bangladesh had weathered a succession of crises in the course of the year. By August basic food supplies for the year were assured and preliminary estimates of the *aman* crop, which is harvested in November and December and accounts for more than half of domestic grain production, were encouraging. There were many imponderables, but there was more than a little hope and it seemed likely, at least to optimists, that UNROD would achieve its primary objectives by the end of the year and be able to withdraw as planned or even earlier. By October the situation had completely changed. The failure of the monsoon and of the *aman* harvest dashed hopes that the relief operation could be brought to an early end, and made its continuation in 1973 essential.

Earlier in the year, the secretary-general had suggested that, circumstances permitting, UNROD's relief work should be terminated on 31 March 1973. The date had been carefully chosen. It was reasonable to hope that by then there would be no more need for emergency rehabilitation and relief assistance and that the flow of international aid through normal channels would be sufficient to finance the reconstruction and development of the economy. The country would have reaped its first postwar *aman* harvest and should, with luck and good management, have built up food grain stocks to a level that would permit it to rely on ordinary imports to alleviate the chronic shortage. With imports reduced to a more manageable level and with the transport system at least partially reconstructed, UNROD could withdraw and allow the government to stand on its own.

By mid-1972 senior members of the UNROD staff in Dacca were persuaded that an earlier date could and should be set for ending the relief operation. The subject was repeatedly discussed at staff meetings, the collective view being that the terminal date should be 31 December 1972. There were many reasons for this proposal. Although progress was undeniably being made, success would never be complete, and there was an obvious danger that the longer UNROD's support was available the more the government would come to rely on it. Psychologically at any rate there was a strong case for moving from relief to reconstruction sooner rather than later.

The possibility of an early switch to reconstruction was very much in the minds of the international aid community in Dacca. It was being actively discussed, for example, by the international voluntary organizations working in Bangladesh, and one of the most important, the Christian Organization for Relief and Rehabilitation, decided in September 1972 to undertake no new relief projects and to concentrate its resources on development. Its Protestant counterpart, the Bangladesh Ecumenical Relief and Rehabilitation Service, followed suit by winding up its affairs and transferring its activities in January 1973 to a Bangalee successor organization, the Christian Council for Development in Bangladesh. A further argument was furnished by the views of a State Department inspector of foreign assistance, D. Formel, who visited Bangladesh in June and recommended that UNROD should move as rapidly as possible to an advisory rather than an operating role.

Headquarters took a different view. From his experience with relief operations in various parts of the world, including Bengal some thirty years previously, Jackson was not prepared to accept the proposal that UNROD should wind up at the end of the year before the results of the *aman* harvest were known. He believed the risks to Bangladesh and to the reputation of the United Nations were unacceptable and the benefits uncertain. Nor did he believe that UNROD could safely be divested of its operational responsibilities.

In principle the inspector's suggestion was unexceptionable. In practice it was dubious. UNROD's operational role was crucial to the survival of Bangladesh as an organized society at something

UNROD—The Last Six Months   157

more than a simple subsistence level. UNROD's logistic support could not safely be withdrawn until the need for it was demonstrably ended. For the time being that was not the case. "I doubt," Jackson wrote, commenting on the inspector's suggestion, "if there is any deeper administrative and practical problem facing us than to find ways and means of transferring successful operational responsibility to the appropriate authorities in Bangladesh."

By force of circumstances UNROD had become the de facto manager of Bangladesh's ports and of many of the vessels and trucks used to move supplies from them. UNROD arranged for stevedoring, lightering, transshipment, and the delivery of grain and other relief goods to the interior. Without UNROD's active participation, the ports would have choked and the relief effort would have stopped. It was one thing for a voluntary organization to decide that the relief phase had come to an end. It was quite another for the secretary-general to withdraw the services UNROD was providing and to imperil the flow of imported food grains on which the lives of millions of Bangladeshis depended.

The discussion soon ceased to be of more than theoretical interest. On 14 October, after discussions with Jackson and Umbricht, Prime Minister Sheikh Mujib formally requested from the secretary-general continued United Nations relief assistance after the planned termination of UNROD at the end of March 1973. The assistance requested was to be mainly in the food grain and transport sectors, in which United Nations help would be required to meet the difficulties expected in 1973 in carrying out the heavy import program necessitated by the failure of the *aman* harvest.

In any circumstances, food grain imports would have been necessary. The question was in what quantities and how and when they were to be provided. The decisive element was the size of the *aman* harvest. A good *aman* harvest would have reduced import needs to a level at which they might have been met without special United Nations assistance. A poor harvest coming at a time when stocks had still not been built up to prudent levels would require imports on a scale Bangladesh could not hope to achieve without further international aid of the kind UNROD had provided in 1972. For this reason, the secretary-general, in cooperation with the director-general of FAO, suggested as early as August that a survey of the *aman* crop should be made by a mission of experts from the Bangladesh government and the international organizations concerned, under the leadership of an expert of international authority. The government accepted the proposal, and Professor Robert Chandler of the Rockefeller Foundation, an internationally recognized agricultural expert and former director of the International Rice Research Institute in the Philippines, agreed to head the mission. He visited Bangladesh in October and again in November.

At the time of his first visit in October, it was clear the monsoon had failed in Bangladesh and throughout southeast Asia. The total rainfall for the months of June, July, August, September, and October was 40 percent below normal. For October alone it was 61 percent below normal. The results were disastrous. Because of the lack of rain, compounded by fertilizer shortages at the time of transplanting the rice seedlings, and unusually heavy attacks by pests, it was certain the *aman* harvest would be seriously depleted. At a senior staff meeting during his first visit, Professor Chandler made a preliminary estimate that the shortfall would be a million tons.

The findings were nevertheless sufficiently certain and sufficiently forbidding to call for immediate action. In the light of the facts available, UNROD, in consultation with the government, made a short-term forecast of food grain requirements for the first quarter of 1973, and on this basis the secretary-general made an interim appeal in November for 700,000 tons of grain to be delivered in the first three months of 1973. There could be no question of waiting for a more definitive estimate. The lead-time was already short. In a matter of a few weeks, donor governments had to be found, commitments had to be made, grain had to be allocated and moved to the ports for loading, shipping had to be arranged, and preparations had to be made in Bangladesh to receive the cargoes when they arrived at Chittagong and Chalna.[1]

Professor Chandler's report, presented in December,[2] was the result of an intensive three-week survey. Using UNROD's Pilatus

Porter aircraft and helicopters, the members of the mission—Professor Chandler, three government experts, and four international specialists—visited all the country's main rice-growing areas. On the basis of their firsthand observations, talks with farmers, and consultations with district agricultural officers and officials of the ministry of agriculture and planning commission, they concluded that the *aman* harvest would yield 5.57 million tons, almost 1.5 million tons less than the figure for 1969/1970, the last normal crop. The most important reason for the shortfall was the drought, the severest for a decade and, the mission reported, "probably for much longer." The mission reported also that less land had been planted than usual, and that some land had been planted too late to get a good crop. Insufficient fertilizer had been available, and much of it had reached the farmers in October, too late to be used to best advantage. The mission's forecast was low, but it was 300,000 tons higher than that of a ministry of agriculture team. The difference was, the mission suggested, "within the expected margin of error." The report noted the figures would, in any case, have to be revised after the crop was harvested and recorded.

The mission was asked also to estimate the outturn of the 1973 *boro* and *aus* crops. It believed that the government's estimate of the *boro* crop was optimistic and suggested that it should be reduced to allow for likely irrigation difficulties and the probability that farmers would not apply sufficient fertilizer, if it were provided. Production was not, the mission thought, likely to exceed 2.1 million tons. It predicted the *aus* crop might produce 2.5 million tons. A strong effort by the Bangladesh government to increase rice production in the *boro* and *aus* crops could, the mission said, increase the figures somewhat. On the other hand, unfavorable weather could easily nullify the predictions. The *aus* yield in particular could be sharply reduced by insufficient rainfall during sowing or excessive flooding during the growing season.

The mission's estimate of food grain requirements for the crop year December 1972 to November 1973 more than justified the secretary-general's interim appeal. To provide 15 ounces of grain a day a head for 75 million people for one year, Bangladesh needed 11.5 million tons. Government stocks at 1 December 1972 totaled 200,000 tons, and on the basis of the mission's estimates no more than 9.44 million tons would become available from domestic production during the crop year. To alleviate the shortage and provide a carry-over stock of 500,000 tons, 2.56 million tons would have to be imported. The figures were staggering, higher than the total imported in the previous year.

A period of intensive discussions with the Bangladesh government and representatives of donor governments in Dacca and New York followed. The government and the United Nations were both anxious that the period of relief should be ended as soon as possible, but the estimated shortage revealed by Professor Chandler's report imposed a burden the government could not hope to shoulder alone.

The government nevertheless informed the secretary-general that it would commit approximately one-third of its meager foreign currency reserves to buy grain abroad. This was the most that could be prudently spent on current needs. Any greater expenditure would have been self-defeating since it would make inroads on the foreign currency needed to buy equipment for the agricultural and other sectors in 1973, and would thus prolong the need for larger-scale grain imports. The government also announced its determination to do its best to buy grain from the local harvest. At the best of times, this would be a difficult undertaking in a country with millions of small farmers who used most of the harvest to feed themselves and normally marketed only a small fraction of their output.

The secretary-general concentrated on mobilizing world support to provide the balance of 1,700,000 tons that would be needed to supplement the 800,000 tons to be purchased by the government.

In many ways, the food problem in Bangladesh was, the secretary-general pointed out in making his appeal for further contributions, likely to be even more difficult in 1973 than in 1972. Crops had been below normal in many countries and the world grain market was under heavy pressure. Grain reserves were sinking fast. Shipping was also likely to be inadquate, and there

UNROD—The Last Six Months 161

would be distribution and transport problems in Bangladesh. The government and UNROD were, he noted, in a position to forecast how essential food grain needs would be met in the first three months of the year and could plan internal transport arrangements. If, however, further contributions for the remainder of the year were not pledged, in cash or in kind, before 1 March 1973, the government and UNROD would be unable to work out the coordinated plan of delivery necessary to move massive imports from the ports to the points of consumption in the remainder of 1973.

During the closing months of 1972 the main preoccupation was to find means to provide Bangladesh with the food aid it needed for survival in 1973. It was obvious that continued United Nations relief assistance would be necessary after 31 March 1973. The form it should take and the mechanisms through which it should be provided had still to be decided. These questions were the subject of repeated discussion with the various governments interested in assisting Bangladesh. Privately and in the regular semiformal meetings of donor governments, several governments voiced doubts and misgivings about the prime minister's request that United Nations relief assistance should continue to be provided after the planned termination of UNROD in March 1973. In Sir Robert Jackson's phrase, UNROD had equipped the government of Bangladesh with a powerful pair of crutches. No one wished to see the crutches become permanent. On the other hand the needs of the situation were plain, and the prime minister's assurance that he would commit a third of his country's foreign currency reserves to buy grain on the world market was evidence of his government's determination to stand on its own. Doubts were dispelled or at least silenced and donor governments accepted the secretary-general's proposal that UNROD should be continued in modified form after 31 March until the end of 1973. The details were still undecided, but the principle was established. After 31 March, the crutches would be replaced by a walking stick.[3]

In the first quarter of 1973, as preparations were made to reduce the staff and to wind up the first phase of the operation, UNROD continued to be preoccupied with logistics problems.

The transport system was still not fully restored. In 1972, as a result of the efforts of the Bangladesh government's bilateral donors, UNROD and the voluntary agencies, the transport bottleneck had been broken and progress had been made in rebuilding the road and rail networks. The railway signaling system was back in operation. Track had been relaid. Bridges and culverts had been repaired. Ferries had been brought back into service or replaced.

Reconstruction was, however, still incomplete. In particular two major links on the vital north-south rail arteries were not fully operational. The Hardinge Bridge over the Ganges was open to single-track working only, and the King George VI Bridge over the Meghna was not scheduled to be opened until later in 1973.

In one respect the logistical difficulties were greater in 1973 than they had been in 1972. The volume of food grain imports to handle would be roughly the same, about 2.5 million tons. However, there was one important difference. In 1972 the strain on the transport system had been greatly eased by the shipment of over 900,000 tons of grain from India, mainly overland. That assistance could not be repeated in 1973. India, like many other countries, was itself seeking imports of food grains. The volume of food grains to be handled in the ports would be at least a third greater in 1973 than it had been in 1972.

In these circumstances the United Nations inland water transport fleet, the UNROD transportation task force, and the UNROD port offices continued to fulfill an essential function. In the first three months of the year nearly 900,000 tons of grain entered the port of Chittagong, 477,000 tons in March alone, as a result of purchases by the Bangladesh government and grants from donor governments in response to the secretary-general's November appeal. In January, 15 grain-carrying vessels arrived at Chittagong and were unloaded without incurring demurrage. In February there were 11 arrivals. In March there were 24, and for the first time the UNROD port officer at Chittagong was obliged to report a substantial carry-over of cargoes awaiting unloading at the end of the month.[4] In the three-month period, the UNROD fleet of 20 minibulkers and lightering vessels handled nearly half a million tons of grain. This was a remarkable feat, and would be repeated in the following months as the flow of grain imports continued.

At Chalna the clearance operation launched in October 1972 was going ahead. The contractor's diving surveys had been completed in November 1972, and the clearance work proper had begun. Preparations were being made to raise one wreck, a small tanker, the *Shaptadinga*, and divers were beginning to break up the five remaining wrecks so that they could be lifted from the water piecemeal when the heavy lift vessels arrived from Japan and Western Europe. On 15 January the Japanese sheerlegs, *Nippon-Go*, arrived in Bangladesh waters, followed a day later by the Dutch sheerlegs, *Taklift One*. In mid-March they were joined by the German heavy lift vessel, *Magnus IV*. The work of clearance was well under way, in spite of the difficulties—the strong currents that made diving impossible except at slack water, the silting and the darkness that made work underwater unusually hazardous. A German diver, Frank Kupcic, lost his life, but the clearance went on, and section by section the wrecks were removed and placed ashore.

It seemed certain the work would be completed on time before the start of the monsoon, and Jackson and Umbricht could justifiably feel the United Nations was making up for the fumbling that had delayed the start of the salvage operations a year earlier. In contrast to its attitude in early 1972, the Bangladesh government was anxious that the UNROD operation should be extended, and in cooperation with the United Nations was negotiating for bilateral assistance so that two additional wrecks could be removed by the UNROD salvage vessels before they left Bangladesh waters. There was a minor diplomatic triumph also. During a visit to Bangladesh in February, Captain Searle, the salvage specialist attached to UNROD headquarters, invited the admiral in charge of the Soviet salvage vessels at Chittagong to inspect the operations at Chalna. The Soviet admiral accepted. The invitation was a graceful gesture and marked an official departure from the muted resentment with which some members of the UNROD team had viewed the Soviet presence in Chittagong. In April cooperation was carried a stage further, when a Soviet helicopter flew to Chalna to evacuate an injured crew member of *Taklift One*.[5]

As the target date for winding up the first phase of the operation approached, pride of achievement was marred for many staff members in the field by a sense of frustration and uncertainty about the future. The mission had achieved, if not miracles, at least more than could reasonably have been expected and more than any comparable United Nations operation had done. These achievements had never received the public recognition they might have, even in Bangladesh, and to many staff members the mission appeared to be dwindling into obscurity, its solid gains overshadowed by the unfinished business being handed on to UNROD's successor organization. Morale was strengthened by the secretary-general's visit in February. Secretary-General Waldheim's private talk to the senior staff and his address to all the employees of the mission gave them a sense of belonging, of having contributed to an important and valued part of the organization's work.

In its last three months UNROD was also concerned with preparations for the Development Conference which the government planned to convene on 31 March. The conference would symbolize the end of the relief phase and the transition to reconstruction and development.

For the organizations of the United Nations system, the conference was also a landmark. On 31 March the UNROD umbrella under which the agencies and programs had worked for so long would be folded and the individual organizations would resume their normal development role under the leadership of IBRD and UNDP. In the course of preparations for the conference, it became clear that the umbrella was showing signs of wear.

The conference was organized by the Bangladesh planning commission with the very active cooperation of the IBRD and IMF. The bank and fund representatives who had been working with UNROD were reinforced by teams of specialists, and the conference began more and more to take on the coloration of an aid consortium meeting. The UNROD office in Dacca would have preferred a broader conference with the participation of all the countries that had provided assistance to Bangladesh, as would some of the representatives in Dacca of Western donor countries. In the end a narrower formula was accepted, and at least two of the Western missions in Dacca were surprised to find that the planning commission had not extended invitations to all donor countries. In the event, India, the USSR, and other countries that had provided bilateral assistance to Bangladesh did not attend the conference.

All the evidence suggests that the conference was not fully satisfactory to any of the participating governments. The press release at the close of the conference, drafted by a committee "after some discussion," is anodyne, hopeful, appreciative of the efforts of the Bangladesh government, donor governments, and the organizations of the United Nations system, and largely noncommittal. No aid pledges were mentioned. In a brief statement before the drafting committee went to work, the chairman, Dr. Nurul Islam, deputy-chairman of the planning commission, explained why. "In spite of my request to the contrary," he said, "some of the delegates have made conditional pledges and have mentioned as conditions extraneous circumstances or matters which are completely outside the purview of this conference. I must inform you that we cannot take note of those statements."[6] The contentious extraneous matter was the question of settling Bangladesh's share in foreign debts incurred in the past by the government of Pakistan. It was an issue to which several donor governments attached importance, but, in the view of the Bangladesh government, it could not be properly discussed at that point or in that form. It is hard to believe that the wrangle served any useful purpose. The debt issue would have to be faced and solved eventually, one way or another, but its introduction into the discussions in March 1973 was unlikely to promote a solution. The only practical effect was to dampen the success of the conference and to reduce its potential impact as a demonstration of international solidarity and concern.

The conference cannot be written off as a failure. Nevertheless, from UNROD's point of view it was a sorry conclusion to fifteen months of increasingly successful effort. Umbricht and Marcel d'Astugues, the resident representative of UNDP who had served as deputy chief of mission of UNROD, attended the conference, with Francis Lacoste, who was to head the new mission that would replace UNROD on 31 March, and UNROD's senior economists, Subhas Dhar and Bernard Oury. D'Astugues spoke of the future when UNDP would emerge from the UNROD umbrella and try to weld the preinvestment activities of the United Nations system into a coherent country program. Umbricht was the first speaker after the opening statements by the minister of finance, Tajuddin Ahmad, and by the chairman of the conference. His position on the speakers' list was symbolic both of the crucial part UNROD had played in Bangladesh's first fifteen months of independent existence and of the high regard in which Umbricht and his colleagues were held by the government.

Umbricht summarized for participants what UNROD had been doing. The record was impressive. As part of the relief effort, 2.5 million tons of food grains had been brought into the country in 1972. Transport requirements had been met. Epidemic diseases were under control and reconstruction was well under way.

Of course, the emphasis had been on relief. Nevertheless many of UNROD's activities had, Umbricht pointed out, led into development projects. "For instance, the railways needed signaling equipment; it is difficult to run railways without some green or red lights and although it was an emergency that caused us to bring equipment in, at the same time this was only the beginning of a long-term rehabilitation of the railway system." The same was true of other sectors—the rebuilding of bridges and roads, "the reconstruction and rehabilitation of power plants, of telecommunications, of rural centers, of schools, of hospitals." There had been mistakes, of course. "We brought fertilizer, unfortunately not enough (and that is one of the reasons why the crops in 1973 do not quite show the result we expected). . . . We brought in engineers to repair some of the plants, among them fertilizer plants, but it took a long time, and Ghorosal—the main fertilizer plant—became operative only last September, when it was too late for the *aman* crop." The total effort, however, had been successful. Although the failure of the 1972 *aman* harvest had prolonged the need for United Nations assistance in the food and transport sectors, the emergency relief phase was over and Bangladesh was, as Umbricht put it, "moving into the normal process of development with general and diversified assistance."

The list of problems to be tackled was long. Umbricht mentioned measures to achieve self-sufficiency in food grains, the diversification of food crops, family planning, the strengthening of small-scale and cottage industries, the shortage of managerial capacity and skilled labor, the provision of transport equipment. He believed that with appropriate external assistance the problems could be solved. It was certainly true that in the fifteen months since independence the government, working in partnership with UNROD and the donor governments, had achieved what many observers thought was impossible. The new nation had survived, and administrative planning and budgetary machinery that could face the job of development had been established, in extraordinarily difficult circumstances and with remarkable speed. As Nurul Islam said, the development of Bangladesh would be an uphill task, but the experience of the first fifteen months suggested that it could be successfully undertaken. "It has been, in my view," Umbricht said, "a very fine beginning and I can only hope that it goes on in the same way."[7]

CHAPTER 13

Winding Up the Operation: April-December 1973

On 1 April 1973 UNROB, the United Nations Special Relief Office, Bangladesh, came into being under Ambassador Francis Lacoste as chief of mission and special representative of the secretary-general.[1] In some quarters in Dacca UNROD's departure was viewed with apprehension, as a sign of waning United Nations interest in Bangladesh's problems. The anxieties were groundless. UNROB's establishment was a direct response to the prime minister's request for continued United Nations relief assistance, and its work would be complemented by the World Bank, the International Monetary Fund, UNDP, UNICEF, and the specialized agencies acting in their traditional development roles. The secretary-general's choice of Ambassador Lacoste to head the mission was also significant. Ambassador Lacoste came to Bangladesh after a distinguished diplomatic career, which had included service as permanent representative of France to the United Nations, ambassador in Belgium and Canada, and resident-general in Morocco. His appointment was, as Umbricht said in introducing him at the Development Conference, evidence of the secretary-general's continued keen interest in the destiny of Bangladesh. It also marked the beginning of a new approach in the United Nations' efforts to help solve the political problems of the subcontinent. As chief of mission of UNROB, Ambassador Lacoste was responsible, in partnership with Sir Robert Jackson at headquarters, for continuing the relief functions in the food and transport sectors hitherto undertaken by UNROD. As special representative of the secretary-general, he also had the diplomatic function furthering the secretary-general's efforts to promote normal relations between Bangladesh, India, and Pakistan.

Throughout 1972 and into the first months of 1973, the humanitarian problems on which Under-Secretary-General

Winding Up the Operation

Winspeare had reported to the secretary-general in January and February 1972 remained unresolved.[2] The fate of nearly a million men and women—the beleaguered non-Bangalee minority groups in Bangladesh, the Pakistani prisoners of war in India, and the Bangalee officials and others detained in Pakistan—was apparently irretrievably enmeshed with the political issues that prevented reconciliation between Pakistan and Bangladesh. The most constructive, and possibly the only prospect for a solution was, Winspeare had suggested, direct contacts between the principals involved. Despite the diplomatic efforts of the secretary-general and of interested governments, the breakthrough never came. Bangladesh would not consent to a meeting with Pakistan until Pakistan granted it full and formal de jure recognition. Pakistan would not grant recognition until the prisoner-of-war issue was resolved in accordance with its wishes and Bangladesh abandoned its declared intention of trying a number of the prisoners for war crimes. The diplomatic stalemate seemed complete. The humanitarian problems could not be grappled with until the political deadlock was broken. The deadlock itself was in large part impeding the end to "conflict and confrontation" envisaged by India and Pakistan in the Simla agreement of 3 July 1972.[3]

These issues were not officially the concern of UNROD, which was a relief organization without political functions. By force of circumstance, it nevertheless became involved, indirectly and almost clandestinely, in the international effort to mitigate and eventually to resolve the problem of the non-Bangalee minorities, the 650,000 "nonlocals," most of whom had been driven from their homes and jobs after independence and were crowded into camps and colonies. At the request of the International Committee of the Red Cross, under whose protection the minorities were placed, UNROD agreed to provide assistance. It did so in a variety of ways, by making regular and direct allocations of food grains for the camps and colonies, by persuading the prime minister to set aside plots of land for the erection of shelters and furnishing corrugated iron sheet to roof them, and by providing ICRC with trucks and transport facilities. Politically UNROD's discreet involvement in feeding and sheltering the minorities was risky. It was accepted by the government, but was unpalatable to many members of the central and divisional administrations, in whose view UNROD was ill-advised to give special assistance to minorities while millions of Bangalees were living in even worse conditions. The political risks were worth taking. UNROD's assistance, backed by regular personal visits from the chief of mission to the camps and colonies, brought about some improvement in living conditions. Equally important, it strengthened the position of the ICRC delegates and voluntary agency representatives working with the minorities in their relations with the local authorities, and it helped to remind both the government and the "nonlocals" of the international community's concern with the problem.

As the UNROD chief of mission, Umbricht also found himself drawn, unofficially, into direct discussion on some of the political issues with members of the government, in particular the prime minister and on occasion the president. From time to time, the prime minister and others sought his views on such matters as the prisoner-of-war issue, war crimes trials, the exchange of civilian populations, minority problems, and the like. Umbricht's response could only be personal. Nevertheless, the talks were useful, he believed. Whatever their impact on the course of events, they must at least have served to keep the secretary-general and his senior colleagues informed of some of the twists and turns and hesitations in the government's thinking.

At headquarters the secretary-general and his senior political assistants continued trying to break the deadlock that the Winspeare mission had begun. In early 1973 the first movements toward a solution became apparent. In February, Secretary-General Waldheim, accompanied by Roberto Guyer, visited the subcontinent and talked with government leaders in Islamabad, New Delhi, and Dacca. The results were not immediate. In late March, however, the secretary-general received a request from the prime minister of Bangladesh for United Nations assistance in arranging transportation to repatriate a limited number of Bangalees from Pakistan. The secretary-general asked the high commissioner to act as executing agent for the operation. Sadruddin

Winding Up the Operation

Aga Khan visited Pakistan and Bangladesh to make operational arrangements, and by July a first batch of 425 Bangalees, seamen, students and compassionate cases, was airlifted to Dacca. At the same time, at the request of the Pakistan government, the High Commissioner assisted in moving to Karachi 2,000 Pakistanis stranded in Nepal and began arrangements for a larger operation in which a UNHCR chartered aircraft would be used to move 5,000 Bangalees from Pakistan to Bangladesh and 5,000 Pakistanis from Nepal to Pakistan on a triangular route, Karachi-Dacca-Kathmandu-Karachi. A beginning, however modest, had been made.

In April a second breakthrough came. In a press release issued on 17 April, together with a joint declaration by the governments of India and Bangladesh on humanitarian issues, the Bangladesh government announced it would try only 195 prisoners for war crimes.[4] From the standpoint of the Bangladesh government, the reduction of prisoners to be tried from "ten thousand" to "less than two hundred" was an act of magnanimity and a major concession. So far as the Pakistan government was concerned, the gesture was insufficient. The prisoner-of-war issue had been reduced but not removed. Until it was removed, the greatest obstacle to reconciliation remained.

In August the obstacle was circumvented. The joint Bangladesh-Indian statement of 17 April prepared the way for resuming discussions between India and Pakistan, and on 28 August the negotiations resulted in the New Delhi agreement, which provided for a three-way repatriation that would, as the agreement suggested, enable "the vast majority of the human beings" whose fate had been in suspense for so long to return to their respective countries.[5] The agreement was, as the secretary-general said in a subsequent statement, a milestone in the history of the region.[6] The government of Bangladesh stood pat on the war crimes issue, but at the last moment concurred in the agreement and accepted a compromise formula under which Bangladesh, India, and Pakistan would discuss and settle the question of the 195 prisoners of war after the three-way repatriation had been completed. The compromise was a triumph of Indian diplomacy, in which the

United Nations had no direct part. The agreement was nevertheless a fruit of the efforts the secretary-general had set in motion in January 1972. Lacoste's assessment is convincing. The negotiations, he reported to the secretary-general, "could never have come to a positive conclusion, or perhaps even have begun, without the knowledge of the three parties concerned that they could count on the organization to help them carry out the implementation of the accord, once it was achieved." In the negotiation of the compromise, "the pressure, very discreetly but persistently maintained on the Bangladesh authorities by the United Nations officials concerned"—the secretary-general and his senior political collaborators, the high commissioner for refugees and the special representative of the secretary-general in Dacca—had, Lacoste said, "played a significant role, probably greater than can ever be ascertained." The successes of quiet diplomacy are less spectacular than those of shuttle diplomacy and less easily identified, but in the end no less important.

The New Delhi agreement provided that in making logistic arrangements for repatriation the governments might seek the assistance of international humanitarian organizations and others. The ICRC had already prepared lists of would-be repatriates and applications for clearance by the governments concerned, and the high commissioner's limited repatriation program clearly provided the framework for a broader undertaking. Within days of the signature of the agreement, the secretary-general received requests for assistance from both Bangladesh and Pakistan. Both went beyond purely logistical assistance. Sheikh Mujibur asked for help in dealing with "the enormous problem of rehabilitating the Bangalees returning from Pakistan" as well as assistance in their repatriation. Foreign Minister Aziz Ahmed of Pakistan similarly drew attention to rehabilitation needs. The repatriation of the Pakistanis returning from Bangladesh and the rehabilitation of the refugees would, he wrote, entail a considerable expenditure that Pakistan could ill afford, particularly in the wake of the recent disastrous floods. Neither government was specific about its assistance needs, but obviously these would be great, and if the assistance was to extend to resettlement and rehabilitation as well as

Winding Up the Operation 173

repatriation, might be very large indeed. While expressing sympathy with the request and his appreciation of "the magnitude of the practical consequences" of implementing the agreement, the secretary-general accordingly informed the two governments that he had asked Sir Robert Jackson and Sadruddin Aga Khan to consider ways and means in which the United Nations could provide logistical assistance and assess the resources and contributions that might be forthcoming from member states. For the time being the question of rehabilitation assistance was set aside.

On 5 September during a brief stopover at Zurich airport on his way from the Middle East to Algiers to attend the conference of nonaligned nations, the secretary-general met for two and a half hours with Under-Secretary-General Winspeare, Sadruddin Aga Khan, and Jackson and gave his approval to steps to ensure a coordinated response to the requests for assistance in implementing the New Delhi agreement.[7]

A week later on his return to headquarters, the secretary-general issued a statement asking support for the assistance requested by the governments concerned.[8] The appeal called for assistance in three broad sectors: repatriation, resettlement, and disaster relief. In the latter sector, the secretary-general, following an assessment by the office of the disaster-relief coordinator, had already appealed to the international community to help the Pakistan government repair the devastation caused by the August floods, and once again stressed the gravity of the situation and the ongoing needs. So far as repatriation was concerned, the secretary-general announced that the high commissioner would continue his efforts and would inform governments of the detailed requirements for assistance. Concerning rehabilitation, the secretary-general had requested Sir Robert Jackson to examine, in consultation with those concerned, the most effective ways to provide assistance; assistance should be woven into the considerable efforts already being made, using existing United Nations programs to maximum advantage. Jackson had also been asked to make the necessary arrangements for coordinating the assistance effort, in agreement with all concerned.

The three-pronged assistance program started well. By November the office of the disaster-relief coordinator was phasing out its immediate flood-relief operation in Pakistan. Cooperating closely with the government, the office had provided information on specific relief needs to some ninety donors, and approximately $75,000,000 had been contributed by the international community for emergency assistance.[9] At the request of Pakistani Prime Minister Zulfikar Ali Bhutto, who visited headquarters in September, the secretary-general arranged for a joint United Nations/IBRD mission to visit Pakistan and make recommendations for the assistance that would be needed in repairing the flood damage. The mission, led by Victor Umbricht as special representative of the secretary-general, and Bernard Chadenet, vice-president of the World Bank, presented its report in November. The report was immediately submitted to the government of Pakistan and circulated to all diplomatic missions in Islamabad and to delegations at headquarters. It provided a detailed and documented assessment of the needs that remained to be met after the emergency-relief program coordinated by the office of the disaster-relief coordinator and was reported by the resident representative of UNDP in Islamabad to have been accepted by donor governments as a useful tool in mobilizing appropriate external assistance.[10]

Repatriation under the high commissioner for refugees was also moving ahead swiftly and more smoothly than might have been expected in so large and complex an undertaking. By the end of November some 70,000 people had been transferred between Bangladesh and Pakistan. It was estimated that approximately 130,000 more would eventually be included in the repatriation operation. There was one ominous setback, however. On 19 September Sadruddin Aga Khan informed governments that the cost of the operation would be about $14,300,000.[11] By the end of November he had received only $7,200,000 in cash contributions. These contributions had been supplemented by contributions in kind by a number of governments, but there was a risk that the high commissioner's target would not be met and that the completion of the operation would be delayed.

The assessment of the requirements for international assistance for the rehabilitation or, as it came to be known, resettlement, was complex from the beginning and became increasingly so. The governments of Pakistan and Bangladesh each provided the secretary-general estimates of their rehabilitation needs.[12] The Pakistani estimate was large—roughly $14,000,000 to resettle an estimated 40,000 destitute repatriates—but manageable. The request from Bangladesh called for more-massive assistance. The Bangladesh authorities estimated that between 150,000 and 200,000 Bangalees would return to Bangladesh from Pakistan, and their resettlement could not, the government argued, be considered apart from the larger problem of rehabilitating the million or so destitute Bangalees whose homes had been destroyed during the war and who were still subsisting miserably on government charity, as well as the substantial number of "nonlocals" who would remain in Bangladesh after the completion of the repatriation movement. Lacoste reported the total rehabilitation load amounted to the staggering figure of 1,500,000 persons. The government's arguments were powerful, but the chances of mobilizing assistance on the scale requested were obviously slim. In Bangladesh, resettlement, except in the narrowest and most limited sense, could not be successfully abstracted from the general and still intractable problem of reconstruction and development.

The difficulties in Bangladesh would have been eased, although not removed, if Pakistan had been willing or able to accept a larger number of "nonlocals." Under the New Delhi agreement, Pakistan had agreed to receive a "substantial number" of non-Bangalees from Bangladesh immediately and to discuss with Bangladesh at a later date "what additional number" of persons might be allowed to emigrate to Pakistan. The issue was a difficult one, for both practical and political reasons, and any hope of an early solution was jeopardized by a newspaper story in October. Walter Schwarz, the *Guardian*'s correspondent in the subcontinent, reported from Rawalpindi that a United Nations proposal to settle the bulk of the Biharis on uncultivated land in Sind was to be put before Prime Minister Bhutto by Umbricht, who had "upgraded his mission" with an attempt to solve the Bihari problem by massive emigration to Pakistan while the repatriation airlift was operating.[13] The report was unfounded. Umbricht had heard of a scheme, apparently suggested by local officials, of the kind described. It was, he recognized, "a visionary scheme" and was not a proposal to be put to the prime minister. It was an idea he intended to convey privately to the secretary-general so that the latter could in due course, if the scheme seemed workable and politically feasible, initiate discussions with the Pakistan government. Whatever the merits of the scheme, its immediate reception was bad. On instructions, the permanent representative of Pakistan protested at headquarters. He was satisfied by the explanations he received, but the scheme was dead for the foreseeable future.

The incident was an unfortunate eddy in the mainstream of events and served only to complicate an already confused situation. By November it was becoming evident that the resettlement problem could not readily be kept within manageable limits as had been originally hoped. Many governments believed assistance should be given, but there was general agreement that the United Nations should not be drawn into an open-ended commitment such as existed with the Palestine refugees. Without specific proposals for resettlement assistance on a scale and for a time period that donor governments could be expected to support, the approach implicit in the secretary-general's appeal of 13 September would clearly have to be reshaped. Meanwhile, at the final meeting on 9 November of governments interested in assisting Bangladesh, Jackson could only refer to the problem of resettlement in general terms.[14]

On 12 December the secretary-general issued a statement on humanitarian activities in the subcontinent embodying the results of the policy review undertaken since November. The statement made no specific appeal, but instead summarized the action that had been taken since September, drew attention to the needs that remained to be met, and urged member states to provide practical assistance "to consolidate in all possible ways the progress represented by the Delhi agreement." The new policy was not, as the governments most closely concerned realized, an indication of flagging interest in the subcontinent's problems. There was no

Winding Up the Operation 177

doubt of the secretary-general's sympathy and understanding. The statement of 12 December was not the end of the matter. The governments concerned knew it would be followed, as earlier appeals had been, by direct contacts with governments known to be sympathetic to the problems of the subcontinent. In the circumstances this was the procedure most likely to generate practical assistance. With new crises and disasters elsewhere in the world crowding themselves upon the attention of the international community, a further appeal for assistance was almost bound to fail; even the appeal for funds to finance the high commissioner's repatriation operation had produced only half the amount required. The problems of the subcontinent remained a matter of deep concern to the secretary-general and his colleagues in New York and Geneva who were familiar with the situation, but in the circumstances, there was, as Lacoste explained to the Bangladesh government, "really nothing else, for the time being, that could be done with any hope of success."[15]

On paper at least, UNROB's functions were straightforward. In his formal response of 4 December 1972 to the prime minister's request for further assistance, the secretary-general informed him that, while many of the responsibilities UNROD had assumed would be transferred by 31 March 1973 to the Bangladesh government or the appropriate international organizations, the United Nations would maintain a reduced office in Dacca to help the government deal with the problem of food and transport. The office had four functions: to participate in the continuous surveillance of the food needs; to coordinate action with the government in arranging for supplies of food grains from overseas; to aid, when requested by the government, in stimulating any action necessary to obtain food supplies essential to preserve life; and to assist, when requested by the government, in the operational management of the infrastructure.

The secretary-general considered that the first three of these functions should end by 31 December 1973, and that the fourth should be phased out by 30 September 1973. These functions were successfully discharged and the mission completed its work as planned on 31 December 1973.[16]

In the food sector, it was reasonably clear by the beginning of April that Bangladesh would come close to obtaining the grain imports needed to meet the food shortage in 1973. After his second survey in March, Professor Chandler estimated that the amount required would be 2.42 million tons. This was somewhat lower than his previous forecast. The *boro* crop was better than expected. More lift pumps were in operation for irrigation, the distribution of fertilizer had been better than in 1972, the rains had come in February and March at just the right time, and high prices had encouraged farmers to grow more rice, unfortunately at the expense of jute. The external supply position was also hopeful. As a result of the action taken by UNROD in the closing months of 1972, imports of roughly 1.7 million tons were assured. Over a million tons had been purchased by the government of Bangladesh and 572,000 tons committed by donor countries in response to the secretary-general's appeals of October 1972 and January 1973. Further pledges were in sight, and by the end of the year the import target had been met.

With total imports reasonably well assured, UNROB concentrated on maintaining an even flow of food grain arrivals during the remainder of the year. Because of the pressure on the world grain market and the shortage of shipping, this was not easy, and a potentially dangerous situation developed in May when food grain arrivals fell below the rate of offtake from government stocks. Twice, Ambassador Lacoste as chief of mission urged caution on the food minister; although aggregate imports would be sufficient, there was no way of knowing whether shipping schedules would permit timely delivery. UNROB believed the government should reduce the ration level and the rate of offtake from government stocks. The government considered that reducing the ration would be politically undesirable. Instead, it raised the ration price by 35 percent in the belief this would serve to regulate offtake.[17] The crisis was surmounted. Local supplies increased and lessened the pressure on official stocks. At the same time the government of Bangladesh and UNROB, through continuous contacts with the missions of donor governments in Dacca and at headquarters, made successful efforts to speed up

Winding Up the Operation 179

grain deliveries. The flow of grain was maintained by the United States, Australia, Canada, Japan, and other donors, and at the request of the prime minister the USSR agreed to divert to Bangladesh 200,000 tons of wheat in transit to the USSR from exporting countries.

By September the supply was satisfactory. The *boro* and *aus* crops were good, and the *aman* crop, harvested at the end of the year, was equally promising. The weather had been kind. There had been no major natural catastrophes, and the introduction of high-yield rice varieties, improved irrigation, and the better distribution of fertilizers and pesticides were beginning to produce results. Bangladesh had been tided over 1973 and, for the first time since the emergencies of 1970 and 1971, could face the new crop year with reasonable confidence. With good fortune and good management, Lacoste reported to the secretary-general, there was a good prospect that the food deficit for 1974 would be less than 500,000 tons.

The massive grain imports in the first half of the year severely strained port facilities. UNROD's fleet of 20 minibulkers and 6 to 8 lightering vessels[18] eliminated the build-up of supplies at Chittagong that had resulted from heavy grain arrivals early in the year. In April over 280,000 tons were discharged and lightered. In May the total was 335,000 tons, the largest volume of imports ever handled at Chittagong in a single month. By early June the inflow of grain was moving normally, and in July the fleet was cut back to 15 minibulkers and 3 to 6 lightering vessels, the level at which it remained for the rest of the year.

UNROB's reduced air component was also active. The chartered Pilatus Porter and Skyvan continued providing passenger and freight services for UNROB itself, for government and diplomatic officials, for UNICEF and the specialized agencies, and for the ICRC and the many voluntary agencies working in Bangladesh.

At Chalna the first phase of the clearance operation was completed on 9 May, six days ahead of schedule and appreciably below the estimated cost.[19] Six wrecks had been removed. In the meantime the Bangladesh government requested the United Nations to assist in clearing away two other wrecks, which had not been included in the original operation because their removal was considered desirable, but not essential. The additional work was to be financed bilaterally. The government of Sweden agreed to meet the estimated costs—$1,500,000—but there were delays. A decision to undertake the operation had to be made before the salvage vessels left Bangladesh waters. However, the United Nations could not commit itself to the operation until funds were on hand. After complicated three-cornered negotiations in New York, Dacca, and Stockholm, a solution was found. At the end of April, the Bangladesh government deposited $1,500,000 with the United Nations, which arranged to retain the heavy lift vessel *Taklift One* and its supporting craft in Bangladesh after the first phase of the clearance operation was completed. Work was begun in mid-August after the monsoon and finished on 2 December, on time and within the cost estimates. A sunken barge, not included in the plan of operations, was lifted from the river at no additional cost, and as a further good-will gesture the barge *Zeeleeuv*, which had been used as a diving tender, was presented to the government.

In April the operation began winding up. Over 700 trucks, some 60 light vehicles, 6 inflatable warehouses, and 2 tugboats were transferred to the government. Staff was reduced, from 47 international staff members on 1 April to 25 at the beginning of December. The United Nations umbrella had been folded on 31 March, but cooperation between UNROB and the specialized agencies was maintained. The regular meetings of the senior representatives of UNROB, UNDP, UNICEF, WHO, ILO, IMF, and IBRD were continued, although with decreasing frequency.

The handover of UNROB's operational responsibility for lightering and shipping operations was successfully completed on 1 September as planned. Members of the Bangladesh transport group formed by the government to assume the functions hitherto discharged by UNROD and UNROB had been working with the United Nations since March, and optimists hoped the handover could be completed earlier. For practical reasons this was impossible. In the situation that existed in April, with over 200,000 tons

Winding Up the Operation 181

of grain awaiting unloading at Chittagong, a change of management would have been dangerous. It would also have been inconsistent with the organization's obligation to ensure donor governments that contributions were used effectively. The delay was disappointing to the members of the Bangladesh transport task group, but the reasons were understood and accepted. The task group staff continued to work side by side with their UNROB counterparts, and the additional experience they gained must have helped toward a smooth transition when they took over on 1 September. Under an agreement with the Bangladesh government, concluded by UNROB with the approval of the secretary-general, the task group assumed full responsibility for unloading and lightering food grains at Chittagong's port and outer anchorage and Chalna, as well as their movement upcountry. The task group undertook to pay all stevedoring charges—which UNROB had been paying on behalf of the government on a reimbursable basis—as well as fresh water and fuel costs, port charges, and charges for other services that would normally be borne by the charterers. UNROB made its vacuvators and some radio equipment available to the task group until 31 December. As charter costs until the end of the year were met out of contributions from donor governments, UNROB also maintained a small liaison staff at Dacca, Chittagong, and Khulna to monitor the operation.

By the end of the year the phase-out was completed and, with no flourish of trumpets, the United Nations Special Relief Office in Bangladesh was formally closed. Administratively there were, of course, minor matters that remained to be completed. There were legal claims and counterlcaims, to be expected in so large an operation. Payments were still outstanding from contractors, shippers, and the government of Bangladesh. These matters were being handled by headquarters and by the small staff left in Dacca and would apparently be resolved in good time. Headquarters had made adequate provision to meet all contingencies and hoped, with the consent of donor governments, to transfer any remaining credit balance after claims had been settled to the United Nations Development Program for use in Bangladesh. In the event, virtually all claims were settled in the United Nations' favor, and the

United Nations was able to make the better part of $10 million available to the government of Bangladesh. The operation had attained its objectives. It had achieved, as Francis Lacoste commented in his final report to the secretary-general, all that it had set out to do, and even more. The adventure that began with U Thant's offer of assistance in March 1971 had come to an auspicious close.

CHAPTER 14

How the Operation Worked

The fundamental purpose of the relief operation was to mobilize and harmonize the efforts of governments, the international voluntary organizations, and the organizations and programs of the United Nations system to assist Bangladesh. This objective was achieved. The volume of aid mobilized was unprecedented. On 31 January 1973 the total aid committed from all external sources since 16 December 1971 stood at $1,318.85 million.[1] The total was made up as follows:

AID TO BANGLADESH,
31 JANUARY 1973-16 DECEMBER 1971

	Value in millions of U.S. dollars	As percentage of total
Bilateral	$ 868.45	65.85
Multilateral (UN system)	342.65	25.98
Voluntary agencies	107.75	8.17
	$1,318.85	100.00

As the table shows, the greater part of the aid committed—65.85 percent of the total—was pledged bilaterally. From the beginning some major donor countries, most notably India and the USSR, preferred to furnish assistance on a bilateral basis. Others came increasingly to use bilateral rather than multilateral channels. The United States is one example. It is noteworthy, however, that a quarter of the aid furnished was channeled through organizations of the United Nations system, in particular UNROD and UNICEF. The fact that many contributors were prepared to make their assistance available multilaterally on this scale greatly facilitated coordination of the overall effort. It also provided the funds needed to undertake direct operational activities and emergency relief actions. The contribution of the voluntary agencies is also remarkable. The amount provided—over $100 million—is large in itself and is an impressive expression of the practical good will and concern of individuals and associations in many countries.

The table shows the total of all aid committed between 16 December 1971 and 31 January 1973, and includes $378.58 million, or 28.70 percent, pledged for food aid and $940.27 million, or 71.80 percent, for nonfood aid. The rate of delivery was high. It was estimated that on 31 December 1972, 52.47 percent of all aid committed at that date had been implemented or delivered. The percentage of food aid deliveries at the same time was higher, with 86.84 percent of all food pledges delivered. The rate of disbursement of nonfood aid was slower, which was understandable. Nonfood aid included project aid relating to schemes for development as well as for rehabilitation and was disbursed over a longer period.

The provision of external aid on this scale is evidence primarily of the generosity and solidarity of the international community—donor governments, voluntary agencies and individuals, and international institutions—and of their concern for Bangladesh. It is also a measure of the success of the United Nations operation. The mobilization of resources was greatly facilitated by the presence of UNROD and by UNROD's action taken both at headquarters and in the field.

Appeals were made with the full authority of the secretary-general. They were infrequent and frank. Potential donors could be sure that needs had been carefully weighed and that supplies could, if provided, be effectively delivered. Through the regular meetings of donor countries at headquarters, delegations, including those of governments that preferred to make their contributions bilaterally, were kept informed of needs, particularly in the food and transport sectors, and of the progress being made in meeting them. The lapidary briefing notes circulated at the meetings gave participants a continuous picture of the state of the operation and found their way to capitals and even to the missions of donor countries in Dacca. As the operation went on, general appeals were largely replaced by specific requests, addressed directly

How the Operation Worked 185

in most cases to governments in a position to meet them and based upon careful, sympathetic but hardheaded analysis.

Ambassador Sailer's report provided an initial authoritative estimate of aggregate needs and a framework of priorities. It was, Victor Umbricht later said, the bible of UNROD's activities. It was reviewed and adjusted as the operation proceeded but remained a valuable guide and tool for the coordination of aid. The Sailer report was supplemented by subsequent expert studies. The reports by Professor Chandler on his missions to Bangladesh in November 1972 and March 1973 gave expert backing to the secretary-general's appeals for food grains and fully documented the requirements. The two nutritional assessments undertaken by UNROD and the government of Bangladesh[2] similarly provided an objective measurement of needs and of the real, but inadequate, progress being made in meeting them.

One factor was crucial but difficult to assess. Delegations and the governments they represented had confidence in the new secretary-general, the under-secretary-general he had appointed to head the operation, and the chief of mission in Dacca. They knew that if a million dollars was requested to operate minibulkers, that sum was needed and the minibulkers could be effectively employed. They knew also that the operation was being economically and prudently managed. The staff at headquarters was small—at the peak it consisted of the under-secretary-general and three professional assistants—primarily because it freely exploited the energies and expertise of existing headquarters services, most notably field operations service, and the purchase and transportation and communications services. The mission in Dacca was similarly kept within manageable proportions and made the fullest use of local staff.[3] At the donor meetings, delegations regularly received financial statements that showed them how UNROD's funds were being expended and what preparations were being made for the future. The operation was "open" in the fullest sense.

In carrying out fund-raising, UNROD served as a clearinghouse, collecting, collating, and disseminating information on relief needs and the action being taken to meet them. At headquarters the information room designed by Captain Brocklehurst of the Canadian Army provided delegations with a continuous display of readily assimilated information in visual form on the progress of the operation. Sir Robert Jackson suggested that the effectiveness of the information room was responsible for much of the support UNROD was able to generate. The information room was, however, more than a public-relations exercise. It also provided tools for analysis of data that would otherwise have been lacking. The maps and displays were, as the representative of a donor government commented, the outward and visible signs of first-class staff work.

In Dacca, as the operation progressed and the relief and rehabilitation effort increased in complexity, the clearinghouse function became increasingly important. From May 1972 on, UNROD's small staff of economists[4] prepared a monthly aid situation report, which became an essential tool of all concerned with aid to Bangladesh. The report was an innovation. It was compiled in active collaboration with the planning commission of the Bangladesh government and the representatives in Dacca of donor governments and organizations. It became increasingly comprehensive and by September 1972 was being actively supported by all the Dacca missions of donor governments. The report was widely circulated and the accompanying wall chart—the size of a bed sheet—was both a status symbol displayed on the walls of offices in Dacca and a useful tool for officials, national as well as international, concerned with the provision of external assistance. For the first time in an operation of this kind, prospective donors had at their disposal a detailed valuation and analysis of all aid from all sources—bilateral, multilateral, and through the voluntary agencies.

This was useful in itself. It was also an important element in the work of coordination, which was one of UNROD's main functions and one of its most considerable achievements. UNROD came increasingly to play a role in coordinating relief activities as a whole. One important factor in this aspect of UNROD's work was a volume of aid—about 25 percent of the total—furnished on a multilateral basis. The fact that a large—

and in the food and transport sectors—crucial share of the relief effort was being directly coordinated by UNROD also provided a base for a more comprehensive coordinating role. The excellent relationships with the government of Bangladesh established by Sir Robert Jackson and Victor Umbricht were no less important. Through their constant contacts with the prime minister, the planning commission, and other government departments, Umbricht and his senior colleagues in UNROD were able to supplement and support the machinery set up by the government to coordinate external assistance. The scheme of priorities established in the Sailer report and refined through discussions at headquarters and in Dacca furnished a valuable framework for coordination, as well as for the collation of aid information, of which coordination was an aspect.

UNROD was also able to help solve specific problems. On one occasion a donor government provided Bangladesh with large quantities of nylon for clothing. The offer was embarrassing. In a humid monsoon climate, nylon is not a desirable fabric. By exercising commercial and diplomatic skill, Umbricht was able to dispose of it and to replace it with cotton without offending the donor. In other cases, UNROD's statement of needs directed the attention of donors to the types of assistance most required.

As a matter of policy, UNROD subcontracted operations wherever possible to the most efficient and economical agencies, partly because of the United Nations system's limitations for direct action and partly because of the reduction of overhead this permitted. In two sectors, food grains and transport, however, UNROD undertook direct operational responsibilities. The two sectors were linked and formed the core of the relief operation.

Under Peter Wheeler, a New Zealander of many years' experience in the area with the World Food Program and FAO, the food section was mainly responsible for assessing food import needs. This was a complex process. Domestic production was estimated by field observation of crops and by information from local agricultural officers and district commissioners. The estimates were then discussed with the interested government departments. Sometimes there were differences of opinion. The food ministry's estimates were usually on the low side. Those of the planning commission and the ministry of agriculture were sometimes higher than UNROD's. The differences were debated at meetings between Umbricht, the food section, the UNROD economist, and the secretaries of the ministries of food and agriculture and the planning commission. In the end an agreed estimate was invariably arrived at, and an agreed statement of food import needs was prepared for presentation to potential donors.

The food section was also responsible for monitoring the arrival of food grain shipments and their movement upcountry and the availability of stocks. This enabled UNROD to pinpoint areas where shortages existed and to arrange for emergency deliveries where necessary. The food ministry was normally responsible for distribution and decided when and where commodities would be delivered. The food section, with the assistance of the transportation task force, saw that the deliveries were made, distribution to the centers of consumption being the responsibility of the Bangladesh authorities.

The food section's business was exacting and essential to the operation's success. Without a mechanism capable of bringing together disparate forecasts and combining them in an agreed estimate based on the best available information, the appeals for food grains launched by the secretary-general would have lacked precision and carried much less conviction. It is also unlikely they could have been made early enough to ensure timely delivery in Bangladesh. This was of cardinal importance, considering the long lead time needed to bring bulk supplies from overseas. The monitoring system worked well. Within Bangladesh it ensured that stocks were maintained at reasonable levels and that action to replenish them was taken in good time. Externally it enabled the secretary-general to call for additional pledges to meet anticipated needs and avert disaster and to make coordinated arrangements in cooperation with donor governments for the shipment of supplies and their movement within Bangladesh.

UNROD's transport operations, air, road, and marine, were managed by a transportation task force. The task force was set up in February 1972, in the period of heroic improvisation, and re-

How the Operation Worked 189

tained some of the aura of those days to the end. It discharged its responsibilities with energy, enthusiasm, and much success. The transport bottleneck was broken, the ports did not choke up, and the relief goods were kept moving. The cost, however, was high. An American transport expert in Dacca said that the operation demonstrated the first law of transport economics: if you put enough cash on the barrel head, you can move anything anywhere. The comment was unfair. Costs might have been reduced and management might have been improved, but the crisis was overcome by the application of energy rather than of money.

In the road sector, the task force was not particularly successful and was able to do little more than attempt to keep a record of the vehicles imported through UNROD and supplied to the government. This was not easy. Many of the vehicles were imported in the chaotic days of 1971 and early 1972. Some records were lost. Others were poor, and staff was never plentiful. Nevertheless, by the end of the operation, a satisfactory accounting had been undertaken. In other areas there were difficulties. A vehicle maintenance project initiated by UNICEF in 1971 collapsed. The international mechanics lost heart and could not cope with the unending difficulties. The project was transferred to UNROD and an interim scheme was set up with three maintenance centers in Chittagong, Khulna, and Dacca. It fared little better. The food ministry, which operated the trucks, could not recruit mechanics or get an imprest account to buy minor spares or even cotton waste. A working group of the planning commission, with UNROD participation, proposed a new scheme to be placed under bilateral auspices.

The task force's air operations were more successful. The heterogeneous air fleet was effectively employed. The fleet varied in size, beginning with two wrecked Pilatus Porter light aircraft and a Short Skyvan in January 1972 and reaching a peak in August with two Pilatus Porters, one Skyvan, three C-130s, and two Bell helicopters. The fleet was active. It carried over 9,000 passengers in 1972 and 40,000,000 pounds of cargo, most of it during the monsoon airlifts and airdrop. UNROD's air fleet flew the first scheduled air service in Bangladesh and throughout the period provided passenger services for international and government officials, experts, and visiting dignitaries.

The heart of the task force's activities was the management of the UNROD fleet. At its peak it consisted of 25 minibulkers, 8 river tugs, 3 ferry barges with pusher tugs, 3 fuel barges, 4 fuel tankers, 1 water tender, 6 lightering ships, 3 LCTs, 5 ocean tugs, and 18 hatch barges. The task force was in radio communication with most of the vessels and controlled their movements.

Through the port officers in Chittagong and Chalna, the task force was responsible for the discharge of all aid consignments and, in many cases, for their onward movement. In particular, UNROD handled all food grain shipments, bilateral and multilateral, on behalf of the government and was responsible for their delivery to the quay side at Chittagong or to inland ports and silos. This was a huge task, and it was successfully performed. The port of Chittagong acquired a reputation, to UNROD's credit, for handling ships rapidly. As a result, the World Food Program reported that it had less difficulty persuading shipowners to accept cargoes consigned to Bangladesh.

There were endless other difficulties. Some of them were removed in the course of continuous contacts and regular weekly meetings with the Bangladesh authorities concerned, the ministry of communications, the coordination division for external assistance, the ministry of food, the Bangladesh Agricultural Development Corporation, the Inland Water Transport Authority, and the Inland Water Transport Corporation. Others could only be dealt with by unremitting effort, cajolery, and even threats. Customs officers were sometimes intransigent, and their procedures were always cumbersome. Stevedores were sometimes hard to find. Pilots were often balky. Consignments were frequently obscurely labeled and ship arrivals were often announced at the last moment. Nevertheless, the system worked, and worked well, with only a minimum staff.

There were shortcomings in the task force itself, whose staff were mostly amateurs. Many of them, a British expert said, later became professionals, but the level of performance would have been higher if the staff had been built around transport specialists.

How the Operation Worked

The transport experts available to UNROD tended, however, to be employed as advisers rather than as operational managers.

One curious lapse in the work of the task force was that it apparently concentrated its attention on the minibulkers. These were the most important and the most expensive part of the fleet, but they were well managed and should have required little supervision. The task force tended in contrast to neglect the motley fleet of tugs and barges. As a result, periods during which the tugs and barges were unserviceable and off hire were not reported to the chief administrative officer. Substantial overpayments were made to the owners and had to be recovered later.

The reasons for this lapse are not clear. Lack of specialist knowledge may have been one factor. Fascination with the minibulkers and concentration on the main object of the operation, the movement of grains from the ports to the points of consumption, may have been another. The division of responsibilities between the chief administrative officer and the chief of the task force seems also to have been important. In UNROD, as traditionally in the United Nations, administration—accounts, budget, payroll, personnel—was in a separate compartment from management. During the early months of UNROD at any rate, the chief of the task force and his administrative counterpart appear to have gone their own ways, the one concerned with the movement of ships, the other concerned with more abstract questions of finance. The difficulty seems to have been fairly general. Despite the efforts of Sir Robert Jackson at headquarters and Victor Umbricht in the field, the operational and administrative sides of the undertaking tended to move apart. In August 1972, for example, UNROD's deputy chief of mission complained that headquarters had paid a contractor without Dacca's prior certification of the invoices. Whatever the merits of his complaint, the fact seems to be that techniques of bifurcated management adequate to cope with the ordinary work of the United Nations are insufficient to tackle operational requirements. The operational goals were met, but less economically and less tidily than might have been the case.

UNROD was an operation by the combined organizations of

the United Nations system. In UNROD, the activities of the system were not simply coordinated. In accordance with the one-voice principle accepted by ACC in April 1972, the agencies and programs of the system agreed to combine their efforts in a single program under the United Nations umbrella. The agencies and programs retained their separate identities, but their staff in Bangladesh worked as members of the UNROD team and were, for the most part, financed by UNROD. Under these arrangements, staff from UNICEF, FAO, and WHO worked with UNROD from the beginning. IBRD and IMF assisted through their representatives in Dacca, and specialists were brought in from various agencies to advise on specific relief problems requiring immediate attention. These included experts from ICAO, the ILO, ITU, FAO, WFP, UNIDO, WHO, the United Nations Office for Technical Cooperation, and the United Nations Fund for Population Activities. The experts were attached to UNROD, some more firmly than others. A few appear to have done little more than pay courtesy calls on the chief of mission and seek information and logistical assistance from the UNROD staff. Others, especially those on long-term assignments, were to all intents and purposes members of the UNROD staff. The representative of UNDP served as deputy chief of the mission.

The one-voice principle was effective and welcomed by governments. So far as the organizations that formed the hard core of UNROD were concerned—UNICEF, FAO/WFP, and WHO—the operation was in the fullest sense a joint undertaking in which funds, equipment, and expertise were pooled and molded into an integrated effort. There were differences of opinion and of emphasis. There were times, for instance, when UNICEF believed that higher priority should be given to the shipment of tube-well spares and other items needed for its programs.[5] The differences were minor and activities were harmonized and integrated, by meetings, discussions, and a system of common reporting, into a coordinated effort designed to meet the priority requirements established by the government in cooperation with UNROD.

Acceptance of the principle was, of course, made easier by the fact that the United Nations had funds at its disposal and that

How the Operation Worked   193

Bangladesh was not a member of any of the organizations of the system. It continued to work, however, even after Bangladesh had been admitted to membership in most of the agencies and the latter had less need of UNROD's umbrella. UNROD could still provide leadership, funds, services—transport and communications in particular—and a unique knowledge of the Bangladesh government and its problems.

In one respect the one-voice principle began to fail toward the end of UNROD's life. The earlier agency advisory missions were clearly directed toward priority problems requiring immediate solutions. In the latter stages, some, at any rate, seem to have been principally concerned with identifying areas in which the government might be induced to request assistance rather than finding ways to meet the government's priority needs. One mission, for example, suggested possible projects in twelve sectors that happened to correspond fairly closely to the rubrics in its organization's program budget. The habits of international civil servants die hard.

The voluntary agencies' contribution to the relief and rehabilitation effort in Bangladesh was remarkable in many ways.[6] It was large—$116,500,000 at mid-March 1973. It was prompt. It was flexible and untrammeled by bureaucratic constraints and was able to meet needs that could not easily have been satisfied by governments or intergovernmental agencies. It was also effectively coordinated with other external assistance and directed toward the priorities established by the government. It was remarkable also for the high degree of cooperation among the agencies themselves.

This achievement resulted from a series of measures by the Bangladesh government, UNROD, and the voluntary agencies themselves. The first step toward a coordinated voluntary agency program was taken in January 1972 when Toni Hagen, then serving as chief of mission in Dacca, convened a meeting of agencies to consider ways of coordinating the operations and pooling the resources of the nongovernmental and the international agencies involved and to review policies and programs. The meeting was a success and regular meetings followed. These were at first under the chairmanship of the UNROD chief of mission and later under that of Rab Chaudhuri, the government coordinator for external assistance, relief, and rehabilitation. The coordinator was assisted by an UNROD liaison officer and worked from an office close to UNROD headquarters.

The government coordinator's approach was somewhat unorthodox. At an early meeting, he told the voluntary agency representatives that all relief operations, including those channeled through the Bangladesh Red Cross, must be integrated with the government's program. Agencies unwilling to accept this should, he said, leave. None did. The agencies welcomed this approach. They responded as they had done to Hagen's earlier brusque appeal to abandon the traditional blankets-and-baby-food approach to relief, in favor of getting the economy and the transport system moving, and began to discuss projects directly related to the country's priority needs. These were not in the areas in which the voluntary agencies normally worked and required a rather radical revision of agency practices. This was promptly undertaken. One major agency put up $900,000 to buy ferries, in order to remove one of the most frustrating transport bottlenecks. Another large agency bought ten coastal and smaller vessels. Other voluntary agencies turned their attention to priority needs that they were better equipped to meet than slower-moving, more cumbersome, less personal, and more inhibited official agencies. A number of voluntary agencies, for example, began to work on projects to rehabilitate the large numbers of women who had been raped and otherwise ill-treated by the Pakistan Army during the crackdown and subsequently rejected by their families. This was not the kind of problem that an intergovernmental international organization could successfully undertake. Voluntary agencies were also active in nutritional and preventive-health programs, child care, the promotion of cooperatives for cottage and small industries, including handloom weavers and fishermen, and integrated rural development. Under a rural housing program, twenty voluntary agencies combined their efforts to build 364,000 houses in 1972. They did so with the assistance of UNROD, which provided corrugated iron and delivered it as near as possible to the construc-

How the Operation Worked 195

tion sites scattered throughout the country. These programs were valuable in themselves and were the more effective because they were carried out by enthusiastic, dedicated agency personnel working side by side with Bangalees.

The voluntary agency programs were planned in a series of subcommittees consisting of representatives of agencies with similar interests. This guaranteed a high degree of cooperation, in which voluntary agencies exchanged staff and resources and assisted each other in meeting the country's needs.

By mid-May 1972, when the planning was completed, the subcommittee meetings were discontinued. Their place was taken by a fortnightly voluntary agency meeting, which had, as the UNROD liaison officer put it, no fixed terms of reference, conducted no business, and made no recommendations. It was, nevertheless, a valuable meeting, which enabled agency representatives to exchange ideas among themselves and with the government. Representatives of government agencies were brought to the meeting by the government coordinator and informed the agency representatives of their needs. The agencies responded rapidly, sometimes in the course of the meeting. For observers accustomed to the slower responses of international organizations, the process was encouraging and refreshing. At one meeting, for example, representatives of the Bangladesh Agricultural Development Corporation discussed the prospects for the coming *aus* harvest and told the agencies of the need for mechanics and spare parts to repair irrigation pumps. They were followed by representatives of a large United Nations advisory mission who outlined, at some length, their intricate plans for studies, investigation and, eventually, recommendations. While this exposition went on, field workers from two voluntary agencies conferred with the representatives of the Agricultural Development Corporation and undertook to supply volunteer mechanics who would be flown in from Europe in time to repair the irrigation pumps needed for the *aus* crop. In the long run, the recommendations promised by the United Nations mission may prove more important than the action taken by the voluntary agencies. In the short run, there is no doubt where the advantage lay. The volume of aid the two agencies supplied in this case was small, but it was immediate and practical.

The voluntary agencies' achievements in Bangladesh and UNROD's contribution to them through its liaison officer, Tom Haighton, were impressive. They were also instructive. On the basis of their experience in Bangladesh, the voluntary agencies, with the encouragement of Haighton, made a number of recommendations that call for the extension to other disaster situations of the procedures which were found effective in Bangladesh.

The recommendations were:

(i) A planned alerting procedure for disasters should be set up under international auspices. It could be entrusted to the United Nations Disaster Relief Office in Geneva, if this body were equipped to carry the function, but voluntary agency representatives should assist in preparing it and be associated with its operation. The procedure might include:

—an emergency fund to cover dispatch of an investigating team to a disaster area;

—regional stockpiles of emergency relief supplies;

—preparing an 'operations manual' or 'guidelines to action by voluntary agencies' for disaster situations.

(ii) The greatest need for coordinating action in a disaster situation is within the stricken country, and it is the government's responsibility to take the lead and bear the main burden, with the assistance of the concerned UNDP resident representative and specialized agencies, Red Cross and other voluntary agencies. For this purpose governments in disaster-prone areas should be encouraged to set up 'emergency cells' within their administrative structure.

(iii) A 'guidelines' or 'model rules' agreement between governments and voluntary agencies, worked out at international level and preferably under the auspices of the United Nations would be helpful to all concerned. It should include what the government can require from voluntary agencies by way of program approval and reporting; rules governing the type of relief goods which can be imported duty free, and for what period of time; the government's responsibility for internal transportation, etc.

(iv) There is a critical need for government at the start of a relief operation to appoint a relief coordinator with effective powers to overcome procedural bottlenecks and authorize unorthodox emergency actions. The need for this function should be kept under review and it should be terminated when the government departments concerned have reorganized themselves to cope with the emergency. (In Bangladesh, one voluntary agency commented that "The 1972 relief operation was remarkably free of red tape, thanks initially to the coordination division, then to the ministry of relief and rehabilitation which took over effectively later on. . . .")

(v) Since relief is temporary and exceptional help to meet temporary, exceptional requirements, a "cut-off" date should be fixed as early as the situation allows, to obviate encouragement of the so-called relief syndrome and to enable the authorities, and voluntary agencies, to take up or resume rehabilitation and development work.

(vi) Where by arrangement with governments or other donors, the sale of donated food is authorized to set up a counterpart fund to be used for relief and development purposes, whether under the control of the government or of the United Nations or jointly, provision should be made to allow relief projects by voluntary agencies of proved capacity to be assisted from the fund for their local expenditures.[7]

The recommendations are interesting and may well prove useful to those concerned with the provision of relief in future disaster situations. They are also evidence of the voluntary agencies' satisfaction with the arrangements instituted and successfully operated by the government and UNROD in Bangladesh. In material ways UNROD assisted the agencies by giving them access to transport and communications facilities and in some cases by providing supplies. It also furnished a central reference point in the person of Haighton, the UNROD liaison officer, who was able in countless ways to encourage and help forward the agencies' plans for cooperation and ensure that they were constantly aware of the government's priorities. As a result, the efforts of the fifty or so voluntary agencies in Bangladesh were welded into a single, substantial, and outstandingly effective component of the entire relief effort.

As a mechanism for mobilizing resources, as an instrument for coordinating aid, and as an operating agency in the transport and food sectors, UNROD was immensely successful. Looking back on the operation after the conclusion of his assignment, Victor Umbricht analyzed some of the reasons for its success and some of the causes of its shortcomings.

The main priorities had been properly assessed and had been acted upon "with celerity and imagination." Of course, some things could have been done better. Urgently required relief items, for example, had been held at the ports too long because of customs delays. The unloading of minibulkers at inland ports had not always been properly organized, making it impossible to operate the minibulker fleet at peak efficiency. These and similar difficulties could, he thought, have been reduced if UNROD intervention had been more insistent and if there had been daily conferences with the port authorities. He felt strongly that UNROD should have been equipped with experienced port officers and with a highly qualified specialist in marine transport. "What was missing," he said, "was a sea captain. . . . The gimmicks of the shipping trade are much too tricky to be left to nonprofessionals." He was inclined, also, to believe that transport operations would have been improved if UNROD had employed more local professionals.

He regretted, too, that the priority given to the importation of pumps, tube wells, fertilizers, and spare parts for pumps and trucks had not resulted in the needed equipment being brought in soon enough to be used for the 1972 *aman* harvest. "We erred in not keeping pressure on the government at an early stage to emphasize this need in their bilateral associations with donor countries." He thought the situation would have been helped if UNROD in the field had had sufficient funds to make direct purchases from sources that could have effected speedy deliveries.

This would, he recognized, have required modification of United Nations rules for administering funds and the limitations on the delegation of financial authority. "These rules, however, were not conceived for emergency relief operations like Bangladesh," he said, "but for classical procurement practices." Although headquarters in New York had done well in supplying the mission in Bangladesh with the goods requested, it had been hamstrung by cumbersome rules that should, he suggested, be reviewed in the light of UNROD's experience.

On the positive side, Umbricht believed that the one-voice principle had been "fundamental to the effectiveness of our operation." The Bangladesh experience had provided the model for future operations and shown that it was possible to coordinate effectively the operations of the specialized agencies, the voluntary agencies, and the bilateral efforts of donor countries. "If," he said, "the principle is to be faulted at all, it is that the principle was not always observed stringently enough and that, for successor operations, an even stricter approach might be adopted."

There were two other aspects of UNROD's work that were, in Umbricht's opinion, crucial to the success of the operation: cooperation with donor governments and with the government of Bangladesh and local authorities. Close cooperation had, he noted, been established with all donor countries, bilateral and multilateral. This was "based on their confidence in the coordinating role of UNROD." In Dacca, UNROD had daily contacts with the diplomatic missions of donor countries and visiting delegations and was "often in a position to assist them with advice and information on the urgent requirements of Bangladesh and to help avoid project duplications." UNROD was also able to assist the various missions by providing them with transport whenever needed. Without access to UNROD's ships, light aircraft, and helicopters, delegations of donor countries would have met with great difficulty in visiting outlying parts of the country.

Cooperation with the government of Bangladesh and local authorities was extremely close. "All my senior colleagues and I myself," Umbricht reported, "had daily contact with the various Bangladesh representatives at the different levels. On many occasions, I had meetings with several cabinet members at various times on the same day and quite often I dropped into the office of one or other of the ministers simply because I chanced to be nearby. I had a cup of tea with them and we talked about generalities, but this was a major factor in establishing the atmosphere of mutual trust that was essential to the close working relationship which characterized UNROD's activities. I believe that this human relationship should be given more attention than it normally receives."

What Umbricht wrote of UNROD in Dacca was equally true of UNROD headquarters in New York. The operation was efficient, economical, and vigorous. It was also an outstandingly successful exercise in cooperation, with the government of Bangladesh, with donor governments, with agencies and programs of the United Nations system, with the voluntary agencies, and with the many sections of the secretariat able to contribute to its work. Without that cooperation and the policy of consistently limiting UNROD's direct involvement in operational functions to the minimum by subcontracting wherever possible to existing efficient agencies, the operation could not have accomplished so much with so small an administrative infrastructure.[8]

Commenting on the operation in 1973, Sir Robert Jackson suggested that much of its success resulted from the "three umbrellas" with which it had provided the international community.

The first umbrella was one that the secretary-general could offer to extend over the United Nations system as a whole and thus help it to speak with "one voice." The principle had worked well. The process had, of course, been made easier by the fact that the United Nations itself had had funds at its disposal. It proved most helpful to the specialized agencies, including the World Bank and IMF, before Bangladesh had become a member of the organizations concerned.

The second umbrella was more voluntary in character but had proved to be equally effective. This was the umbrella offered to all the voluntary agencies working in Bangladesh. The voluntary agencies had very quickly responded when they saw that the

How the Operation Worked

United Nations arrangements assured that the resources were used to the best advantage.

The third umbrella was also essentially voluntary and was extended to the many governments providing bilateral assistance. In the early days before some of the principal donor governments had recognized Bangladesh, the United Nations had provided a channel through which they could offer assistance. As the operation progressed and more aid was provided bilaterally, UNROD's umbrella continued to be useful. In the end, virtually all donor governments, either formally or informally, made use of the third umbrella because they saw its advantages. As a result of UNROD's efforts, donors, governmental and nongovernmental, had been provided with a comprehensive picture of all external assistance to Bangladesh.

The operation had, Jackson said, achieved its fundamental objective "as a result of much help by many people and many governments and organizations." He suggested it had also demonstrated that the United Nations is "a very suitable instrument to use as a catalyst and political coordinator." The political initiatives taken by U Thant in 1971 and Kurt Waldheim in 1972 and 1973 had been matched by the creation of a successful, supple, and innovative organization. The organization was temporary. With the end of the emergency it was disbanded, but the experience it had accumulated and the lessons it provided remain.

APPENDIX 1

UNEPRO, UNROD, UNROB:
A Chronology

1971	
1 April	Secretary-general publicly offers UN humanitarian assistance to the government of Pakistan
22 April	Secretary-general makes formal offer of UN humanitarian assistance for the relief of suffering in East Pakistan
29 April	Secretary-general designates UNHCR as focal point for UN assistance to refugees from East Pakistan
22 May	Pakistan formally accepts the secretary-general's offer of humanitarian assistance
3 June	Assistant secretary-general Kittani visits Pakistan to make arrangements for relief operation
7 June	Representative of secretary-general, El-Tawil, and small field staff arrive in East Pakistan to coordinate emergency aid
16 June	Secretary-general appeals for contributions for emergency assistance in East Pakistan
21 June	S. Tripp appointed headquarters coordinator for UN humanitarian assistance to East Pakistan
16 July	ECOSOC endorses the action taken by the secretary-general
20 July	Secretary-general addresses memorandum to the president of the Security Council on the situation in the subcontinent
13 August	Secretary-general convenes meeting of potential donor governments
23 August	Paul-Marc Henry appointed assistant secre-

Appendix 1

	tary-general in charge of East Pakistan relief operation (UNEPRO) at headquarters
September-October	Contributions beginning to be delivered, including first 100 trucks
22 October	Secretary-general offers his good offices to the governments of India and Pakistan
15-16 November	Agreement between government of Pakistan and UN on conduct of operation
18 November	Paul-Marc Henry reports to the Third Committee of the General Assembly on the operation
24 November	Movement of staff and supplies to East Pakistan halted. Supplies diverted to Singapore
4-6 December	Security Council considers situation in the subcontinent
6 December	General Assembly adopts resolution 2790 (XXVI) endorsing the secretary-general's initiative in establishing UNEPRO
7 December	General Assembly adopts resolution 2793 (XXVI) calling for cease-fire
12-21 December	Security Council again considers situation and adopts resolution 307 (1971)
21 December	Secretary-general informs General Assembly and Security Council of establishment of UNROD
22 December	Evacuation of staff completed, leaving small nucleus in Dacca
27 December	Toni Hagen arrives in Dacca as officer in charge of UNROD
1972	
12 January	First informal meeting of potential UNROD donor governments
20 January	Paul-Marc Henry meets prime minister of Bangladesh
14 February	Secretary-general appeals for contributions in support of UNROD

Appendix 1

5 March	The Sailer mission arrives in Dacca to survey needs
23 March	Sir Robert Jackson appointed as under-secretary-general in charge of the operation
10 April	ACC endorses the one-voice principle for the conduct of the operation
14 April	Dr. Victor Umbricht appointed chief of mission in Dacca
28 April	Report of Sailer mission published
31 May	Secretary-general makes further appeal for contributions. Donor meeting
11 July	Donor meeting
5 August	S.S. *Manhattan* arrives in Bangladesh waters for use as a floating silo
August	UNROD airdrop and airlift of food supplies
11 August	Donor meeting
8 September	Government of Bangladesh requests UN to undertake clearance of Chalna anchorage
14 September	Donor meeting
14 October	Prime minister of Bangladesh requests continued UN relief assistance after the planned termination of UNROD
18 October	Donor meeting
20 October	UN signs Chalna clearance contract
16 November	Salvage equipment begins to arrive at Chalna
23 November	S.S. *Manhattan* leaves Bangladesh waters
1 December	Donor meeting

1973

5 January	Donor meeting
2 February	Donor meeting
February	Secretary-general visits subcontinent
16 March	Donor meeting
31 March	UNROD terminated
1 April	UNROB established under Francis Lacoste as chief of mission and special representative of the secretary-general

Appendix 1

1 May	Donor meeting
11 May	Chalna clearance completed
22 June	Donor meeting
14 August	Contract for second Chalna clearance operation signed
24 August	Donor meeting
1 September	Operational responsibility for shipping operations transferred to Bangladesh transport task group
13 September	Secretary-general appeals for support of UN humanitarian operations in the subcontinent
9 November	Final donor meeting
23 November	Work under second Chalna clearance contract completed
31 December	UNROB terminated as planned

APPENDIX 2

Published United Nations Material

Reports of the Secretary-General

Between December 1971 and December 1973 the secretary-general made a series of formal reports to the General Assembly and the Security Council on the work of UNEPRO, UNROD, and UNROB under the general title "Report of the Secretary-General concerning the implementation of General Assembly resolution 2790 (XXVI) and Security Council resolution 307 (1971)." The dates of issue and document numbers were: S/10466, 21 Dec. 1971; S/10539, 15 Feb. 1972; S/10539/add. 1, 28 Apr. 1972; S/10539/add. 2, 31 May 1972; S/10539/add. 3, 11 Aug. 1972; S/10853, 1 Jan. 1973; S/10853/add. 1, 15 Jan. 1973; S/10853/add. 2, 13 Mar. 1973; S/10853/add. 3, 26 Apr. 1973; and S/10853/add. 4, 5 Dec. 1973. The reports are reprinted in the official records of the United Nations Security Council.

UNROD Publications

The UNROD office in Dacca published the following numbered information papers:

1. Field reports compiled from 2 January to 12 February 1972, Toni Hagen, 12 February 1972
2. Labour intensive schemes and food imports, Peter Wheeler, 13 February 1972
3. Blunt facts on relief and rehabilitation in Bangladesh, Toni Hagen, 13 February 1972
4. Bridges and ferries (Bangladesh), W. K. Cross, 29 February 1972
5. What Bangladesh needs (a brief note), S. K. Dey, 3 March 1972
6. Rural works programme, Peter Wheeler, 3 March 1972
7. Report on rehabilitation of groundwater irrigation equipment, S. R. Vasudev, 7 March 1972

8. Plight of weavers in Bangladesh, S. K. Dey, 15 March 1972

9. Report on Chittagong port, Rex Dodson, 17 March 1972

10. Note on relief materials and services pledged to Bangladesh up to March 1972, T. Haighton, 17 March 1972

11. Bangladesh today and tomorrow, S. K. Dey, 23 March 1972

12. Situation and relief in Bangladesh as of 7 May 1972, Toni Hagen, 7 May 1972

13. Bangladesh health nutrition survey, Dr. M. S. Lowenstein, Dr. Alfred Sommer, and Dr. James Sprague, 23 June 1972

14. The health situation in Bangladesh—The great outreach, Dr. Sam Street, June 1972

15. UNROD—The first six months, January-June 1972, 26 July 1972

16. The work of the voluntary agencies in Bangladesh, January-June 1972, 14 August 1972

17. Bangladesh: A survey of damage and repairs, two vols., S. K. Dey, 13 October 1972

18. Rehabilitation of the disabled in Bangladesh, Esko Kosunen, 6 November 1972

19. Food storage management (rats), P. M. Thomas, 16 November 1972

20. Study of ferry crossings in Bangladesh, S. Haque, 15 December 1972

21. Second Bangladesh national nutritional assessment, Dr. James B. Sprague, 22 December 1972

22. A report on telecommunications in Bangladesh, John F. Boag, 9 January 1973

23. Health in Bangladesh—WHO country review, Dr. Sam Street, 14 February 1973

24. Bangladesh—A broad survey of institutions, S. K. Dey, 28 February 1973

25. Aid situation report, Bernard Oury, March 1973

26. The work of the voluntary agencies in Bangladesh, 1972 (projected to June 1973), 15 March 1973

Other publications were:

A. Report of the civil aviation mission/Bangladesh, John R. Houghton, April 1972

Appendix 2

B. Supplemental report of the civil aviation mission, May 1972

C. Report of the special agricultural mission to assess import requirements of food grains for the calendar year 1973, Dr. Robert Chandler, December 1972

D. Further report of the special agricultural mission, March 1973

E. Some social aspects of development planning in Bangladesh: Report prepared under the sponsorship of UNROD, three vols., December 1972

Notes

In addition to the published sources cited in the notes, unpublished archival material and information derived from interviews have been used. As the archival material is not readily accessible and many of the persons interviewed preferred to remain anonymous, such sources are not identified. Where no sources are supplied, the sources are internal, unpublished papers or interviews.

Introduction

1. Abdur Rab Chaudhury, *The Saga of Bangladesh*, Dacca, Bangladesh Government Press, 1972, p. 1.
2. Azizur Rahman Khan, *The Economy of Bangladesh*, London, Macmillan, 1972, p. 4.
3. Statement by Dr. Marcus F. Franda, *Political Trends in India and Bangladesh*, Washington, U.S. Government Printing Office, 1973, p. 9.
4. S. K. Dey, *Bangladesh: A Survey of Damages and Repairs*, Dacca, UNROD, 1972, vol. 1, p. v.
5. Abdur Rab Chaudhury, *op. cit.*, p. 10.
6. *Morning News*, Dacca, 2 Feb. 1973.

Chapter 1

1. *Pakistan Horizon*, Pakistan Institute of International Affairs, Karachi, vol. 24, no. 2, pp. 107-110.
2. United Nations Security Council, Official Records, document S/10410, 3 Dec. 1971, para. 3.
3. *Bangla Desh Documents*, Ministry of External Affairs, New Delhi, 1971, vol. 1, pp. 669 and 672.
4. The note was quoted by Ambassador Sen in a speech to the General Assembly on 7 December 1971. United Nations General Assembly, Plenary Meetings, meeting 2003, 7 Dec. 1971, para. 156.
5. A Pakistan foreign office statement on 6 May 1971 maintained that Indian Army sappers were sabotaging communications in East Pakistan to create artificial scarcities of essential goods. *Pakistan Horizon*, vol. 24, no. 2, p. 117.

6. United Nations press release SG/SM/1474, 12 May 1971.
7. President Podgorny's letter and Chou En-lai's note are reproduced in *Pakistan Horizon*, vol. 24, no. 2, pp. 148 and 153.
8. United Nations press release SG/SM/1474, 12 May 1971.
9. *New York Times*, 20 May 1971, p. 6.
10. United Nations press release SG/SM/1484, 26 May 1971.
11. United Nations press release SG/SM/1478, 19 May 1971. The work of UNHCR as focal point for the assistance of the refugees in India is described in A *Story of Anguish and Action*, Geneva, UNHCR, 1972, and in the secretary-general's report to the Security Council, United Nations Security Council, Official Records, document S/10539/add. 3, 11 Aug. 1972.
12. *New York Times*, 30 May 1971, p. 1.

Chapter 2

1. *Bangla Desh Documents*, Ministry of External Affairs, New Delhi, 1971, vol. 1, pp. 672-675.
2. United Nations press release SG/SM/1493, 3 June 1971, p. 11.
3. Great Britain, Parliamentary Debates, Commons, vol. 818, col. 1066, 10 June 1971.
4. *Bangla Desh Documents*, vol. 1, p. 707.
5. United Nations press release SG/SM/1531, 16 Sept. 1971.
6. United Nations Economic and Social Council, *Assistance in Cases of Natural Disaster: Comprehensive Report of the Secretary-General* (E/4994), 13 May 1971. The arrangements in force were set out in a manual on the resources and procedures of the United Nations family prepared by the UN Office of Technical Cooperation in 1966 and revised in June 1971.
7. United Nations note to correspondents no. 3669, 5 June 1971.
8. United Nations press release SG/1756, 9 June 1971.
9. United Nations press release SG/SM/1498, 16 June 1971.
10. United Nations press release IHA/1, 21 June 1971.
11. Pakistan government press release GAIV/174/71, 18 June 1971.
12. United Nations press release IHA/20, 15 July 1971.
13. United Nations Economic and Social Council, Records of Meetings, meeting 1783, 16 July 1971.
14. United Nations General Assembly, *Introduction to the Report of the Secretary-General on the Work of the Organization* (A/8401/add. 1), Sept. 1971, para. 180.

Notes   213

15. The United States representative, Ambassador Bernard Zagorin, suggested that the high commissioner's work to assist the refugees in India and the parallel effort in East Pakistan illustrated the possibility of permanent arrangements to deal with emergency situations. United Nations Economic and Social Council, Records of Meetings, meeting 1783, 16 July 1971, para, 85.

Chapter 3

1. *New York Times*, 13 July 1971, pp. 1 and 8. The excerpts from the report printed in the *Times* speak of military repression, widespread fear among the population, economic stagnation, the breakdown of administration, and the dislocation of transport and communications facilities. In contrast the United Nations press release of 15 July (IHA/20) states:

   Reports from the secretary-general's representative in East Pakistan indicate that there has been considerable movement of population to rural areas causing an as yet uncalculated loss of crops and purchasing power as well as disruption of transportation. These situations will complicate food and relief operations now and in the near future. However, no mass concentrations of displaced persons has been reported.
   Preliminary assessments suggest that the problem is primarily one of distribution of food and other relief supplies. . . . However, railway and road transportation capacities have been reduced by an estimated 65 to 75 percent. The government of Pakistan is working on the restoration of these facilities but it is clear that reliance must be placed on water transport for food and relief supplies.

2. *New York Times*, 22 July 1971, p. 4.
3. Great Britain, Parliamentary Debates (Commons), vol. 819, col. 1436, 23 June 1971.
4. *New York Times*, 20 July 1971, p. 3.
5. *New York Times*, 1 Aug. 1971, p. 1.
6. United Nations note to correspondents no. 3675, 2 Aug. 1971.
7. United Nations press release SG/SM/1516, 2 Aug. 1971.
8. *Bangla Desh Documents*, Ministry of External Relations, New Delhi, 1971, vol. 1, pp. 660-663.
9. United Nations Security Council, Official Records, meeting 1329, official communiqué, 2 Dec. 1966.

10. In a lecture to the Royal Central Asian Society in October 1972, Professor Wilcox of Columbia University suggested with some plausibility that United States policy in the crisis resulted from the "very weak" level of concern and willingness to play a major role in Washington. "Official Washington faithfully reflected South Asia's modest position in US foreign policy in its staffing positions in the major agencies. No principal officer in the White House, Treasury, or departments of State and Defense had any deep experience in the region. Only the Agency for International Development had any high level of institutional commitment and expertise relating to the region and AID was a very weak player in Washington politics. Instead, during the period of the crisis its very existence was being challenged." The lecture is reproduced in *Political Trends in India and Bangladesh*, Washington, U.S. Government Printing Office, 1973, pp. 66-74.
11. *Pakistan Horizon*, vol. 24, no. 3, pp. 131-139.
12. United Nations press release IHA/2, 23 June 1971.
13. Honor Tracy, *The Straight and Narrow Path*, London, Methuen, 1956.
14. United Nations note to correspondents no. 3678, 10 Aug. 1971.
15. *Pakistan Horizon*, vol. 24, no. 3, p. 139.

Chapter 4

1. United Nations press release SG/SM/1523, 13 Aug. 1971.
2. United Nations notes to correspondents no. 3675, 2 Aug. 1971, no. 3676, 6 Aug. 1971, and no. 3680, 11 Aug. 1971.
3. Additional contributions were received by 13 August, when the total was $4 million.
4. United Nations press release IHA/46, 24 Aug. 1971.
5. This was a major difficulty. Some donors were reluctant to meet requests that were not endorsed by the United Nations. On 30 August Ambassador Shahi forwarded a note to the headquarters coordinator which Pakistan had received from a West European government. It said in part "as soon as requests for assistance to the population in East Pakistan are received through appropriate UN channels, we stand ready to comply with such requests to the extent possible." Other prospective donors took a similar position.
6. United Nations press release IHA/93, 17 Nov. 1971. The text of the agreement is as follows:

Notes

A. A chief of mission shall be appointed by the secretary-general, who shall exercise full authority, on behalf of the secretary-general, over the conduct of UNEPRO. In selecting the chief of mission, the secretary-general shall take into consideration the views of the government of Pakistan.

B. UNEPRO shall consist of such officials as the secretary-general may assign or appoint for the purpose of discharging the operation's functions, namely, international officials of the United Nations, its programs, and specialized agencies, and officials locally recruited for the purposes of UNEPRO. Such officials, with the exception of those locally recruited and employed at hourly rates, shall be accorded the privileges and immunities specified in article V of the Convention on the Privileges and Immunities of the United Nations and article VI of the Convention on the Privileges and Immunities of the Specialized Agencies, to both of which instruments Pakistan is a party. UNEPRO personnel shall respect the laws and regulations of Pakistan and shall refrain from any action incompatible with their status as officials of the United Nations or of the specialized agencies.

C. UNEPRO associated personnel shall consist of persons, other than those referred to in paragraph 2 above, who are not of Pakistan nationality and who are engaged in relief activities forming part of UNEPRO. UNEPRO associated personnel shall, in particular, include international members of the crews of vessels engaged in activities forming part of UNEPRO and such additional categories of personnel (other than those covered under paragraph 2 above) as may be agreed between the government of Pakistan and the United Nations. The secretary-general shall provide to the government of Pakistan at its request lists of UNEPRO associated personnel, and shall from time to time inform it of any changes in those lists. The government of Pakistan shall grant UNEPRO associated personnel immunity from legal process in respect of words spoken or written and all acts performed by them in the course of such activities, UNEPRO associated personnel shall respect the laws and regulations of Pakistan and shall refrain from any action incompatible with their functions.

D. UNEPRO personnel and associated personnel shall enjoy freedom of access to, and freedom of movement within East Pakistan. In particular they shall have free access to the places and facilities where relief supplies brought in by, or under the auspices of, the

United Nations, are discharged, stored, transported or distributed. Such freedom of access and movement shall include the use of motor vehicles, vessels used for sea and river navigation, and equipment, required in connection with UNEPRO activities. The freedom of access and movement envisaged in this paragraph may be subject to temporary restriction for security reasons. The chief of mission shall be informed when such restrictions are imposed and shall be consulted with a view to ensuring that activities forming part of UNEPRO can continue to be conducted so far as possible without interruption.

E. (1) All property, equipment and forms of transport used as part of UNEPRO, as well as all relief supplies brought in by, or under the auspices of, the United Nations, shall be afforded free entry into Pakistan and expeditious handling. They shall not be diverted to any purpose incompatible with the functions of UNEPRO.

(2) The government of Pakistan shall provide free storage facilities for relief supplies brought in by, or under the auspices of, the United Nations. Arrangements shall be made for regular on-the-spot consultations between officials of the government of Pakistan and UNEPRO personnel and associated personnel regarding customs formalities and similar matters.

F. UNEPRO personnel and associated personnel shall enjoy an unrestricted right of communication, by radio, telephone, telegraph or other means, when performing duties forming part of UNEPRO. The United Nations may, for this purpose, establish a system of radio communication in East Pakistan connected with the UN radio network, which shall be operated in accordance with such international agreements, conventions and regulations as may be in force.

G. The United Nations flag, markings and emblem may be used in connection with UNEPRO as the chief of mission shall determine.

H. The government of Pakistan shall take all necessary measures to ensure the security and safety of UNEPRO personnel and associated personnel and of all premises, facilities, means of transport and equipment used in connection with UNEPRO activities.

I. The United Nations and the government of Pakistan shall extend to each other the fullest possible cooperation in order that activities forming part of UNEPRO may fulfill the strictly humanitarian purposes of the operation.

7. *Ibid.*
8. Government of East Pakistan, Food Plan for East Pakistan, Aug. 1971.
9. *New York Times*, 19 Aug. 1971, p. 35 and 28 Aug. 1971, p. 24.
10. United Nations note to correspondents no. 3685, 1 Sept. 1971.
11. United Nations press release IHA/76, 13 Oct. 1971, and IHA/81, 15 Oct. 1971.
12. United Nations note to correspondents no. 3701, 22 Oct. 1971.
13. United Nations General Assembly, Official Records, Third Committee, meeting 1877, 18 Nov. 1971.

Chapter 5

1. *New York Times*, 13 Oct. 1971, p. 1.
2. United Nations press release SG/SM/1530, 14 Sept. 1971.
3. United Nations press release SG/SM/1566, 27 Oct. 1971. In Indian circles it was suggested that the leaks were intended to embarrass India.
4. *New York Times*, 14 Oct. 1971, p. 1.
5. United Nations Security Council, Official Records, document S/10410, 3 Dec. 1971, para. 6.
6. United Nations General Assembly, Official Records, Plenary, meeting 1940, 27 Sept. 1971.
7. *Bangla Desh Documents*, vol. 2, p. 250.
8. *Ibid.*, p. 263.
9. *Ibid.*, p. 269.
10. United Nations Security Council, Official Records, document S/10410, 3 Dec. 1971, para. 7.
11. *Ibid.*, para. 8.
12. *Ibid.*, para. 9.
13. *Ibid.*, para. 10.
14. *Ibid.*, para. 12.
15. *Ibid.*, para. 13.
16. United Nations Security Council, Official Records, document S/10412, 4 Dec. 1971.
17. Lt. Commander Ravi Kaul, Indian Navy (Ret.), *The Indo-Pakistani War and the Changing Balance of Power in the Indian Ocean*, U.S. Naval Institute, Proceedings, May 1973.

Chapter 6

1. The name is odd. The humanitarian operation had been neutral from the beginning.
2. United Nations Security Council, Official Records, document S/10433, 7 Dec. 1971.

Chapter 7

1. United Nations Security Council, Official Records, document S/10410, 3 Dec. 1971.
2. *Ibid.*, document S/10410/add. 1, 4 Dec. 1971.
3. *Ibid.*, document S/10412 and addenda, 4, 5, and 6 Dec. 1971.
4. The debate is summarized in the *Report of the Security Council 16 June 1971-15 June 1972*, General Assembly, Official Records, document A/8702, pp. 59-62.
5. United Nations Security Council, Official Records, document S/10416, 4 Dec. 1971.
6. *Ibid.*, document S/10418, 4 Dec. 1971.
7. *Ibid.*, document S/10419, 4 Dec. 1971.
8. United Nations Security Council, Resolutions, resolution 303 (1971).
9. United Nations General Assembly, Official Records, Plenary, meetings 2002 and 2003, 7 Dec. 1971.
10. *Ibid.*, meeting 2003, para. 3.
11. *Bangladesh Observer*, Dacca, 16 Dec. 1972.
12. *Evening Post*, Dacca, 10 Feb. 1973.
13. United Nations Security Council, Official Records, document S/10444, 12 Dec. 1971.
14. *Ibid.*, document S/10445, 12 Dec. 1971. Pakistan's acceptance of the resolution was communicated by Ambassador Shahi on 9 December (document S/10440).
15. India recognized the government of Bangladesh on 6 December 1971.
16. United Nations General Assembly, Official Records, *Report of the Security Council 16 June 1971-15 June 1972* (document A/8702), pp. 69-79.
17. United Nations Security Council, Official Records, document S/10467, 22 Dec. 1971.
18. By prescience or good fortune, the field service staff assigned to

Notes   219

UNEPRO included an officer, Masaichi Nagai, who had served as a pilot in Japan. One of the remarkable features of the operation was field service's knack of producing staff with useful previous experience. It would be gratifying to report that this was the result of planning. In fact, there is nothing to suggest that Nagai was assigned to UNEPRO because someone thought his previous training would be useful. It seems to have been a stroke of luck. It was, of course, made possible by the fact that field service officers constitute a rather large pool of highly varied skills.

Chapter 8

1. United Nations Security Council, Official Records, document S/10466, 21 Dec. 1971.
2. United Nations General Assembly, Official Records, Plenary, meeting 2001, 6 Dec. 1971, para. 97.
3. *New York Times*, 9 Jan. 1972, p. 4.
4. United Nations Security Council, Official Records, document S/10473, 25 Dec. 1971.
5. *Ibid.*, document S/10512, 17 Jan. 1972.
6. *Field Reports Compiled from 2 January to 12 February 1972*, Dacca, UNROD, 12 Feb. 1972.
7. United Nations Security Council, Official Records, document S/10539, 15 Feb. 1972.
8. The United Nations secretariat was more punctilious than governments. On 22 March Ambassador George Bush announced that the United States was making a contribution of $35 million "in further response" to the secretary-general's February appeal "for the UN relief program in Bangladesh." The United States did not recognize Bangladesh until April 1972. United Nations press release IHA/144, 29 Mar. 1972.
9. The Annual Plan, Planning Commission, People's Republic of Bangladesh, June 1972.
10. United Nations Security Council, Official Records, document S/10539/add. 1, 28 Apr. 1972.
11. *Ibid.*, document S/10512/add. 1, 26 Feb. 1972, para. 18.
12. *Ibid.*, document S/10512/add. 1, 26 Feb. 1972, para, 16.
13. *New York Times*, 13 Feb. 1972, p. 17.
14. The second letter was delivered in a correctly addressed envelope.

Chapter 9

1. The UNROD office in Dacca was a remarkably prolific producer of published material, some useful, some not. The publications include a three-volume study on some social aspects of development planning, an essay on rats, and more mundane reports on war damages and relief. See appendix 2.
2. *New York Times*, 10 Mar. 1972, p. 5.
3. *Morning News*, Dacca, 19 Mar. 1972.
4. *New York Times*, 30 Mar. 1972, p. 3.
5. *New York Times*, 31 Mar. 1972, p. 9.
6. Headquarters opposed the use of military personnel. It relented when it was agreed that the soldiers would wear civilian clothes. Indian army engineers were also helping to restore the rail network.
7. Government of the People's Republic of Bangladesh, Food for Works Programme 1971-72, circular 183 (483), 4 Apr. 1972.
8. United Nations Security Council, Official Records, document S/10539/add. 1 (part I), 28 Apr. 1972, para. 23. The appeal was made at a private meeting of ACC and the discussion was unrecorded. The appeal and the response were not mentioned in the report of ACC to the Economic and Social Council. The omission is remarkable. ACC had been criticized in the Economic and Social Council for lack of candor and for the ineffective coordination of many activities of the United Nations system. Information about the decision to strengthen coordination in the conduct of UNROD would, it may be supposed, have gone some way to offset these criticisms. Delegations knew of the decision, of course, but seem to have chosen not to relate it to the Council's annual discussion of coordination matters. It is difficult to see what, other than the compartmentalization of United Nations activities in delegations and in the secretariat, prevented them from doing so.
9. United Nations press release IHA/118, 14 Apr. 1972.

Chapter 10

1. United Nations Security Council, Official Records, document S/10539/add. 1 (part II), 28 Apr. 1972. Only the first volume is reproduced in the Security Council records. The second volume consisting of sectoral reports was distributed informally and could be consulted in the UNROD offices in New York and Dacca.
2. *Ibid.*, document S/10539/add. 1 (part II), para. 26.

Notes   221

3. United Nations, A *Study of the Capacity of the United Nations Development System*, Geneva, 1969.
4. United Nations Security Council, Official Records, document S/10539/add. 1 (part I), para. 27-29.

Chapter 11

1. UNROD press release, Dacca, 20 May 1972.
2. United Nations Security Council, Official Records, document S/10539/add. 2, 31 May 1972, para. 4.
3. *The People*, Dacca, 15 June 1972.
4. *Morning News*, Dacca, 12 June 1972.
5. Government of the People's Republic of Bangladesh, The Annual Plan 1972-73.
6. The sea trucks were light, fiberglass boats supplied by the British government and used to ferry supplies.
7. *The People*, Dacca, 5 Aug. 1972.

Chapter 12

1. United Nations Security Council, Official Records, document S/10853, 1 Jan. 1973, paras. 79-82.
2. *Report of the Special Agricultural Mission*, Dacca, UNROD, Dec. 1972.
3. United Nations Security Council, Official Records, document S/10853, 1 Jan. 1973, paras. 79-82.
4. UNROD schedule of food shipments, Dacca, 31 Mar. 1972.
5. "United Nations Shipwreck Clearance of Chalna Port Anchorage and Approaches, Lower Pusr River, Bangladesh," final report prepared by the contractors, Smit Tak International Bergingsbedrijf NV, Rotterdam, 1974.
6. Verbatim report of Meeting on the Development of Bangladesh, Dacca, 31 Mar.-1 Apr. 1973.
7. *Ibid.*

Chapter 13

1. United Nations press release IHA/169, 14 Mar. 1973.
2. United Nations Security Council, Official Records, document S/10512 and add. 1, 17 Jan. and 26 Feb. 1973.
3. For the text of the agreement, see Mohammed Ayoob, *India, Paki-*

stan and Bangladesh—Search for a new relationship, New Delhi, Indian Council of World Affairs, 1975, pp. 151-153.
4. Ibid., pp. 165-166.
5. Ibid., pp. 167-169.
6. United Nations press release SG/SM/1878, 30 Aug. 1973.
7. United Nations note to correspondents UNPSS/377, 6 Sept. 1973.
8. United Nations press release SG/SM/1888, 14 Sept. 1973.
9. The assistance contributed directly through the office of the disaster-relief coordinator included $250,000 from the secretary-general's Fund for Displaced Persons in Pakistan. The fund had been set up under Bradford Morse, under-secretary-general for political and general assembly affairs, in 1972 in response to the request of the Pakistan government, and had been successfully assisting the government in resettling persons displaced by the Indo-Pakistan war of 1971.
10. The report was circulated informally and was not distributed officially.
11. United Nations press release IHA/94, 19 Sept. 1973.
12. Memorandum on Repatriation of Homeless Repatriates from Bangla Desh/India, Government of Pakistan, Cabinet Division, and Programme for Relief and Rehabilitation of Bangalee Repatriates from Pakistan, Government of Bangladesh. The requests were not published.
13. *The Guardian*, London, 26 Oct. 1973.
14. United Nations press release IHA/201, 12 Nov. 1973.
15. The repatriation operation was successfully concluded in mid-1974. It was, the high commissioner commented, significant that so many governments had helped and had joined forces under the insignia of a strictly nonpolitical international organization to carry out one of the largest population movements of recent times. United Nations press release REF/706, 1 July 1974.
16. United Nations Security Council, Official Records, document S/10853/add. 4, 6 Dec. 1973.
17. The United Nations was charged in articles in *The Economist* (13 Oct. 1973) and the *Christian Science Monitor* (6 Nov. 1973) with forcing an unrealistically high ration level on the government. A ration of less than 13 ounces would, the articles argued, have been sufficient, would have released resources, and would have enabled the government to provide transport for the export of jute. The criticism was unfounded. UNROB urged the government to reduce the

Notes

ration level. In any case, the 13-ounce figure was not strictly speaking a ration, but a planning figure used in calculating total food grain requirements, and was less than that used in the earliest forecasts. In fact, UNROD's estimates of grain needs seem to have been remarkably accurate.
18. The lightering vessels were on short-term charter and the number was varied to meet requirements.
19. United Nations press release SG/1776, 7 Dec. 1973.

Chapter 14

1. United Nations Security Council, Official Records, document S/10853, 1 Jan. 1973. The total at the end of 1973 when UNROB terminated was $1,324,000,000.
2. UNROD information papers no. 13 and no. 21, June and Oct. 1972.
3. One mystery of the operation is how the staff, beginning with Sir Robert Jackson, fitted all they did into a twenty-four-hour day. The time budgets of the officials most actively involved, such as George Lansky of field operations service and Albert Contreras-Suarez of communications, would make interesting reading.
4. The report was largely the work of one international economist and his Bangalee assistant.
5. UNICEF's programs are described in *UNICEF Meets an Emergency*, New York, UNICEF, Nov. 1973.
6. UNROD information papers nos. 16 and 26, Aug. 1972 and Mar. 1973.
7. UNROD information paper no. 26.
8. On the basis of Umbricht's analysis and subsequent discussions at headquarters, Sir Robert Jackson's office prepared a series of suggestions for the organization of future relief operations. The points emphasized were:
   A. The preparation of contingency plans;
   B. The preparation of a "skeleton" plan for dealing with specific disasters (a "disaster relief manual");
   C. The effective application of the one-voice principle through, *inter alia*:
      1. the selection of a central point in the UN system for preparing the plans mentioned in A and B above (presumably UNDRO);

2. the establishment of focal points in all relevant organizations of the UN system for coordinating each agency's participation in emergency operations;
   3. strict coordination of all appeals above $500,000, which should only emanate from the secretary-general;
   4. clear definition of which part of the UN or which agency is to be responsible for dealing with each specific emergency as it arises (to be endorsed by the secretary-general and communicated to the UN system, and all governments);
   5. strict observance of those arrangements by all concerned in the operational phase.
D. Further consideration of financial arrangements and procedures to be applied in cases of emergency operations:
   1. the availability of funds for emergencies under standing arrangements;
   2. the delegation of financial authority either by:
      i. a special set of emergency financial procedures automatically applied when the secretary-general declares an "emergency operation";
      or by
      ii. bestowing an ad hoc special authority in specific instances.
   3. more flexible procedures for handling contracts (e.g. by local contracts committees).
E. Ensuring the prompt fielding of competent and experienced *administrative support* personnel of high personal caliber by:
   1. maintenance by both the UN and relevant agencies (through the focal point in each case) of roster comprising:
      i. those who have served effectively in previous emergency operations, with full record of their performance;
      ii. those who would be ready to serve at short notice, thus enabling screening to take place in advance.
   2. keeping a small cadre of trained headquarters and field service personnel available for further missions (instead of the present policy of releasing most of them at the end of each operation).
F. Ensuring the prompt fielding of experienced *professional* personnel of high personal caliber by asking:
   1. governments
   and

2. all relevant components of the UN system to provide lists of suitably qualified and experienced people (a checklist of the main fields usually required could be provided) who could be made available at short notice.
G. Encouraging governments in disaster-prone areas to draw up lists of their own professional and administrative support personnel qualified to occupy key posts in case of emergency.
H. The establishment of basic organizational principles to be applied to emergency operations, including:
   1. full application of the one-voice principle: the chief of mission must be the focal point of the UN system on the spot;
   2. adequate delegation of authority to the chief of mission while still
   3. pinpointing overall responsibility on the headquarters made responsible for that particular operation;
   4. maximum decentralization to the field, keeping the headquarters unit to a bare minimum, yet ready to provide service around the clock, seven days a week;
   5. efficient logistical planning;
   6. frequent provision of adequate and accurate information to donor governments;
   7. at the local level, appointing an "executive officer" who would be second in command and responsible for organization;
   8. guidelines for setting up an information/intelligence unit to collect information systematically and provide it in readily usable form.

   A corollary of all this is the urgent need to train more UN personnel in these techniques.
I. Providing adequate and effective OPI facilities for informing the general public of successful UN emergency operations.
J. The policy implications of the Chalna clearance operation for future emergency relief operations.

In separate documents, Jackson emphasized that, apart from efficient "operational" personnel, nothing is more important than the provision of first class communication facilities throughout any particular operation.

Index

Administrative Committee on Coordination, 128, 129, 134, 192
Ahmed, Aziz, 172
Ahmed, M. M., 10
Ahmed, Tajuddin, 100, 166
aid mobilized, xviii, 183
airdrop, 73, 150-52
airlift, 73, 147, 150
Algeria, 81
Ali, Mansoor, 117
Amin Dada, Idi, 40
appeals by secretary-general: for refugees, 11; for East Pakistan relief, 22; for Bangladesh relief, 108, 143, 160; for repatriation, resettlement, and disaster relief, 173
Argentina, 43, 80, 81, 89
Aurora, General, 86
Australia, 179
Austria, 43
Awami League, 3, 40, 61, 68

Bangalees in Pakistan, 103, 170-71
Bangladesh: development conference, 164-65; establishment of administration, xvii; international recognition, xviii, 102, 112; republic proclaimed, 8
Bangladesh Agricultural Development Corporation, 195
Bangladesh Ecumenical Relief and Rehabilitation Service, 156
Bangladesh Red Cross, 194
Bangladesh Rehabilitation Assistance Committee, 126
Beer, Henrik, 82
Belgium, 43, 80, 81
Bhutto, Zulfikar Ali, 84, 89, 111, 174
Biharis, 92, 103, 111-12, 113, 169-70. *See also* minorities
blankets, 114-15

Boe, Johan, 99
Brazil, 43, 81
Britain (United Kingdom), 18, 33, 43, 44, 78, 80-81, 90, 114, 123, 147
Brocklehurst, Captain, 186
Burundi, 80, 81, 89
Bush, George, 22, 123

Cameroon, 81
Canada, 43, 44, 99, 179
Canadian International Development Agency, 72
Chad, 81
Chadenet, Bernard, 174
Chalna clearance. *See* salvage operations
Chandler, Robert, 158-59, 178, 185
Charter, United Nations, 6, 7, 19, 39
Chaudhuri, Rab, 106, 115, 139, 194
China, 80, 87
Chou En-lai, 8
Chowdhury, Abu Syed, 15, 147
Christian Council for Development in Bangladesh, 156
Christian Organization for Relief and Rehabilitation, 126, 156
Colombia, 81
coordination of relief effort, 27, 47, 129, 134-36, 186-87, 191-93
Costa Rica, 81
criticism: of UN reaction to East Pakistan crisis, 16-19; of UNROD performance, 122-23
crop assessment, 158-59, 187-88
cyclone, 3, 17, 21
Czechoslovakia, 43

D'Astugues, Marcel, 153, 166
Denmark, 43
Dhar, Subhas, 166

228　Index

domestic jurisdiction, principle of noninterference in, 6, 39, 82
donor meetings, 43, 102, 185
Douglas-Home, Sir Alec, 10, 18, 32
Driss, Rachid, 29

Earley, Colonel, 148
Economic and Social Council (United Nations), 16, 19, 20, 28, 31
Ecuador, 81
El-Tawil, Bahgat, 14, 21, 25-26, 34, 47, 53-55, 61
emergencies, UN machinery for dealing with, 20-21, 31
evacuation of UNEPRO staff from East Pakistan, 74, 76-79, 95

famine, xvii, 27, 29, 36, 51
Farman Ali, General, 83, 84, 85, 86
Finland, 43
Food and Agriculture Organization, 13, 28, 47, 59, 119, 158, 192
food distribution system, East Pakistan, 52
food needs, 26-27, 51-52, 120, 158-61
food ration, Bangladesh, 178
Formel, D., 156
Foundation for Airborne Relief, 150
Foy, Louis, 17
France, 43, 44, 81
Fulcheri, Gualtiero, 57, 100

Gandhi, Indira, 5, 16, 63, 64, 65, 66, 68, 71, 89, 121
General Assembly (United Nations), 58-60, 81-82, 98
Germany, Federal Republic of, 43, 114
Ghana, 81
good offices mission, 102-4, 110-12
Greece, 76
Guatemala, 81
guerilla activity, 55, 72. *See also* Mukti Bahini

Guyer, Roberto, 9, 48, 65, 70, 95, 101, 170

Hagen, Toni, 95, 100-102, 104, 105, 113-18, 120-21, 128, 193
Haighton, Tom, 196, 197
Haiti, 81
Haydon, Glen, 27
Heath, Edward, 10
Henry, Paul-Marc, 48-51, 56-60, 68, 72-73, 75-79, 82-97, 99, 101, 106-7, 119, 126
Honduras, 81
Hungary, 43

India: condemns Pakistan actions in East Bengal, 5; requests UN assistance for refugees, 8; rejects U Thant's proposal on repatriation of refugees, 35; concludes treaty of friendship with USSR, 39; rejects U Thant's offer of good offices, 65-67; announces cease-fire, 89; ships grain to Bangladesh, 121, 148-49
Indonesia, 81
International Bank for Reconstruction and Development, 9, 10, 12, 32, 47, 107, 119, 136, 164, 168, 180, 192
International Civil Aviation Organization, 136, 192
International Committee of the Red Cross, 6, 82, 83, 91, 93, 103, 147, 169, 172, 179
International Labor Organization, 136, 192
International Monetary Fund, 10, 13, 107, 119, 136, 164, 168, 180, 192
International Telecommunication Union, 192
Iran, 43
Islam, Nurul, 165
Italy, 43, 81
Ivory Coast, 81

Index

Jackson, Sir Robert, 133, 141, 145, 147, 153, 173, 176, 186, 187, 191: appointed under-secretary-general in charge of UNROD, 127-29, 134; defines UNROD strategy, 138, 140; and continuation of UNROD, 156, 157, 161; comments on the operation, 200
Japan, 43, 80, 81, 89, 115, 179
Jensen, Erik, 47, 112
Jordan, 81

Karatzas, Captain, 105
Kelly, John, 85-86
Kiser, Charles, 74
Kissinger, Henry, 10, 39, 68
Kittani, Ismat, 12-15, 29, 46, 48, 135
Kupcic, Frank, 163

Lacoste, Francis, 166, 168, 172, 175, 178, 182
League of Red Cross Societies, 13, 47, 59, 82, 112
Liberia, 81
Libya, 43, 81

Malik, A. M., 61, 83, 85, 103
Manhattan operation, 144-46
McCaw, William, 57, 72-75, 114
McNamara, Robert S., 9, 10, 107, 119
mediation, 40
Mexico, 43
minibulkers, 57, 73-76, 92, 149-50
minorities, xvii. *See also* Biharis
monsoon, 129, 147-48, 155
Morocco, 81
Mujibur Rahamn, Sheikh, xvii, 3, 4, 15, 41-42, 61, 68, 100, 106, 112, 127, 146, 157, 172
Mukti Bahini, 59, 62, 91, 93-94. *See also* guerilla activity
Murray, Richard, 145

Netherlands, 43, 60, 81, 114
neutral zones, 75, 82-83
New Delhi agreement, 171, 173
New Zealand, 30, 60
Niazi, General, 86
Nicaragua, 80, 81, 89
Nixon, Richard M., 10, 39
Norway, 43

observer group in East Pakistan, 33-34
obstacles to UN action in East Pakistan, 62
Office for Technical Cooperation, UN, 192
operation neutral, 73, 102
Oury, Bernard, 166

Pakistan: rejects U Thant's offer of assistance, 9; accepts offer of assistance, 10; accepts U Thant's proposal on repatriation of refugees, 34; accepts U Thant's offer of good offices, 64; rehabilitation needs, 172
Pakistan Aid Consortium, 10, 41
Pakistani forces, surrender in Dacca, 84-88
Pakistani prisoners of war in India, 103, 171
Panama, 81
Paraguay, 81
Pfeifer, Captain, 118
Podgorny, Nikolai, 8
Poland, 43, 81, 89

refugees from East Pakistan, xvii, 8, 11, 16, 34-35, 105
repatriation, under New Delhi agreement, 170-73
Rogers, William, 10, 45, 68
Romania, 43
Ruhul Quddus, 95

Sadruddin Aga Khan, 11, 35, 170, 173, 174

230 Index

Sailer, Erna, 119, 120-21, 130, 132, 139
Sales, Pierre, 106, 116
salvage operations, 109, 115-19, 152-54, 163-64, 179-80
Samad, Abdus, xix
Schoellkopf, Jacques, 56, 82
Searle, Captain W., 118, 153-54, 163
Secretary-General, UN. *See* Thant, U and Waldheim, Kurt
Secretary-General, UN, obstacles to action by, 5
Security Council, UN, 19, 35, 38-39, 80-81, 88-89, 98
self-determination, right of, 5, 39, 81
Sen, Samar, 5, 8, 35, 63, 65, 66, 67, 83
Shahi, Agha, 4, 6, 9, 10, 12, 41, 63, 83
Sierra Leone, 81, 89
Sikoutris, Captain, 76
Simla agreement, 169
Singh, General, 94-95
Singh, Swaran Sardar, 19, 42, 65, 88
smuggling of supplies from Bangladesh, 101, 134, 143
Somalia, 80, 81, 89
Spain, 43
strategy, UNROD, 137-41
Sudan, 81
surveillance of use of relief supplies, 11, 13, 23, 27, 45, 53-55, 58-59
Sweden, 43, 60, 114, 180
Switzerland, 43, 147

territorial integrity, principle of, 5, 39, 82
Thant, U, xiii, 4, 17, 41-42, 103, 201: offers humanitarian assistance for East Pakistan, 6-7; appeals for aid for refugees, 11; proposes measures for repatriation of refugees, 34; calls for Security Council action, 35-38; offers good offices, 62-68; makes statement to General Assembly, 98

Thorner, Alice, 55
Tikka Khan, General, 14
Timm, Father, 56, 91, 94-95
Tripp, Stephen R., 24-25, 27-28, 114
Tunisia, 60, 80, 81

Umbricht, Victor, 114, 133-34, 145, 146, 148, 154, 157, 174, 175-76, 185, 187, 188, 191: appointed UNROD chief of mission in Dacca, 128; and UNROD strategy, 139, 140-41; addresses development conference, 166-67; analyzes UNROD's success and shortcomings, 198-200
UNDP, 47, 119, 164, 168, 174, 180, 192
UNDRO, 174, 196
UNEPRO: established, 43; organization, 44; agreement with Pakistan government, 51, 215-16n; plan of action, 57; supplies diverted to Singapore, 73; disbanded, 95
UNESCO, 119, 136
UNFPA, 192
UNHCR, 11, 13, 29, 34, 40, 47, 59, 114, 171
UNICEF, 11, 25, 28, 47, 58, 59, 104, 114, 119, 136, 168, 180, 192
UNIDO, 192
UNMOGIP, 63, 70, 80, 90
UNROB: established, 157, 168; functions, 177; closed, 181
UNROD: established, 95; relations with Bangladesh government, 107; information papers, 113; transportation unit, 123-24; field stations, 124-25; logistical assistance, 144, 157; clearing-house functions, 185-86; operational responsibilities, 187-92; concluded, 161, 166-67
United States, 18, 33, 43, 44, 80, 88, 89, 115, 141, 179
Urquhart, Brian, 48, 101

Index

Uruguay, 81
USAID, 26, 51, 53, 56, 145, 147, 149, 150
USSR, 39, 43, 46, 80, 81, 89, 115, 116, 141, 179, 183

voluntary agencies, 183-84, 193-97, 200

Waldheim, Kurt, 99, 128, 171, 173, 201: appeals for aid to Bangladesh, xiii, 119, 160; visits subcontinent, xix, 164, 170; makes statement on humanitarian activities in subcontinent, 176
Walker, Robert, 93, 95, 99
WFP, 11, 13, 25, 28, 47, 59, 136, 190, 192

Wheeler, General Raymond, 118, 153
Wheeler, Peter, 95, 187
WHO, 13, 28, 47, 59, 136, 192
Wiis, Paul, 125
Winspeare Guicciardi, Vittorio, 45, 83, 91, 102-4, 110-12, 169, 173
World Bank. *See* International Bank for Reconstruction and Development

Yahya Khan, 3, 4-6, 15, 33, 41, 50, 61, 63, 64, 69, 70
Yemen, 81
Yugoslavia, 43

Zagorin, Bernard, 213n
Zaire, 81
Zambia, 81

Library of Congress Cataloging in Publication Data

Oliver, Thomas W
    The United Nations in Bangladesh.

    Includes bibliographical references and index.
    1. United Nations—Bangladesh.   2. International relief—Bangladesh.   I. Title.
JX1977.2.B27057   341.23'549'2   77-85554
ISBN 0-691-07593-X